FATHER AND SON

FATHER AND SON

A STUDY OF
TWO TEMPERAMENTS

By EDMUND GOSSE, C.B.

Der Glaube ist wie die Liebe:
er lässt sich nicht erzwingen.
SCHOPENHAUER

BOOKLOVER'S EDITION

WILLIAM HEINEMANN LTD
MELBOURNE :: LONDON :: TORONTO

First Published October 1907
New Impressions: December 1907, *January, April* 1908
Booklovers' Edition, November 1912, *January* 1948

Popular Edition, October 1909
New Impressions: December 1909, *April, December* 1910,
November 1912, *March* 1916, *September* 1922, *January* 1925

New Edition, Windmill Library 1928
New Impressions; October 1928, *August* 1929, *February* 1930,
January 1932, *July* 1933, *January* 1936, *October* 1937

New Leather-bound Edition 1935

PRINTED IN GREAT BRITAIN AT THE WINDMILL PRESS
KINGSWOOD, SURREY

PREFACE

AT the present hour, when fiction takes forms so ingenious and so specious, it is perhaps necessary to say that the following narrative, in all its parts, and so far as the punctilious attention of the writer has been able to keep it so, is scrupulously true. If it were not true, in this strict sense, to publish it would be to trifle with all those who may be induced to read it. It is offered to them as a *document*, as a record of educational and religious conditions which, having passed away, will never return. In this respect, as the diagnosis of a dying Puritanism, it is hoped that the narrative will not be altogether without significance.

It offers, too, in a subsidiary sense, a study of the development of moral and intellectual ideas during the progress of infancy. These have been closely and conscientiously noted, and may have some value in consequence of the unusual conditions in which they were produced. The author has observed that those who have written about the facts of their own childhood have usually delayed to note them down until age has dimmed their recollections. Perhaps an even more common fault in such

PREFACE

autobiographies is that they are sentimental, and are falsified by self-admiration and self-pity. The writer of these recollections has thought that if the examination of his earliest years was to be undertaken at all, it should be attempted while his memory is still perfectly vivid and while he is still unbiased by the forgetfulness or the sensibility of advancing years.

At one point only has there been any tampering with precise fact. It is believed that, with the exception of the Son, there is but one person mentioned in this book who is still alive. Nevertheless, it has been thought well, in order to avoid any appearance of offence, to alter the majority of the proper names of the private persons spoken of.

It is not usual, perhaps, that the narrative of a spiritual struggle should mingle merriment and humour with a discussion of the most solemn subjects. It has, however, been inevitable that they should be so mingled in this narrative. It is true that most funny books try to be funny throughout, while theology is scandalised if it awakens a single smile. But life is not constituted thus, and this book is nothing if it is not a genuine slice of life. There was an extraordinary mixture of comedy and tragedy in the situation which is here described, and those who are affected by the pathos of it will not need to have it explained to them that the comedy was superficial and the tragedy essential.

September 1907

CHAPTER I

THIS book is the record of a struggle between two temperaments, two consciences and almost two epochs. It ended, as was inevitable, in disruption. Of the two human beings here described, one was born to fly backward, the other could not help being carried forward. There came a time when neither spoke the same language as the other, or encompassed the same hopes, or was fortified by the same desires. But, at least, it is some consolation to the survivor, that neither, to the very last hour, ceased to respect the other, or to regard him with a sad indulgence.

The affection of these two persons was assailed by forces in comparison with which the changes that health or fortune or place introduce are as nothing. It is a mournful satisfaction, but yet a satisfaction, that they were both of them able to obey the law which says that ties of close family relationship must be honoured and sustained. Had it not been so, this story would never have been told.

The struggle began soon, yet of course it did not begin in early infancy. But to familiarise my readers with the conditions of the two persons (which were unusual) and with the outlines of their temperaments (which were, perhaps innately, antagonistic), it is needful to

I

A*

open with some account of all that I can truly
and independently recollect, as well as with
some statements which are, as will be obvious,
due to household tradition.

My parents were poor gentlefolks ; not young ;
solitary, sensitive and, although they did not
know it, proud. They both belonged to what
is called the Middle Class, and there was this
further resemblance between them that they
each descended from families which had been
more than well-to-do in the eighteenth century,
and had gradually sunken in fortune. In both
houses there had been a decay of energy which
had led to decay in wealth. In the case of my
Father's family it had been a slow decline ; in
that of my Mother's, it had been rapid. My
maternal grandfather was born wealthy, and in
the opening years of the nineteenth century,
immediately after his marriage, he bought a
little estate in North Wales, on the slopes of
Snowden. Here he seems to have lived in a
pretentious way, keeping a pack of hounds and
entertaining on an extravagant scale. He had
a wife who encouraged him in this vivid life, and
three children, my Mother and her two brothers.
His best trait was his devotion to the education
of his children, in which he proclaimed himself
a disciple of Rousseau. But he can hardly
have followed the teaching of " Émile " very
closely, since he employed tutors to teach his
daughter, at an extremely early age, the very
subjects which Rousseau forbade, such as history,
literature and foreign languages.

My Mother was his special favourite, and his
vanity did its best to make a blue-stocking of
her. She read Greek, Latin and even a little
Hebrew, and, what was more important, her
mind was trained to be self-supporting. But
she was diametrically opposed in essential matters
to her easy-going, luxurious and self-indulgent
parents. Reviewing her life in her thirtieth
year, she remarked in some secret notes : " I
cannot recollect the time when I did not love
religion." She used a still more remarkable
expression : " If I must date my conversion
from my first wish and trial to be holy, I may
go back to infancy ; if I am to postpone it till
after my last wilful sin, it is scarcely yet begun."
The irregular pleasures of her parents' life were
deeply distasteful to her, as such were to many
young persons in those days of the wide revival
of Conscience, and when my grandfather, by his
reckless expenditure, which he never checked
till ruin was upon him, was obliged to sell his
estate, and live in penury, my Mother was the
only member of the family who did not regret
the change. For my own part, I believe I
should have liked my reprobate maternal grandfather, but his conduct was certainly very
vexatious. He died, in his eightieth year, when
I was nine months old.

It was a curious coincidence that life had
brought both my parents along similar paths
to an almost identical position in respect to
religious belief. She had started from the
Anglican standpoint, he from the Wesleyan,

and each, almost without counsel from others, and after varied theological experiments, had come to take up precisely the same attitude towards all divisions of the Protestant Church, that, namely, of detached and unbiased contemplation. So far as the sects agreed with my Father and my Mother, the sects were walking in the light ; wherever they differed from them, they had slipped more or less definitely into a penumbra of their own making, a darkness into which neither of my parents would follow them. Hence, by a process of selection, my Father and my Mother alike had gradually, without violence, found themselves shut outside all Protestant communions, and at last they met only with a few extreme Calvinists like themselves, on terms of what may almost be called negation—with no priest, no ritual, no festivals, no ornament of any kind, nothing but the Lord's Supper and the exposition of Holy Scripture drawing these austere spirits into any sort of cohesion. They called themselves " the Brethren," simply ; a title enlarged by the world outside into " Plymouth Brethren."

It was accident and similarity which brought my parents together at these meetings of the Brethren. Each was lonely, each was poor, each was accustomed to a strenuous intellectual self-support. He was nearly thirty-eight, she was past forty-two, when they married. From a suburban lodging, he brought her home to his mother's little house in the north-east of London without a single day's honeymoon.

My Father was a zoologist, and a writer of books on natural history ; my Mother also was a writer, author already of two slender volumes of religious verse—the earlier of which, I know not how, must have enjoyed some slight success, since a second edition was printed—afterwards she devoted her pen to popular works of edification. But how infinitely removed in their aims, their habits, their ambitions from " literary " people of the present day, words are scarcely adequate to describe. Neither knew nor cared about any manifestation of current literature. For each there had been no poet later than Byron, and neither had read a romance since, in childhood, they had dipped into the Waverley Novels as they appeared in succession. For each the various forms of imaginative and scientific literature were merely means of improvement and profit, which kept the student " out of the world," gave him full employment, and enabled him to maintain himself. But pleasure was found nowhere but in the Word of God, and to the endless discussion of the Scriptures each hurried when the day's work was over.

In this strange household the advent of a child was not welcomed, but was borne with resignation. The event was thus recorded in my Father's diary :

" E. delivered of a son. Received green swallow from Jamaica."

This entry has caused amusement, as showing that he was as much interested in the bird as in the boy. But this does not follow ; what the wording exemplifies is my Father's extreme punctilio. The green swallow arrived later in the day than the son, and the earlier visitor was therefore recorded first ; my Father was scrupulous in every species of arrangement.

Long afterwards, my Father told me that my Mother suffered much in giving birth to me, and that, uttering no cry, I appeared to be dead. I was laid, with scant care, on another bed in the room, while all anxiety and attention were concentrated on my Mother. An old woman who happened to be there, and who was unemployed, turned her thoughts to me, and tried to awake in me a spark of vitality. She succeeded, and she was afterwards complimented by the doctor on her cleverness. My Father could not—when he told me the story— recollect the name of my preserver. I have often longed to know who she was. For all the rapture of life, for all its turmoils, its anxious desires, its manifold pleasures, and even for its sorrow and suffering, I bless and praise that anonymous old lady from the bottom of my heart.

It was six weeks before my Mother was able to leave her room. The occasion was made a solemn one, and was attended by a species of Churching. Mr. Balfour, a valued minister of the denomination, held a private service in the parlour, and " prayed for our child, that he may be the Lord's." This was the opening act of that " dedication " which was never henceforward forgotten, and of which the following pages will endeavour to describe the results. Around my tender and unconscious spirit was flung the luminous web, the light and elastic but impermeable veil, which it was hoped would keep me " unspotted from the world."

Until this time my Father's mother had lived in the house and taken the domestic charges of it on her own shoulders. She now consented to leave us to ourselves. There is no question that her exodus was a relief to my Mother, since my paternal grandmother was a strong and masterful woman, buxom, choleric and practical, for whom the interests of the mind did not exist. Her daughter-in-law, gentle as she was, and ethereal in manner and appearance—strangely contrasted (no doubt), in her tinctures of gold hair and white skin, with my grandmother's bold carnations and black tresses—was yet possessed of a will like tempered steel. They were better friends apart, with my grandmother lodged hard by, in a bright room, her household gods and bits of excellent eighteenth-century furniture around her, her miniatures and sparkling china arranged on shelves.

Left to my Mother's sole care, I became the centre of her solicitude. But there mingled with those happy animal instincts which sustain the strength and patience of every human mother, and were fully present with her—there mingled with these certain spiritual determinations which can be but rare. They are, in their outline, I suppose, vaguely common to many

religious mothers, but there are few indeed who
fill up the sketch with so firm a detail as she did.
Once again I am indebted to her secret notes, in
a little locked volume, seen until now, nearly
sixty years later, by no eye save her own.   Thus
she wrote when I was two months old :

"We have given him to the Lord ; and we
trust that He will really manifest him to be His
own, if he grow up ; and if the Lord take him
early, we will not doubt that he is taken to
Himself.   Only, if it please the Lord to take
him, I do trust we may be spared seeing him
suffering in lingering illness and much pain.
But in this as in all things His will is better than
what we can choose.   Whether his life be
prolonged or not, it has already been a blessing
to us, and to the saints, in leading us to much
prayer, and bringing us into varied need and
some trial."

The last sentence is somewhat obscure to me.
How, at that tender age, I contrived to be a
blessing "to the saints" may surprise others
and puzzles myself.   But "the saints" was the
habitual term by which were indicated the
friends who met on Sunday mornings for Holy
Communion, and at many other times in the
week for prayer and discussion of the Scriptures,
in the small hired hall at Hackney, which my
parents attended.   I suppose that the solemn
dedication of me to the Lord, which was repeated in public in my Mother's arms, being by

no means a usual or familiar ceremony even among the Brethren, created a certain curiosity and fervour in the immediate services, or was imagined so to do by the fond, partial heart of my Mother. She, however, who had been so much isolated, now made the care of her child an excuse for retiring still further into silence. With those religious persons who met at the Room, as the modest chapel was called, she had little spiritual and no intellectual sympathy. She noted

" I do not think it would increase my happiness to be in the midst of the saints at Hackney. I have made up my mind to give myself up to Baby for the winter, and to accept no invitations. To go when I can to the Sunday morning meetings and to see my own Mother."

The monotony of her existence now became extreme, but she seems to have been happy. Her days were spent in taking care of me, and in directing one young servant. My Father was for ever in his study, writing, drawing, dissecting ; sitting, no doubt, as I grew afterwards accustomed to see him, absolutely motionless, with his eye glued to the microscope, for twenty minutes at a time. So the greater part of every week-day was spent, and on Sunday he usually preached one, and sometimes two extempore sermons. His work-day labours were rewarded by the praise of the learned world, to which he was indifferent, but by very little money, which he needed more. For over three years after their marriage, neither of my parents left London for a single day, not being able to afford to travel. They received scarcely any visitors, never ate a meal away from home, never spent an evening in social intercourse abroad. At night they discussed theology, read aloud to one another, or translated scientific brochures from French or German. It sounds a terrible life of pressure and deprivation, and that it was physically unwholesome there can be no shadow of a doubt. But their contentment was complete and unfeigned. In the midst of this, materially, the hardest moment of their lives, when I was one year old, and there was a question of our leaving London, my Mother recorded in her secret notes :—

"We are happy and contented, having all things needful and pleasant, and our present habitation is hallowed by many sweet associations. We have our house to ourselves and enjoy each other's society. If we move we shall no longer be alone. The situation may be more favourable, however, for Baby, as being more in the country. I desire to have no choice in the matter, but as I know not what would be for our good, and God knows, so I desire to leave it with Him, and if it is not His will we should move, He will raise objections and difficulties, and if it is His will He will make Henry [my Father] desirous and anxious to take the step, and then, whatever the result, let us leave all to Him and not regret it."

No one who is acquainted with the human heart will mistake this attitude of resignation for weakness of purpose. It was not poverty of will, it was abnegation, it was a voluntary act. My Mother, underneath an exquisite amenity of manner, concealed a rigour of spirit which took the form of a constant self-denial. For it to dawn upon her consciousness that she wished for something, was definitely to renounce that wish, or, more exactly, to subject it in every thing to what she conceived to be the will of God.

This is perhaps the right moment for me to say that at this time, and indeed until the hour of her death, she exercised, without suspecting it, a magnetic power over the will and nature of my Father. Both were strong, but my Mother was unquestionably the stronger of the two ; it was her mind which gradually drew his to take up a certain definite position, and this remained permanent although she, the cause of it, was early removed. Hence, while it was with my Father that the long struggle which I have to narrate took place, behind my Father stood the ethereal memory of my Mother's will, guiding him, pressing him, holding him to the unswerving purpose which she had formed and defined. And when the inevitable disruption came, what was unspeakably painful was to realise that it was not from one, but from both parents that the purpose of the child was separated.

My Mother was a Puritan in grain, and never a word escaped her, not a phrase exists in her diary, to suggest that she had any privations to put up with. She seemed strong and well, and so did I ; the one of us who broke down was my Father. With his attack of acute nervous dyspepsia came an unexpected small accession of money, and we were able, in my third year, to take a holiday of nearly ten months in Devonshire. The extreme seclusion, the unbroken strain, were never repeated, and when we returned to London, it was to conditions of greater amenity and to a less rigid practice of "the world forgetting by the world forgot." That this relaxation was more relative than positive, and that nothing ever really tempted either of my parents from their cavern in an intellectual Thebaïd, my recollections will amply prove. But each of them was forced by circumstances into a more or less public position, and neither could any longer quite ignore the world around.

It is not my business here to re-write the biographies of my parents. Each of them became, in a certain measure, celebrated, and each was the subject of a good deal of contemporary discussion. Each was prominent before the eyes of a public of his or her own, half a century ago. It is because their minds were vigorous and their accomplishments distinguished that the contrast between their spiritual point of view and the aspect of a similar class of persons to-day is interesting and may, I hope, be instructive. But this is not another memoir of public individuals, each of whom has had more than

one biographer. My serious duty, as I venture
to hold it, is other ;

> that's the world's side,
> Thus men saw them, praised them, thought they knew them !
> There, in turn, I stood aside and praised them !
> Out of my own self, I dare to phrase it.

But this is a different inspection, this is a
study of

> the other side, the novel
> Silent silver lights and darks undreamed of,

the record of a state of soul once not uncommon
in Protestant Europe, of which my parents were
perhaps the latest consistent exemplars among
people of light and leading.

The peculiarities of a family life, founded
upon such principles, are, in relation to a little
child, obvious ; but I may be permitted to re-
capitulate them. Here was perfect purity, perfect intrepidity, perfect abnegation ; yet there
was also narrowness, isolation, an absence of
perspective, let it be boldly admitted, an absence
of humanity. And there was a curious mixture
of humbleness and arrogance ; entire resignation to the will of God and not less entire disdain
of the judgment and opinion of man. My
parents founded every action, every attitude,
upon their interpretation of the Scriptures, and
upon the guidance of the Divine Will as revealed
to them by direct answer to prayer. Their
ejaculation in the face of any dilemma was,
" Let us cast it before the Lord ! "

So confident were they of the reality of their

intercourse with God, that they asked for no other guide. They recognised no spiritual authority among men, they subjected themselves to no priest or minister, they troubled their consciences about no current manifestation of "religious opinion." They lived in an intellectual cell, bounded at its sides by the walls of their own house, but open above to the very heart of the uttermost heavens.

This, then, was the scene in which the soul of a little child was planted, not as in an ordinary open flower-border or carefully tended social parterre, but as on a ledge, split in the granite of some mountain. The ledge was hung between night and the snows on one hand, and the dizzy depths of the world upon the other ; was furnished with just soil enough for a gentian to struggle skywards and open its stiff azure stars ; and offered no lodgment, no hope of salvation, to any rootlet which should stray beyond its inexorable limits.

CHAPTER II

OUT of the darkness of my infancy there comes only one flash of memory. I am seated alone, in my baby-chair, at a dinner-table set for several people. Somebody brings in a leg of mutton, puts it down close to me, and goes out. I am again alone, gazing at two low windows, wide open upon a garden. Suddenly, noiselessly, a large, long animal (obviously a greyhound) appears at one window-sill, slips into the room, seizes the leg of mutton and slips out again. When this happened I could not yet talk. The accomplishment of speech came to me very late, doubtless because I never heard young voices. Many years later, when I mentioned this recollection, there was a shout of laughter and surprise :—

"That, then, was what became of the mutton ! It was not you, who, as your Uncle A. pretended, ate it up, in the twinkling of an eye, bone and all ! "

I suppose that it was the startling intensity of this incident which stamped it upon a memory from which all other impressions of this early date have vanished.

The adventure of the leg of mutton occurred, evidently, at the house of my Mother's brothers, for my parents, at this date, visited no other. My uncles were not religious men, but they had

an almost filial respect for my Mother, who was
several years senior to the elder of them.   When
the catastrophe of my grandfather's fortune had
occurred, they had not yet left school.   My
Mother, in spite of an extreme dislike of teaching,
which was native to her, immediately accepted
the situation of a governess in the family of an
Irish nobleman.   The mansion was only to be
approached, as Miss Edgeworth would have
said, " through eighteen sloughs, at the imminent peril of one's life," and when one had
reached it, the mixture of opulence and squalour,
of civility and savagery, was unspeakable.   But
my Mother was well paid, and she stayed in this
distasteful environment, doing the work she
hated most, while with the margin of her salary
she helped first one of her brothers and then the
other through his Cambridge course.   They
studied hard and did well at the university.   At
length their sister received, in her " ultima
Thule," news that her younger brother had taken
his degree, and then and there, with a sigh of
intense relief, she resigned her situation and
came straight back to England.

It is not to be wondered at, then, that my
uncles looked up to their sister with feelings of
especial devotion.   They were not inclined, they
were hardly in a position, to criticise her modes
of thought.   They were easy-going, cultured and
kindly gentlemen, rather limited in their views,
without a trace of their sister's force of intellect
or her strenuous temper.   E. resembled her in
person, he was tall, fair, with auburn curls ; he

cultivated a certain tendency to the Byronic type,
fatal and melancholy. A. was short, brown and
jocose, with a pretension to common sense ;
bluff and chatty. As a little child, I adored my
Uncle E., who sat silent by the fireside, holding
me against his knee, saying nothing, but looking
unutterably sad, and occasionally shaking his
warm-coloured tresses. With great injustice, on
the other hand, I detested my Uncle A., because
he used to joke in a manner very displeasing to
me, and because he would so far forget himself
as to chase, and even, if it will be credited, to
tickle me. My uncles, who remained bachelors
to the end of their lives, earned a comfortable
living, E. by teaching, A. as '' something in the
City,'' and they rented an old rambling house
in Clapton, that same in which I saw the greyhound. Their house had a strange, delicious
smell, so unlike anything I smelt anywhere else,
that it used to fill my eyes with tears of mysterious
pleasure. I know now that this was the odour
of cigars, tobacco being a species of incense
tabooed at home on the highest religious
grounds.

It has been recorded that I was slow in learning to speak. I used to be told that having met
all invitations to repeat such words as '' Papa ''
and '' Mamma '' with gravity and indifference,
I one day drew towards me a volume, and said
'' book '' with startling distinctness. I was not
at all precocious, but at a rather early age, I
think towards the beginning of my fourth year,
I learned to read. I cannot recollect a time

when a printed page of English was closed to me.
But perhaps earlier still my Mother used to
repeat to me a poem which I have always
taken for granted that she had herself com-
posed, a poem which had a romantic place in
my early mental history. It ran thus, I
think :

> O pretty Moon, you shine so bright !
> I'll go to bid Mamma good-night,
> And then I'll lie upon my bed
> And watch you move above my head.
>
> Ah ! there, a cloud has hidden you !
> But I can see your light shine thro' ;
> It tries to hide you—quite in vain,
> For—there you quickly come again !
>
> It's God, I know, that makes you shine
> Upon this little bed of mine ;
> But I shall all about you know
> When I can read and older grow.

Long, long after the last line had become an
anachronism, I used to shout this poem from
my bed before I went to sleep, whether the night
happened to be moon-lit or no.

It must have been my Father who taught me
my letters. To my Mother, as I have said, it
was distasteful to teach, though she was so
prompt and skilful to learn. My Father, on the
contrary, taught cheerfully, by fits and starts.
In particular, he had a scheme for rationalising
geography, which I think was admirable. I was
to climb upon a chair, while, standing at my

side, with a pencil and a sheet of paper, he was
to draw a chart of the markings on the carpet.
Then, when I understood the system, another
chart on a smaller scale of the furniture in the
room, then of a floor of the house, then of the
back-garden, then of a section of the street.
The result of this was that geography came to
me of itself, as a perfectly natural miniature
arrangement of objects, and to this day has
always been the science which gives me least
difficulty.   My Father also taught me the simple
rules of arithmetic, a little natural history, and
the elements of drawing ; and he laboured long
and unsuccessfully to make me learn by heart
hymns, psalms and chapters of Scripture, in
which I always failed ignominiously and with
tears.   This puzzled and vexed him, for he himself had an extremely retentive textual memory.
He could not help thinking that I was naughty,
and would not learn the chapters, until at last he
gave up the effort.   All this sketch of an education began, I believe, in my fourth year, and was
not advanced or modified during the rest of my
Mother's life.

Meanwhile, capable as I was of reading, I
found my greatest pleasure in the pages of books.
The range of these was limited, for story-books
of every description were sternly excluded.   No
fiction of any kind, religious or secular, was
admitted into the house.   In this it was to my
Mother, not to my Father, that the prohibition
was due.   She had a remarkable, I confess to
me still somewhat unaccountable impression,

that to "tell a story," that is, to compose fictitious narrative of any kind, was a sin. She carried this conviction to extreme lengths. My Father, in later years, gave me some interesting examples of her firmness. As a young man in America, he had been deeply impressed by "Salathiel," a pious prose romance by that then popular writer, the Rev. George Croly. When he first met my Mother, he recommended it to her, but she would not consent to open it. Nor would she read the chivalrous tales in verse of Sir Walter Scott, obstinately alleging that they were not "true." She would read none but lyrical and subjective poetry. Her secret diary reveals the history of this singular aversion to the fictitious, although it cannot be said to explain the cause of it. As a child, however, she had possessed a passion for making up stories, and so considerable a skill in it that she was constantly being begged to indulge others with its exercise. But I will, on so curious a point, leave her to speak for herself :

"When I was a very little child, I used to amuse myself and my brothers with inventing stories, such as I read. Having, as I suppose, naturally a restless mind and busy imagination, this soon became the chief pleasure of my life. Unfortunately, my brothers were always fond of encouraging this propensity, and I found in Taylor, my maid, a still greater tempter. I had not known there was any harm in it, until Miss Shore [a Calvinist governess], finding it

out, lectured me severely, and told me it was
wicked. From that time forth I considered
that to invent a story of any kind was a sin.
But the desire to do so was too deeply rooted in
my affections to be resisted in my own strength
[she was at that time nine years of age], and
unfortunately I knew neither my corruption nor
my weakness, nor did I know where to gain
strength. The longing to invent stories grew
with violence ; everything I heard or read
became food for my distemper. The simplicity
of truth was not sufficient for me ; I must needs
embroider imagination upon it, and the folly,
vanity and wickedness which disgraced my heart
are more than I am able to express. Even now
[at the age of twenty-nine], tho' watched,
prayed and striven against, this is still the sin
that most easily besets me. It has hindered my
prayers and prevented my improvement, and
therefore has humbled me very much.''

This is, surely, a very painful instance of the
repression of an instinct. There seems to have
been, in this case, a vocation such as is rarely
heard, and still less often wilfully disregarded
and silenced. Was my Mother intended by
nature to be a novelist ? I have often thought
so, and her talents and vigour of purpose,
directed along the line which was ready to form
" the chief pleasure of her life,'' could hardly
have failed to conduct her to great success. She
was a little younger than Bulwer Lytton, a little
older than Mrs. Gaskell,—but these are vain and
trivial speculations !

My own state, however, was, I should think, almost unique among the children of cultivated parents. In consequence of the stern ordinance which I have described, not a single fiction was read or told to me during my infancy. The rapture of the child who delays the process of going to bed by cajoling " a story " out of his mother or his nurse, as he sits upon her knee, well tucked up, at the corner of the nursery fire,—this was unknown to me. Never, in all my early childhood, did any one address to me the affecting preamble, " Once upon a time ! " I was told about missionaries, but never about pirates ; I was familiar with humming-birds, but I had never heard of fairies. Jack the Giant-Killer, Rumpelstiltskin and Robin Hood were not of my acquaintance, and though I understood about wolves, Little Red Ridinghood was a stranger even by name. So far as my " dedication " was concerned, I can but think that my parents were in error thus to exclude the imaginary from my outlook upon facts. They desired to make me truthful ; the tendency was to make me positive and sceptical. Had they wrapped me in the soft folds of supernatural fancy, my mind might have been longer content to follow their traditions in an unquestioning spirit.

Having easily said what, in those early years, I did not read, I have great difficulty in saying what I did read. But a queer variety of natural history, some of it quite indigestible by my undeveloped mind ; many books of travels,

mainly of a scientific character, among them
voyages of discovery in the South Seas, by which
my brain was dimly filled with splendour ; some
geography and astronomy, both of them sincerely
enjoyed ; much theology, which I desired to
appreciate but could never get my teeth into
(if I may venture to say so), and over which my
eye and tongue learned to slip without penetrating, so that I would read, and read aloud, and
with great propriety of emphasis, page after
page without having formed an idea or retained
an expression. There was, for instance, a writer
on prophecy called Jukes, of whose works each
of my parents was inordinately fond, and I was
early set to read Jukes aloud to them. I did it
glibly, like a machine, but the sight of Jukes's
volumes became an abomination to me, and I
never formed the outline of a notion what they
were about. Later on, a publication called
"The Penny Cyclopædia" became my daily,
and for a long time almost my sole study ;
to the subject of this remarkable work I may
presently return.

It is difficult to keep anything like chronological order in recording fragments of early
recollection, and in speaking of my reading I
have been led too far ahead. My memory does
not, practically, begin till we returned from
certain visits, made with a zoological purpose, to
the shores of Devon and Dorset, and settled,
early in my fifth year, in a house at Islington, in
the north of London. Our circumstances were
now more easy ; my Father had regular and

well-paid literary work ; and the house was larger and more comfortable than ever before, though still very simple and restricted. My memories, some of which are exactly dated by certain facts, now become clear and almost abundant. What I do not remember, except from having it very often repeated to me, is what may be considered the only " clever " thing that I said during an otherwise unillustrious childhood. It was not startlingly " clever," but it may pass. A lady—when I was just four— rather injudiciously showed me a large print of a human skeleton, saying, " There ! you don't know what that is, do you ? " Upon which, immediately and very archly, I replied, " Isn't it a man with the meat off ? " This was thought wonderful, and, as it is supposed that I had never had the phenomenon explained to me, it certainly displays some quickness in seizing an analogy. I had often watched my Father, while he soaked the flesh off the bones of fishes and small mammals. If I venture to repeat this trifle, it is only to point out that the system on which I was being educated deprived all things, human life among the rest, of their mystery. The " bare-grinning skeleton of death " was to me merely a prepared specimen of that featherless plantigrade vertebrate, " homo sapiens."

As I have said that this anecdote was thought worth repeating, I ought to proceed to say that there was, so far as I can recollect, none of that flattery of childhood which is so often merely a backhanded way of indulging the vanity of parents. My Mother, indeed, would hardly have been human if she had not occasionally entertained herself with the delusion that her solitary duckling was a cygnet. This my Father did not encourage, remarking, with great affection, and chucking me under the chin, that I was " a nice little ordinary boy." My Mother, stung by this want of appreciation, would proceed so far as to declare that she believed that in future times the F.R.S. would be chiefly known as his son's father ! (This is a pleasantry frequent in professional families.)

To this my Father, whether convinced or not, would make no demur, and the couple would begin to discuss, in my presence, the direction which my shining talents would take. In consequence of my dedication to "the Lord's Service," the range of possibilities was much restricted. My Father, who had lived long in the Tropics, and who nursed a perpetual nostalgia for "the little lazy isles where the trumpet-orchids blow," leaned towards the field of missionary labour. My Mother, who was cold about foreign missions, preferred to believe that I should be the Charles Wesley of my age, " or perhaps," she had the candour to admit, " merely the George Whitefield." I cannot recollect the time when I did not understand that I was going to be a minister of the Gospel.

It is so generally taken for granted that a life strictly dedicated to religion is stiff and dreary, that I may have some difficulty in persuading my readers that, as a matter of fact, in these

B

early days of my childhood, before disease and
death had penetrated to our slender society, we
were always cheerful and often gay. My parents
were playful with one another, and there were
certain stock family jests which seldom failed to
enliven the breakfast table. My Father and
Mother lived so completely in the atmosphere of
faith, and were so utterly convinced of their
intercourse with God, that, so long as that intercourse was not clouded by sin, to which they
were delicately sensitive, they could afford to
take the passing hour very lightly. They would
even, to a certain extent, treat the surroundings
of their religion as a subject of jest, joking very
mildly and gently about such things as an
attitude at prayer or the nature of a supplication.
They were absolutely indifferent to forms. They
prayed, seated in their chairs, as willingly as,
reversed, upon their knees ; no ritual having
any significance for them. . My Mother was
sometimes extremely gay, laughing with a soft,
merry sound. What I have since been told of
the guileless mirth of nuns in a convent has
reminded me of the gaiety of my parents during
my early childhood.

So long as I was a mere part of them, without
individual existence, and swept on, a satellite, in
their atmosphere, I was mirthful when they
were mirthful, and grave when they were grave.
The mere fact that I had no young companions,
no story books, no outdoor amusements, none of
the thousand and one employments provided for
other children in more conventional surroundings,

did not make me discontented or fretful, because
I did not know of the existence of such entertainments. In exchange, I became keenly attentive to the limited circle of interests open to me.
Oddly enough, I have no recollection of any
curiosity about other children, nor of any desire
to speak to them or play with them. They did
not enter into my dreams, which were occupied
entirely with grown-up people and animals. I
had three dolls, to whom my attitude was not
very intelligible. Two of these were female, one
with a shapeless face of rags, the other in wax.
But, in my fifth year, when the Crimean War
broke out, I was given a third doll, a soldier,
dressed very smartly in a scarlet cloth tunic.
I used to put the dolls on three chairs, and
harangue them aloud, but my sentiment to them
was never confidential, until our maid-servant
one day, intruding on my audience, and misunderstanding the occasion of it, said : " What ?
a boy, and playing with a soldier when he's got
two lady-dolls to play with ? " I had never
thought of my dolls as confidants before, but
from that time forth I paid a special attention to
the soldier, in order to make up to him for
Lizzie's unwarrantable insult.

The declaration of war with Russia brought
the first breath of outside life into our Calvinist
cloister. My parents took in a daily newspaper,
which they had never done before, and events in
picturesque places, which my Father and I
looked out on the map, were eagerly discussed.
One of my vividest early memories can be dated

exactly. I was playing about the house, and suddenly burst into the breakfast-room, where, close to the door, sat an amazing figure, a very tall young man, as stiff as my doll, in a gorgeous scarlet tunic. Quite far away from him, at her writing-table, my Mother sat with her Bible open before her, and was urging the gospel plan of salvation on his acceptance. She promptly told me to run away and play, but I had seen a great sight. This guardsman was in the act of leaving for the Crimea, and his adventures,—he was converted in consequence of my Mother's instruction,—were afterwards told by her in a tract, called " The Guardsman of the Alma," of which I believe that more than half a million of copies were circulated. He was killed in that battle, and this added an extraordinary lustre to my dream of him. I see him still in my mind's eye, large, stiff, and unspeakably brilliant, seated, from respect, as near as possible to our parlour door. This apparition gave reality to my subsequent conversations with the soldier doll.

That same victory of the Alma, which was reported in London on my fifth birthday, is also marked very clearly in my memory by a family circumstance. We were seated at breakfast, at our small round table drawn close up to the window, my Father with his back to the light. Suddenly, he gave a sort of cry, and read out the opening sentences from the " Times " announcing a battle in the valley of the Alma. No doubt the strain of national anxiety had been very

great, for both he and my Mother seemed deeply
excited. He broke off his reading when the fact
of the decisive victory was assured, and he and
my Mother sank simultaneously on their knees
in front of their tea and bread-and-butter, while
in a loud voice my Father gave thanks to the
God of Battles. This patriotism was the more
remarkable, in that he had schooled himself, as
he believed, to put his '' heavenly citizenship ''
above all earthly duties. To those who said :
'' Because you are a Christian, surely you are
not less an Englishman ? '' he would reply by
shaking his head, and by saying : '' I am a
citizen of no earthly State.''   He did not realise
that, in reality, and to use a cant phrase not yet
coined in 1854, there existed in Great Britain no
more thorough '' Jingo '' than he.

Another instance of the remarkable way in
which the interests of daily life were mingled,
in our strange household, with the practice of
religion, made an impression upon my memory.
We had all three been much excited by a report
that a certain dark geometer-moth, generated
in underground stables, had been met with in
Islington. Its name, I think, is '' Boletobia
fuliginaria,'' and I believe that it is excessively
rare in England. We were sitting at family
prayers, on a summer morning, I think in 1855,
when through the open window a brown moth
came sailing. My Mother immediately interrupted the reading of the Bible by saying to my
Father, '' O ! Henry, do you think that can be
' Boletobia ? ' ''   My Father rose up from the

sacred book, examined the insect, which had now perched, and replied : "No! it is only the common Vapourer, 'Orgyia antiqua!'", resuming his seat, and the exposition of the Word, without any apology or embarrassment.

In the course of this, my sixth year, there happened a series of minute and soundless incidents which, elementary as they may seem when told, were second in real importance to none in my mental history. The recollection of them confirms me in the opinion that certain leading features in each human soul are inherent to it, and cannot be accounted for by suggestion or training. In my own case, I was most carefully withdrawn, like Princess Blanchefleur in her marble fortress, from every outside influence whatever, yet to me the instinctive life came as unexpectedly as her lover came to her in the basket of roses. What came to me was the consciousness of self, as a force and as a companion, and it came as the result of one or two shocks, which I will relate.

In consequence of hearing so much about an Omniscient God, a being of supernatural wisdom and penetration who was always with us, who made, in fact, a fourth in our company, I had come to think of Him, not without awe, but with absolute confidence. My Father and Mother, in their serene discipline of me, never argued with one another, never even differed ; their wills seemed absolutely one. My Mother always deferred to my Father, and in his absence

spoke of him to me, as if he were all-wise. I
confused him in some sense with God ; at all
events I believed that my Father knew everything and saw everything.   One morning in my
sixth year, my Mother and I were alone in the
morning-room, when my Father came in and
announced some fact to us.   I was standing on
the rug, gazing at him, and when he made this
statement, I remember turning quickly, in embarrassment, and looking into the fire.   The
shock to me was as that of a thunderbolt, for
what my Father had said "was not true."   My
Mother and I, who had been present at the
trifling incident, were aware that it had not
happened exactly as it had been reported to him.
My Mother gently told him so, and he accepted
the correction.   Nothing could possibly have
been more trifling to my parents, but to me it
meant an epoch.   Here was the appalling discovery, never suspected before, that my Father
was not as God, and did not know everything.
The shock was not caused by any suspicion that
he was not telling the truth, as it appeared to
him, but by the awful proof that he was not, as
I had supposed, omniscient.

This experience was followed by another,
which confirmed the first, but carried me a
great deal further.   In our little back-garden,
my Father had built up a rockery for ferns and
mosses, and from the water-supply of the house
he had drawn a leaden pipe so that it pierced
upwards through the rockery and produced,
when a tap was turned, a pretty silvery parasol

of water. The pipe was exposed somewhere
near the foot of the rockery. One day, two
workmen, who were doing some repairs, left
their tools during the dinner-hour in the back-
garden, and as I was marching about I suddenly
thought that to see whether one of these tools
could make a hole in the pipe would be attractive.
It did make such a hole, quite easily, and then
the matter escaped my mind. But a day or two
afterwards, when my Father came in to dinner,
he was very angry. He had turned the tap,
and instead of the fountain arching at the
summit, there had been a rush of water through
a hole at the foot. The rockery was absolutely
ruined.

Of course I realised in a moment what I had
done, and I sat frozen with alarm, waiting to be
denounced. But my Mother remarked on the
visit of the plumbers two or three days before,
and my Father instantly took up the suggestion.
No doubt that was it ; the mischievous fellows
had thought it amusing to stab the pipe and
spoil the fountain. No suspicion fell on me ; no
question was asked of me. I sat there, turned
to stone within, but outwardly sympathetic and
with unchecked appetite.

We attribute, I believe, too many moral ideas
to little children. It is obvious that in this
tremendous juncture, I ought to have been
urged forward by good instincts, or held back by
naughty ones. But I am sure that the fear
which I experienced for a short time, and which
so unexpectedly melted away, was a purely

physical one. It had nothing to do with the
motions of a contrite heart. As to the destruction of the fountain, I was sorry about that, for
my own sake, since I admired the skipping water
extremely, and had had no idea that I was
spoiling its display. But the emotions which
now thronged within me, and which led me, with
an almost unwise alacrity, to seek solitude in the
back-garden, were not moral at all, they were
intellectual. I was not ashamed of having successfully — and so surprisingly — deceived my
parents by my crafty silence ; I looked upon
that as a providential escape, and dismissed all
further thought of it. I had other things to
think of.

In the first place, the theory that my Father
was omniscient or infallible was now dead and
buried. He probably knew very little ; in this
case he had not known a fact of such importance
that if you did not know that, it could hardly
matter what you knew. My Father, as a deity,
as a natural force of immense prestige, fell in my
eyes to a human level. In future, his statements
about things in general need not be accepted
implicitly. But of all the thoughts which rushed
upon my savage and undeveloped little brain at
this crisis, the most curious was that I had found
a companion and a confidant in myself. There
was a secret in this world and it belonged to me
and to a somebody who lived in the same body
with me. There were two of us, and we could
talk with one another. It is difficult to define
impressions so rudimentary, but it is certain that

it was in this dual form that the sense of my individuality now suddenly descended upon me, and it is equally certain that it was a great solace to me to find a sympathiser in my own breast.

About this time, my Mother, carried away by the current of her literary and her philanthropic work, left me more and more to my own devices. She was seized with a great enthusiasm; as one of her admirers and disciples has written, " she went on her way, sowing beside all waters." I would not for a moment let it be supposed that I regard her as a Mrs. Jellyby, or that I think she neglected me. But a remarkable work had opened up before her; after her long years in a mental hermitage, she was drawn forth into the clamorous harvest-field of souls. She developed an unexpected gift of persuasion over strangers whom she met in the omnibus or in the train, and with whom she courageously grappled. This began by her noting, with deep humility and joy, that " I have reason to judge the sound conversion to God of three young persons within a few weeks, by the instrumentality of my conversations with them." At the same time, as another of her biographers has said, " those testimonies to the Blood of Christ, the fruits of her pen, began to be spread very widely, even to the most distant parts of the globe." My Father, too, was at this time at the height of his activity. After breakfast, each of them was amply occupied, perhaps until night-fall; our evenings we still always spent together. Some-

times my Mother took me with her on her
" unknown day's employ " ; I recollect pleasant
rambles through the City by her side, and the
act of looking up at her figure soaring above me.
But when all was done, I had hours and hours of
complete solitude, in my Father's study, in the
back-garden, above all in the garret.

The garret was a fairy place.   It was a low
lean-to, lighted from the roof.   It was wholly
unfurnished, except for two objects, an ancient
hat-box and a still more ancient skin-trunk.
The hat-box puzzled me extremely, till one day,
asking my Father what it was, I got a distracted
answer which led me to believe that it was itself
a sort of hat, and I made a laborious but repeated
effort to wear it.   The skin-trunk was absolutely
empty, but the inside of the lid of it was lined
with sheets of what I now know to have been a
sensational novel.   It was, of course, a fragment,
but I read it, kneeling on the bare floor, with
indescribable rapture.   It will be recollected that
the idea of fiction, of a deliberately invented
story, had been kept from me with entire success.
I therefore implicitly believed the tale in the lid
of the trunk to be a true account of the sorrows
of a lady of title, who had to flee the country,
and who was pursued into foreign lands by
enemies bent upon her ruin.   Somebody had an
interview with a " minion " in a " mask " ; I
went downstairs and looked up these words in
Bailey's " English Dictionary," but was left in
darkness as to what they had to do with the lady
of title.   This ridiculous fragment filled me with

delicious fears ; I fancied that my Mother, who was out so much, might be threatened by dangers of the same sort ; and the fact that the narrative came abruptly to an end, in the middle of one of its most thrilling sentences, wound me up almost to a disorder of wonder and romance.

The preoccupation of my parents threw me more and more upon my own resources. But what are the resources of a solitary child of six ? I was never inclined to make friends with servants, nor did our successive maids proffer, so far as I recollect, any advances. Perhaps, with my '' dedication '' and my grown-up ways of talking, I did not seem to them at all an attractive little boy. I continued to have no companions, or even acquaintances of my own age. I am unable to recollect exchanging two words with another child till after my Mother's death.

The abundant energy which my Mother now threw into her public work did not affect the quietude of our private life. We had some visitors in the day-time, people who came to consult one parent or the other. But they never stayed to a meal, and we never returned their visits. I do not quite know how it was that neither of my parents took me to any of the sights of London, although I am sure it was a question of principle with them. Notwithstanding all our study of natural history, I was never introduced to live wild beasts at the Zoo, nor to dead ones at the British Museum. I can understand better why we never visited a picture-gallery or a concert-room. So far as I can recollect, the only time I was ever taken to any place of entertainment was when my Father and I paid a visit, long anticipated, to the Great Globe in Leicester Square. This was a huge structure, the interior of which one ascended by means of a spiral staircase. It was a poor affair; that was concave in it which should have been convex, and my imagination was deeply affronted. I could invent a far better Great Globe than that in my mind's eye in the garret.

Being so restricted, then, and yet so active, my mind took refuge in an infantile species of natural magic. This contended with the definite ideas of religion which my parents were continuing, with too mechanical a persistency, to force into my nature, and it ran parallel with them. I formed strange superstitions, which I can only render intelligible by naming some concrete examples. I persuaded myself that, if I could only discover the proper words to say or the proper passes to make, I could induce the gorgeous birds and butterflies in my Father's illustrated manuals to come to life, and fly out of the book, leaving holes behind them. I believed that, when, at the Chapel, we sang, drearily and slowly, loud hymns of experience and humiliation, I could boom forth with a sound equal to that of dozens of singers, if I could only hit upon the formula. During morning and evening prayers, which were extremely lengthy and fatiguing, I fancied that one of my two

selves could flit up, and sit clinging to the cornice,
and look down on my other self and the rest of
us, if I could only find the key. I laboured for
hours in search of these formulas, thinking to
compass my ends by means absolutely irrational.
For example, I was convinced that if I could only
count consecutive numbers long enough, without losing one, I should suddenly, on reaching
some far-distant figure, find myself in possession
of the great secret. I feel quite sure that nothing
external suggested these ideas of magic, and I
think it probable that they approached the ideas
of savages at a very early stage of development.

All this ferment of mind was entirely unob-
served by my parents. But when I formed the
belief that it was necessary, for the success of
my practical magic, that I should hurt myself,
and when, as a matter of fact, I began, in extreme
secrecy, to run pins into my flesh and bang my
joints with books, no one will be surprised to
hear that my Mother's attention was drawn to
the fact that I was looking " delicate." The
notice nowadays universally given to the hygienic
rules of life was rare fifty years ago, and among
deeply religious people, in particular, fatalistic
views of disease prevailed. If any one was ill,
it showed that " the Lord's hand was extended
in chastisement," and much prayer was poured
forth in order that it might be explained to the
sufferer, or to his relations, in what he or they
had sinned. People would, for instance, go on
living over a cess-pool, working themselves up

into an agony to discover how they had incurred
the displeasure of the Lord, but never moving
away. As I became very pale and nervous, and
slept badly at nights, with visions and loud
screams in my sleep, I was taken to a physician,
who stripped me and tapped me all over (this
gave me some valuable hints for my magical
practices), but could find nothing the matter.
He recommended,—whatever physicians in such
cases always recommend,—but nothing was
done. If I was feeble it was the Lord's Will,
and we must acquiesce.

It culminated in a sort of fit of hysterics, when
I lost all self-control, and sobbed with tears, and
banged my head on the table. While this was
proceeding, I was conscious of that dual individuality of which I have already spoken, since
while one part of me gave way, and could not
resist, the other part in some extraordinary sense
seemed standing aloof, much impressed. I was
alone with my Father when this crisis suddenly
occurred, and I was interested to see that he was
greatly alarmed. It was a very long time since
we had spent a day out of London, and I said,
on being coaxed back to calmness, that I wanted
"to go into the country." Like the dying
Falstaff, I babbled of green fields. My Father,
after a little reflection, proposed to take me to
Primrose Hill. I had never heard of the place,
and names have always appealed directly to
my imagination. I was in the highest degree
delighted, and could hardly restrain my impatience. As soon as possible we set forth west-

ward, my hand in my Father's, with the liveliest
anticipations. I expected to see a mountain
absolutely carpeted with primroses, a terrestrial
galaxy like that which covered the hill that led
up to Montgomery Castle in Donne's poem.
But at length, as we walked from the Chalk Farm
direction, a miserable acclivity stole into view—
surrounded, even in those days, on most sides
by houses, with its grass worn to the buff by
millions of boots, and resembling what I meant
by "the country" about as much as Poplar
resembles Paradise. We sat down on a bench
at its inglorious summit, whereupon I burst into
tears, and in a heart-rending whisper sobbed,
"Oh! Papa, let us go home!"

This was the lachrymose epoch in a career
not otherwise given to weeping, for I must tell
one more tale of tears. About this time,—the
autumn of 1855,—my parents were disturbed
more than once in the twilight, after I had been
put to bed, by shrieks from my crib. They
would rush up to my side, and find me in great
distress, but would be unable to discover the
cause of it. The fact was that I was half beside
myself with ghostly fears, increased and pointed
by the fact that there had been some daring
burglaries in our street. Our servant-maid, who
slept at the top of the house, had seen, or thought
she saw, upon a moonlight night, the figure of a
crouching man, silhouetted against the sky, slip
down from the roof and leap into her room.
She screamed, and he fled away. Moreover, as
if this were not enough for my tender nerves,

there had been committed a horrid murder, at a baker's shop just round the corner in the Caledonian Road, to which murder actuality was given to us by the fact that my Mother had been "just thinking" of getting her bread from this shop. Children, I think, were not spared the details of these affairs fifty years ago ; at least, I was not, and my nerves were a packet of spilikins.

But what made me scream o' nights was that when my Mother had tucked me up in bed, and had heard me say my prayer, and had prayed aloud on her knees at my side, and had stolen downstairs, noises immediately began in the room. There was a rustling of clothes, and a slapping of hands, and a gurgling, and a sniffing, and a trotting. These horrible muffled sounds would go on, and die away, and be resumed ; I would pray very fervently to God to save me from my enemies ; and sometimes I would go to sleep. But on other occasions, my faith and fortitude alike gave way, and I screamed "Mama ! Mama !" Then would my parents come bounding up the stairs, and comfort me, and kiss me, and assure me it was nothing. And nothing it was while they were there, but no sooner had they gone than the ghostly riot recommenced. It was at last discovered by my Mother that the whole mischief was due to a card of framed texts, fastened by one nail to the wall ; this did nothing when the bed-room door was shut, but when it was left open (in order that my parents might hear me call), the card began to gallop in the draught, and made the most intolerable noises.

Several things tended at this time to alienate my conscience from the line which my Father had so rigidly traced for it. The question of the efficacy of prayer, which has puzzled wiser heads than mine was, began to trouble me. It was insisted on in our household that if anything was desired, you should not, as my Mother said, "lose any time in seeking for it, but ask God to guide you to it." In many junctures of life, this is precisely what, in sober fact, they did. I will not dwell here on their theories, which my Mother put forth, with unflinching directness, in her published writings. But I found that a difference was made between my privileges in this matter and theirs, and this led to many discussions. My parents said : "Whatever you need, tell Him and He will grant it, if it is His will." Very well ; I had need of a large painted humming-top which I had seen in a shop-window in the Caledonian Road. Accordingly, I introduced a supplication for this object into my evening prayer, carefully adding the words : "If it is Thy will." This, I recollect, placed my Mother in a dilemma, and she consulted my Father. Taken, I suppose, at a disadvantage, my Father told me I must not pray for "things like that." To which I answered by another query, "Why?" And I added that he said we ought to pray for things we needed, and that I needed the humming-top a great deal more than I did the conversion of the heathen or the restitution of Jerusalem to the Jews, two objects of my nightly supplication which left me very cold.

I have reason to believe, looking back upon this scene, conducted by candle-light in the front parlour, that my Mother was much baffled by the logic of my argument. She had gone so far as to say publicly that no " things or circumstances are too insignificant to bring before the God of the whole earth." I persisted that this covered the case of the humming-top, which was extremely significant to me. I noticed that she held aloof from the discussion, which was carried on with some show of annoyance by my Father. He had never gone quite so far as she did in regard to this question of praying for material things. I am not sure that she was convinced that I ought to have been checked ; but he could not help seeing that it reduced their favourite theory to an absurdity for a small child to exercise the privilege. He ceased to argue, and told me peremptorily that it was not right for me to pray for things like humming-tops, and that I must do it no more. His authority, of course, was paramount, and I yielded ; but my faith in the efficacy of prayer was a good deal shaken. The fatal suspicion had crossed my mind that the reason why I was not to pray for the top was because it was too expensive for my parents to buy, that being the usual excuse for not getting things I wished for.

It was about the date of my sixth birthday that I did something very naughty, some act

of direct disobedience, for which my Father,
after a solemn sermon, chastised me, sacrificially,
by giving me several cuts with a cane. This
action was justified, as everything he did was
justified, by reference to Scripture—" Spare the
rod and spoil the child." I suppose that there
are some children, of a sullen and lymphatic
temperament, who are smartened up and made
more wide-awake by a whipping. It is largely a
matter of convention, the exercise being endured
(I am told) with pride by the infants of our
aristocracy, but not tolerated by the lower
classes. I am afraid that I proved my inherent
vulgarity by being made, not contrite or humble,
but furiously angry by this caning. I cannot
account for the flame of rage which it awakened
in my bosom. My dear, excellent Father had
beaten me, not very severely, without ill-temper,
and with the most genuine desire to improve
me. But he was not well-advised, especially so
far as the " dedication to the Lord's service "
was concerned. This same " dedication " had
ministered to my vanity, and there are some
natures which are not improved by being
humiliated. I have to confess with shame that
I went about the house for some days with a
murderous hatred of my Father locked within
my bosom. He did not suspect that the chastisement had not been wholly efficacious, and he
bore me no malice ; so that after a while, I
forgot and thus forgave him. But I do not
regard physical punishment as a wise element
in the education of proud and sensitive children.

My theological misdeeds culminated, however, in an act so puerile and preposterous that I should not venture to record it if it did not throw some glimmering of light on the subject which I have proposed to myself in writing these pages. My mind continued to dwell on the mysterious question of prayer. It puzzled me greatly to know why, if we were God's children, and if he was watching over us by night and day, we might not supplicate for toys and sweets and smart clothes as well as for the conversion of the heathen. Just at this juncture, we had a special service at the Room, at which our attention was particularly called to what we always spoke of as " the field of missionary labour." The East was represented among " the saints " by an excellent Irish peer, who had, in his early youth, converted and married a lady of colour ; this Asiatic shared in our Sunday morning meetings, and was an object of helpless terror to me ; I shrank from her amiable caresses, and vaguely identified her with a personage much spoken of in our family circle, the " Personal Devil."

All these matters drew my thoughts to the subject of idolatry, which was severely censured at the missionary meeting. I cross-examined my Father very closely as to the nature of this sin, and pinned him down to the categorical statement that idolatry consisted in praying to any one or anything but God himself. Wood and stone, in the words of the hymn, were peculiarly liable to be bowed down to by the

heathen in their blindness. I pressed my Father
further on this subject, and he assured me that
God would be very angry, and would signify His
anger, if any one, in a Christian country, bowed
down to wood and stone. I cannot recall why
I was so pertinacious on this subject, but I
remember that my Father became a little restive
under my cross-examination. I determined,
however, to test the matter for myself, and one
morning, when both my parents were safely out
of the house, I prepared for the great act of
heresy. I was in the morning-room on the
ground-floor, where, with much labour, I
hoisted a small chair on to the table close to
the window. My heart was now beating as if
it would leap out of my side, but I pursued
my experiment. I knelt down on the carpet
in front of the table and looking up I said
my daily prayer in a loud voice, only substi-
tuting the address "O Chair!" for the habitual
one.

Having carried this act of idolatry safely
through, I waited to see what would happen.
It was a fine day, and I gazed up at the slip of
white sky above the houses opposite, and expected something to appear in it. God would
certainly exhibit his anger in some terrible form,
and would chastise my impious and wilful action.
I was very much alarmed, but still more excited;
I breathed the high, sharp air of defiance. But
nothing happened; there was not a cloud in the
sky, not an unusual sound in the street. Presently I was quite sure that nothing would

happen. I had committed idolatry, flagrantly
and deliberately, and God did not care.

The result of this ridiculous act was not to
make me question the existence and power of
God ; those were forces which I did not dream
of ignoring. But what it did was to lessen still
further my confidence in my Father's knowledge
of the Divine mind. My Father had said,
positively, that if I worshipped a thing made of
wood, God would manifest his anger. I had
then worshipped a chair, made (or partly made)
of wood, and God had made no sign whatever. My Father, therefore, was not really
acquainted with the Divine practice in cases
of idolatry. And with that, dismissing the subject, I dived again into the unplumbed depths of
the " Penny Cyclopædia."

CHAPTER III

THAT I might die in my early childhood was a thought which frequently recurred to the mind of my Mother. She endeavoured, with a Roman fortitude, to face it without apprehension. Soon after I had completed my fifth year she had written as follows in her secret journal :

" Should we be called on to weep over the early grave of the dear one whom now we are endeavouring to train for heaven, may we be able to remember that we never ceased to pray for and watch over him. It is easy, comparatively, to watch over an infant. Yet shall I be sufficient for these things ? I am not. But God is sufficient. In his strength I have begun the warfare, in his strength I will persevere, and I will faint not till either I myself or my little one is beyond the reach of earthly solicitude."

That either she or I would be called away from earth, and that our physical separation was at hand, seems to have been always vaguely present in my Mother's dreams, as an obstinate conviction to be carefully recognised and jealously guarded against.

It was not, however, until the course of my seventh year, that the tragedy occurred, which altered the whole course of our family existence.

48

My Mother had hitherto seemed strong and in
good health ; she had even made the remark to
my Father, that " sorrow and pain, the badges
of Christian discipleship," appeared to be with-
held from her. On her birthday, which was to
be her last, she had written these ejaculations in
her locked diary :

" Lord, forgive the sins of the past, and help
me to be faithful in future ! May this be a
year of much blessing, a year of jubilee ! May
I be kept lowly, trusting, loving ! May I more
have blessing than in all former years combined !
May I be happier as a wife, mother, sister,
writer, mistress, friend ! "

But a symptom began to alarm her and in
the beginning of May, having consulted a local
physician without being satisfied, she went to
see a specialist in a northern suburb in whose
judgment she had great confidence. This occasion I recollect with extreme vividness. I had
been put to bed by my Father, in itself a note-
worthy event. My crib stood near a window
overlooking the street ; my parents' ancient
four-poster, a relic of the eighteenth century,
hid me from the door, but I could see the rest
of the room. After falling asleep on this particular evening, I awoke silently, surprised to
see two lighted candles on the table, and my
Father seated writing by them. I also saw a
little meal arranged.

While I was wondering at all this, the door

opened, and my Mother entered the room ; she emerged from behind the bed-curtains, with her bonnet on, having returned from her expedition. My Father rose hurriedly, pushing back his chair, and greeted her by exclaiming : " Well, what does he say ? " There was a pause, while my Mother seemed to be steadying her voice, and then she replied, loudly and distinctly, " He says it is —" and she mentioned one of the most cruel maladies by which our poor mortal nature can be tormented. Then I saw them fold one another in a silent long embrace, and presently sink together out of sight on their knees, at the further side of the bed, whereupon my Father lifted up his voice in prayer. Neither of them had noticed me, and now I lay back on my pillow and fell asleep.

Next morning, when we three sat at breakfast, my mind reverted to the scene of the previous night. With my eyes on my plate, as I was cutting up my food, I asked, casually, " What is — ? " mentioning the disease whose unfamiliar name I had heard from my bed. Receiving no reply, I looked up to discover why my question was not answered, and I saw my parents gazing at each other with lamentable eyes. In some way, I know not how, I was conscious of the presence of an incommunicable mystery, and I kept silence, though tortured with curiosity, nor did I ever repeat my inquiry.

About a fortnight later, my Mother began to go three times a week all the long way from Islington to Pimlico, in order to visit a certain

practitioner, who undertook to apply a special
treatment to her case. This involved great
fatigue and distress to her, but so far as I was
personally concerned it did me a great deal of
good. I invariably accompanied her, and when
she was very tired and weak, I enjoyed the
pride of believing that I protected her. The
movement, the exercise, the occupation, lifted
my morbid fears and superstitions like a cloud.
The medical treatment to which my poor
Mother was subjected was very painful, and
she had a peculiar sensitiveness to pain. She
carried on her evangelical work as long as she
possibly could, continuing to converse with her
fellow passengers on spiritual matters. It was
wonderful that a woman, so reserved and proud
as she by nature was, could conquer so completely her natural timidity. In those last
months, she scarcely ever got into a railway
carriage or into an omnibus, without presently
offering tracts to the persons sitting within reach
of her, or endeavouring to begin a conversation
with some one on the sufficiency of the Blood
of Jesus to cleanse the human heart from sin.
Her manners were so gentle and persuasive,
she looked so innocent, her small, sparkling
features were lighted up with so much benevolence, that I do not think she ever met with
discourtesy or roughness. Imitative imp that
I was, I sometimes took part in these strange
conversations, and was mightily puffed up by
compliments paid, in whispers, to my infant
piety. But my Mother very properly dis-

couraged this, as tending in me to spiritual pride.

If my parents, in their desire to separate themselves from the world, had regretted that through their happiness they seemed to have forfeited the Christian privilege of affliction, they could not continue to complain of any absence of temporal adversity. Everything seemed to combine, in the course of this fatal year 1856, to harass and alarm them. Just at the moment when illness created a special drain upon their resources, their slender income, instead of being increased, was seriously diminished. There is little sympathy felt in this world of rhetoric for the silent sufferings of the genteel poor, yet there is no class that deserves a more charitable commiseration.

At the best of times, the money which my parents had to spend was an exiguous and an inelastic sum. Strictly economical, proud—in an old-fashioned mode now quite out of fashion —to conceal the fact of their poverty, painfully scrupulous to avoid giving inconvenience to shop-people, tradesmen or servants, their whole financial career had to be carried on with the adroitness of a campaign through a hostile country. But now, at the moment when fresh pressing claims were made on their resources, my Mother's small capital suddenly disappeared. It had been placed, on bad advice (they were as children in such matters), in a Cornish mine, the grotesque name of which, Wheal Maria, became familiar to my ears. One day the river Tamar, in a playful mood, broke into Wheal Maria, and not a penny more was ever lifted from that unfortunate enterprise. About the same time, a small annuity which my Mother had inherited also ceased to be paid.

On my Father's books and lectures, therefore, the whole weight now rested, and that at a moment when he was depressed and unnerved by anxiety. It was contrary to his principles to borrow money, so that it became necessary to pay doctor's and chemist's bills punctually, and yet to carry on the little household with the very small margin. Each artifice of economy was now exercised to enable this to be done without falling into debt, and every branch of expenditure was cut down ; clothes, books, the little garden which was my Father's pride, all felt the pressure of new poverty. Even our food, which had always been simple, now became Spartan indeed, and I am sure that my Mother often pretended to have no appetite that there might remain enough to satisfy my hunger. Fortunately my Father was able to take us away in the autumn for six weeks by the sea in Wales, the expenses of this tour being paid for by a professional engagement, so that my seventh birthday was spent in an ecstasy of happiness, on golden sands, under a brilliant sky, and in sight of the glorious azure ocean beating in from an infinitude of melting horizons. Here, too, my Mother, perched in a nook of the high rocks, surveyed the west, and forgot for a little while her weakness and the gnawing, grinding pain.

But in October, our sorrows seemed to close

in upon us. We went back to London, and for
the first time in their married life, my parents
were divided. My Mother was now so seriously
weaker that the omnibus-journeys to Pimlico
became impossible. My Father could not leave
his work, and so my Mother and I had to take a
gloomy lodging close to the doctor's house. The
experiences upon which I presently entered were
of a nature in which childhood rarely takes a
part. I was now my Mother's sole and ceaseless
companion ; the silent witness of her suffering,
of her patience, of her vain and delusive attempts
to obtain alleviation of her anguish. For nearly
three months I breathed the atmosphere of pain,
saw no other light, heard no other sounds,
thought no other thoughts than those which
accompany physical suffering and weariness.
To my memory these weeks seem years ; I
have no measure of their monotony. The
lodgings were bare and yet tawdry ; out of
dingy windows we looked from a second storey
upon a dull small street, drowned in autumnal
fog. My Father came to see us when he could,
but otherwise, save when we made our morning
expedition to the doctor, or when a slatternly
girl waited upon us with our distasteful meals,
we were alone,—without any other occupation
than to look forward to that occasional abate-
ment of suffering which was what we hoped for
most.

It is difficult for me to recollect how these
interminable hours were spent. But I read
aloud in a great part of them. I have now in

my mind's cabinet a picture of my chair turned
towards the window, partly that I might see
the book more distinctly, partly not to see quite
so distinctly that dear patient figure rocking on
her sofa, or leaning, like a funeral statue, like a
muse upon a monument, with her head on her
arms against the mantelpiece. I read the Bible
every day, and at much length ; also,—with I
cannot but think some praiseworthy patience,—
a book of incommunicable dreariness, called
Newton's "Thoughts on the Apocalypse." Newton bore a great resemblance to my old aversion,
Jukes, and I made a sort of playful compact
with my Mother that if I read aloud a certain
number of pages out of "Thoughts on the
Apocalypse," as a reward I should be allowed
to recite "my own favourite hymns." Among
these there was one which united her suffrages
with mine. Both of us extremely admired the
piece by Toplady which begins :—

> What though my frail eyelids refuoo
> Continual watchings to keep,
> And, punctual as midnight renews,
> Demand the refreshment of sleep.

To this day, I cannot repeat this hymn without
a sense of poignant emotion, nor can I pretend
to decide how much of this is due to its merit
and how much to the peculiar nature of the
memories it recalls. But it might be as rude
as I genuinely think it to be skilful, and I should
continue to regard it as a sacred poem. Among
all my childish memories none is clearer than

my looking up,—after reading, in my high
treble,

> Kind Author and Ground of my hope,
> Thee, Thee for my God I avow ;
> My glad Ebenezer set up,
> And own Thou hast help'd me till now ;
> I muse on the years that are past,
> Wherein my defence Thou hast prov'd,
> Nor wilt Thou relinquish at last
> A sinner so signally lov'd,—

and hearing my Mother, her eyes brimming with
tears and her alabastrine fingers tightly locked
together, murmur in unconscious repetition :

> Nor wilt Thou relinquish at last
> A sinner so signally lov'd.

In our lodgings at Pimlico I came across a
piece of verse which exercised a lasting influence
on my taste. It was called " The Cameronian's
Dream,'' and it had been written by a certain
James Hyslop, a schoolmaster on a man-of-war.
I do not know how it came into my possession,
but I remember it was adorned by an extremely
dim and ill-executed wood-cut of a lake surrounded by mountains, with tombstones in the
foreground. This lugubrious frontispiece positively fascinated me, and lent a further gloomy
charm to the ballad itself. It was in this copy
of mediocre verses that the sense of romance
first appealed to me, the kind of nature-romance
which is connected with hills, and lakes, and
the picturesque costumes of old times. The
following stanza, for instance, brought a revelation to me :

'Twas a dream of those ages of darkness and blood,
When the minister's home was the mountain and wood ;
When in Wellwood's dark valley the standard of Zion,
All bloody and torn, 'mong the heather was lying.

I persuaded my Mother to explain to me
what it was all about, and she told me of the
affliction of the Scottish saints, their flight to
the waters and the wilderness, their cruel
murder while they were singing "their last
song to the God of Salvation." I was greatly
fired, and the following stanza, in particular,
reached my ideal of the Sublime :

The muskets were flashing, the blue swords were gleaming,
The helmets were cleft, and the red blood was streaming,
The heavens grew dark, and the thunder was rolling,
When in Wellwood's dark muirlands the mighty were falling.

Twenty years later I met with the only
other person whom I have ever encountered
who had even heard of "The Cameronian's
Dream." This was Robert Louis Stevenson,
who had been greatly struck by it when he was
about my age. Probably the same ephemeral
edition of it reached, at the same time, each
of our pious households.

As my Mother's illness progressed, she could
neither sleep, save by the use of opiates, nor
rest, except in a sloping posture, propped
up by many pillows. It was my great joy,
and a pleasant diversion, to be allowed to
shift, beat up, and rearrange these pillows, a
task which I learned to accomplish not too
awkwardly. Her sufferings, I believe, were

c

principally caused by the violence of the medicaments to which her doctor, who was trying a new and fantastic " cure," thought it proper to subject her. Let those who take a pessimistic view of our social progress ask themselves whether such tortures could to-day be inflicted on a delicate patient, or whether that patient would be allowed to exist, in the greatest misery, in a lodging with no professional nurse to wait upon her, and with no companion but a little helpless boy of seven years of age. Time passes smoothly and swiftly, and we do not perceive the mitigations which he brings in his hands. Everywhere, in the whole system of human life, improvements, alleviations, ingenious appliances and humane inventions are being introduced to lessen the great burden of suffering.

If we were suddenly transplanted into the world of only fifty years ago, we should be startled and even horror-stricken by the wretchedness to which the step backwards would re-introduce us. It was in the very year of which I am speaking, a year of which my personal memories are still vivid, that Sir James Simpson received the Monthyon prize as a recognition of his discovery of the use of anæsthetics. Can our thoughts embrace the mitigation of human torment which the application of chloroform alone has caused? My early experiences, I confess, made me singularly conscious, at an age when one should know nothing about these things, of

that torrent of sorrow and anguish and terror
which flows under all the footsteps of man.
Within my childish conscience, already, some
dim inquiry was awake as to the meaning of
this mystery of pain—

> The floods of the tears meet and gather ;
> The sound of them all grows like thunder ;
> O into what bosom, I wonder,
> Is poured the whole sorrow of years ?
> For Eternity only seems keeping
> Account of the great human weeping ;
> May God then, the Maker and Father,
> May He find a place for the tears !

In my Mother's case, the savage treatment
did no good ; it had to be abandoned, and a
day or two before Christmas, while the fruits
were piled in the shop-fronts and the butchers
were shouting outside their forests of carcases,
my Father brought us back in a cab through
the streets to Islington, a feeble and languish-
ing company. Our invalid bore the journey
fairly well, enjoying the air, and pointing out
to me the glittering evidences of the season,
but we paid heavily for her little entertainment,
since, at her earnest wish the window of the
cab having been kept open, she caught a cold,
which became, indeed, the technical cause of a
death that no applications could now have long
delayed.

Yet she lingered with us six weeks more,
and during this time I again relapsed, very
naturally, into solitude. She now had the
care of a practised woman, one of the '' saints ''

from the Chapel, and I was only permitted to pay brief visits to her bedside. That I might not be kept indoors all day and every day, a man, also connected with the meeting-house, was paid a trifle to take me out for a walk each morning. This person, who was by turns familiar and truculent, was the object of my intense dislike. Our relations became, in the truest sense, "forced"; I was obliged to walk by his side, but I held that I had no further responsibility to be agreeable, and after a while I ceased to speak to him, or to answer his remarks. On one occasion, poor dreary man, he met a friend and stopped to chat with him. I considered this act to have dissolved the bond; I skipped lightly from his side, examined several shop-windows which I had been forbidden to look into, made several darts down courts and up passages, and finally, after a delightful morning, returned home, having known my directions perfectly. My official conductor, in a shocking condition of fear, was crouching by the area-rails looking up and down the street. He darted upon me, in a great rage, to know "what I meant by it?" I drew myself up as tall as I could, hissed "Blind leader of the blind!" at him, and, with this inappropriate (but very effective) Parthian shot, slipped into the house.

When it was quite certain that no alleviations and no medical care could prevent, or even any longer postpone, the departure of my Mother, I believe that my future conduct be-

came the object of her greatest and her most
painful solicitude. She said to my Father that
the worst trial of her faith came from the
feeling that she was called upon to leave that
child whom she had so carefully trained from
his earliest infancy for the peculiar service of
the Lord, without any knowledge of what his
further course would be. In many conversations, she most tenderly and closely urged my
Father, who, however, needed no urging, to
watch with unceasing care over my spiritual
welfare. As she grew nearer her end, it was
observed that she became calmer, and less
troubled by fears about me. The intensity of
her prayers and hopes seemed to have a pre-
vailing force ; it would have been a sin to doubt
that such supplications, such confidence and
devotion, such an emphasis of will, should not
be rewarded by an answer from above in the
affirmative. She was able, she said, to leave
me " in the hands of her loving Lord," or, on
another occasion, " to the care of her covenant
God."

Although her faith was so strong and simple,
my Mother possessed no quality of the mystic.
She never pretended to any visionary gifts,
believed not at all in dreams or portents, and
encouraged nothing in herself or others which
was superstitious or fantastic. In order to
realise her condition of mind, it is necessary, I
think, to accept the view that she had formed
a definite conception of the absolute, unmodi-
fied and historical veracity, in its direct and

obvious sense, of every statement contained within the covers of the Bible. For her, and for my Father, nothing was symbolic, nothing allegorical or allusive in any part of Scripture, except what was, in so many words, proffered as a parable or a picture. Pushing this to its extreme limit, and allowing nothing for the changes of scene or time or race, my parents read injunctions to the Corinthian converts without any suspicion that what was apposite in dealing with half-breed Achaian colonists of the first century might not exactly apply to respectable English men and women of the nineteenth. They took it, text by text, as if no sort of difference existed between the surroundings of Trimalchion's feast and those of a City dinner. Both my parents, I think, were devoid of sympathetic imagination ; in my Father, I am sure, it was singularly absent. Hence, although their faith was so strenuous that many persons might have called it fanatical, there was no mysticism about them. They went rather to the opposite extreme, to the cultivation of a rigid and iconoclastic literalness.

This was curiously exemplified in the very lively interest which they both took in what is called " the interpretation of prophecy," and particularly in unwrapping the dark sayings bound up in the Book of Revelation. In their impartial survey of the Bible, they came to this collection of solemn and splendid visions, sinister and obscure, and they had no intention

of allowing these to be merely stimulating to
the fancy, or vaguely doctrinal in symbol.
When they read of seals broken and of vials
poured forth, of the star which was called
Wormwood that fell from Heaven, and of
men whose hair was as the hair of women and
their teeth as the teeth of lions, they did not
admit for a moment that these vivid mental
pictures were of a poetic character, but they
regarded them as positive statements, in
guarded language, describing events which were
to happen, and could be recognised when
they did happen. It was the explanation, the
perfectly prosaic and positive explanation, of
all these wonders which drew them to study
the Habershons and the Newtons whose books
they so much enjoyed. They were helped by
these guides to recognise in wild Oriental
visions direct statements regarding Napoleon
III. and Pope Pius IX. and the King of Pied-
mont, historic figures which they conceived
as foreshadowed, in language which admitted
of plain interpretation, under the names of
denizens of Babylon and companions of the
Wild Beast.

My Father was in the habit of saying, in
later years, that no small element in his
wedded happiness had been the fact that my
Mother and he were of one mind in the
interpretation of Sacred Prophecy. Looking
back, it appears to me that this unusual mental
exercise was almost their only relaxation, and
that in their economy it took the place which

is taken, in profaner families, by cards or the
piano. It was a distraction ; it took them
completely out of themselves. During those
melancholy weeks at Pimlico, I read aloud
another work of the same nature as those of
Habershon and Jukes, the "Horæ Apocalyp-
ticæ" of a Mr. Elliott. This was written, I
think, in a less disagreeable style, and certainly
it was less opaquely obscure to me. My recollection distinctly is that when my Mother
could endure nothing else, the arguments of
this book took her thoughts away from her
pain and lifted her spirits. Elliott saw "the
queenly arrogance of Popery" everywhere, and
believed that the very last days of Babylon
the Great were come. Lest I say what may
be thought extravagant, let me quote what
my Father wrote in his diary at the time of my
Mother's death. He said that the thought
that Rome was doomed (as seemed not
impossible in 1857) so affected my Mother
that it "irradiated her dying hours with an
assurance that was like the light of the Morning
Star, the harbinger of the rising sun."

After our return to Islington, there was a
complete change in my relation to my Mother.
At Pimlico, I had been all-important, her only
companion, her friend, her confidant. But
now that she was at home again, people and
things combined to separate me from her.
Now, and for the first time in my life, I no
longer slept in her room, no longer sank to
sleep under her kiss, no longer saw her mild

eyes smile on me with the earliest sunshine.
Twice a day, after breakfast and before I went
to rest, I was brought to her bedside ; but we
were never alone, other people, sometimes
strange people, were there. We had no cosy
talk ; often she was too weak to do more than
pat my hand : her loud and almost constant
cough terrified and harassed me. I felt, as I
stood, awkwardly and shyly, by her high bed,
that I had shrunken into a very small and insignificant figure, that she was floating out of
my reach, that all things, but I knew not what
nor how, were coming to an end. She herself
was not herself ; her head, that used to be held
so erect, now rolled or sank upon the pillow ;
the sparkle was all extinguished from those
bright, dear eyes. I could not understand it;
I meditated long, long upon it all in my infantile darkness, in the garret, or in the little
slip of a cold room where my bed was now
placed ; and a great, blind anger against I knew
not what awakened in my soul.

The two retreats which I have mentioned
were now all that were left to me. In the back-
parlour some one from outside gave me occasional lessons, of a desultory character. The
breakfast-room was often haunted by visitors,
unknown to me by face or name,—ladies, who
used to pity me and even to pet me, until I
became nimble in escaping from their caresses.
Everything seemed to be unfixed, uncertain ; it
was like being on the platform of a railway-
station waiting for a train. In all this time,

the agitated, nervous presence of my Father,
whose pale face was permanently drawn with
anxiety, added to my perturbation, and I became miserable, stupid, as if I had lost my
way in a cold fog.

Had I been older and more intelligent, of
course, it might have been of him and not of
myself that I should have been thinking. As
I now look back upon that tragic time, it is for
him that my heart bleeds,—for them both, so
singularly fitted as they were to support and
cheer one another in an existence which their
own innate and cultivated characteristics had
made little hospitable to other sources of
comfort. This is not to be dwelt on here.
But what must be recorded was the extraordinary tranquillity, the serene and sensible
resignation, with which at length my parents
faced the awful hour. Language cannot utter
what they suffered, but there was no rebellion,
no repining ; in their case even an atheist
might admit that the overpowering miracle of
grace was mightily efficient.

It seems almost cruel to the memory of their
opinions that the only words which rise to my
mind, the only ones which seem in the least
degree adequate to describe the attitude of my
parents, had fallen from the pen of one whom,
in their want of imaginative sympathy, they
had regarded as anathema. But John Henry
Newman might have come from the contemplation of my Mother's death-bed when he wrote :
" All the trouble which the world inflicts upon

us, and which flesh cannot but feel,—sorrow, pain, care, bereavement,—these avail not to disturb the tranquillity and the intensity with which faith gazes at the Divine Majesty." It was "tranquillity," it was not the rapture of the mystic. Almost in the last hour of her life, urged to confess her "joy" in the Lord, my Mother, rigidly honest, meticulous in self-analysis, as ever, replied : "I have peace, but not *joy*. It would not do to go into eternity with a lie in my mouth."

When the very end approached, and her mind was growing clouded, she gathered her strength together to say to my Father, "I shall walk with Him in white. Won't you take your lamb and walk with me ?" Confused with sorrow and alarm, my Father failed to understand her meaning. She became agitated, and she repeated two or three times : "Take our lamb, and walk with me !" Then my Father comprehended, and pressed me forward ; her hand fell softly upon mine and she seemed content. Thus was my dedication, that had begun in my cradle, sealed with the most solemn, the most poignant and irresistible insistence, at the death-bed of the holiest and purest of women. But what a weight, intolerable as the burden of Atlas, to lay on the shoulders of a little fragile child !

CHAPTER IV

CERTAINLY the preceding year, the seventh of my life, had been weighted for us with comprehensive disaster. I have not yet mentioned that, at the beginning of my Mother's fatal illness, misfortune came upon her brothers. I have never known the particulars of their ruin, but, I believe in consequence of A.'s unsuccessful speculations, and of the fact that E. had allowed the use of his name as a surety, both my uncles were obliged to fly from their creditors, and take refuge in Paris. This happened just when our need was the sorest, and this, together with the poignancy of knowing that their sister's devoted labours for them had been all in vain, added to their unhappiness. It was doubtless also the reason why, having left England, they wrote to us no more, carefully concealing from us even their address, so that when my Mother died, my Father was unable to communicate with them. I fear that they fell into dire distress ; before very long we learned that A. had died, but it was fifteen years more before we heard anything of E., whose life had at length been preserved by the kindness of an old servant, but whose mind was now so clouded that he could recollect little or nothing of the past ; and soon he also died. Amiable, gentle, without any species of practical ability, they were quite unfitted to struggle with the world, which had touched them only to wreck them.

The flight of my uncles at this particular juncture left me without a relative on my Mother's side at the time of her death. This isolation threw my Father into a sad perplexity. His only obvious source of income—but it happened to be a remarkably hopeful one—was an engagement to deliver a long series of lectures on marine natural history throughout the north and centre of England. These lectures were an entire novelty ; nothing like them had been offered to the provincial public before ; and the fact that the newly-invented marine aquarium was the fashionable toy of the moment added to their attraction. My Father was bowed down by sorrow and care, but he was not broken. His intellectual forces were at their height, and so was his popularity as an author. The lectures were to begin in March ; my Mother was buried on the 13th of February. It seemed at first, in the inertia of bereavement, to be all beyond his powers to make the supreme effort, but the wholesome prick of need urged him on. It was a question of paying for food and clothes, of keeping a roof above our heads. The captain of a vessel in a storm must navigate his ship, although his wife lies dead in the cabin. That was my Father's position in the spring of 1857; he had to stimulate, instruct, amuse large audiences of strangers, and seem gay, although affliction and loneliness had settled in his heart. He had to do this, or starve.

But the difficulty still remained. During these months what was to become of me? My Father could not take me with him from hotel to hotel and from lecture-hall to lecture-hall. Nor could he leave me, as people leave the domestic cat, in an empty house for the neighbours to feed at intervals. The dilemma threatened to be insurmountable, when suddenly there descended upon us a kind, but little-known, paternal cousin from the west of England, who had heard of our calamities. This lady had a large family of her own at Bristol; she offered to find room in it for me so long as ever my Father should be away in the north, and when my Father, bewildered by so much goodness, hesitated, she came up to London and carried me forcibly away in a whirlwind of good-nature. Her benevolence was quite spontaneous; and I am not sure that she had not added to it already by helping to nurse our beloved sufferer through part of her illness. Of that I am not positive, but I recollect very clearly her snatching me from our cold and desolate hearthstone, and carrying me off to her cheerful house at Clifton.

Here, for the first time, when half through my eighth year, I was thrown into the society of young people. My cousins were none of them, I believe, any longer children, but they were youths and maidens busily engaged in

various personal interests, all collected in a hive
of wholesome family energy. Everybody was
very kind to me, and I sank back, after the
strain of so many months, into mere childhood again. This long visit to my cousins at
Clifton must have been very delightful : I am
dimly aware that it was : yet I remember but
few of its incidents. My memory, so clear
and vivid about earlier solitary times, now in
all this society becomes blurred and vague.
I recollect certain pleasures ; being taken, for
instance, to a menagerie, and having a practical joke, in the worst taste, played upon me
by the pelican. One of my cousins, who was
a medical student, showed me a pistol, and
helped me to fire it ; he smoked a pipe, and I
was oddly conscious that both the firearm and
the tobacco were definitely hostile to my " dedication." My girl-cousins took turns in putting
me to bed, and on cold nights, or when they
were in a hurry, allowed me to say my
prayer under the bed-clothes instead of
kneeling at a chair. The result of this was
further spiritual laxity, because I could not
help going to sleep before the prayer was
ended.

The visit to Clifton was, in fact, a blessed
interval in my strenuous childhood. It probably prevented my nerves from breaking down
under the pressure of the previous months.
The Clifton family was God-fearing, in a quiet,
sensible way, but there was a total absence
of all the intensity and compulsion of our

religious life at Islington. I was not encouraged—I even remember that I was gently
snubbed—when I rattled forth, parrot-fashion,
the conventional phraseology of "the saints."
For a short, enchanting period of respite, I
lived the life of an ordinary little boy, relaps-
ing, to a degree which would have filled my
Father with despair, into childish thoughts
and childish language. The result was that
of this little happy breathing-space I have
nothing to report. Vague, half-blind remem-
brances of walks, with my tall cousins waving
like trees above me, pleasant noisy evenings
in a great room on the ground-floor, faint
silver-points of excursions into the country, all
this is the very pale and shadowy testimony
to a brief interval of healthy, happy child-life,
when my hard-driven soul was allowed to have,
for a little while, no history.

The life of a child is so brief, its impressions
are so illusory and fugitive, that it is as difficult
to record its history as it would be to design
a morning cloud sailing before the wind. It
is short, as we count shortness in after years,
when the drag of lead pulls down to earth
the foot that used to flutter with a winged
impetuosity, and to float with the pulse of
Hermes. But in memory, my childhood was
long, long with interminable hours, hours with
the pale cheek pressed against the window-
pane, hours of mechanical and repeated lonely
"games," which had lost their savour, and
were kept going by sheer inertness. Not un-

happy, not fretful, but long,—long, long. It
seems to me, as I look back to the life in
the motherless Islington house, as I resumed
it in that slow eighth year of my life, that
time had ceased to move. There was a
whole age between one tick of the eight-
day clock in the hall, and the next tick.
When the milkman went his rounds in our
grey street, with his eldritch scream over the
top of each set of area railings, it seemed as
though he would never disappear again. There
was no past and no future for me, and the
present felt as though it were sealed up in
a Leyden jar. Even my dreams were interminable, and hung stationary from the nightly
sky.

At this time, the street was my theatre,
and I spent long periods, as I have said, leaning against the window. I feel now the
coldness of the pane, and the feverish heat
that was produced, by contrast, in the orbit
round the eye. Now and then amusing things
happened. The onion-man was a joy long
waited for. This worthy was a tall and bony
Jersey protestant with a raucous voice, who
strode up our street several times a week,
carrying a yoke across his shoulders, from the
ends of which hung ropes of onions. He used
to shout, at abrupt intervals, in a tone which
might wake the dead :

> Here's your rope. . . .
> To hang the Pope. . . .
> And a penn'orth of cheese to choke him.

The cheese appeared to be legendary; he sold only onions. My Father did not eat onions, but he encouraged this terrible fellow, with his wild eyes and long strips of hair, because of his "godly attitude towards the Papacy," and I used to watch him dart out of the front door, present his penny, and retire, graciously waving back the proffered onion. On the other hand, my Father did not approve of a fat sailor, who was a constant passer-by. This man, who was probably crazed, used to walk very slowly up the centre of our street, vociferating with the voice of a bull,

Wa-a-atch and pray-hay!
Night and day-hay!

This melancholy admonition was the entire business of his life. He did nothing at all but walk up and down the streets of Islington exhorting the inhabitants to watch and pray. I do not recollect that this sailor-man stopped to collect pennies, and my impression is that he was, after his fashion, a volunteer evangelist.

The tragedy of Mr. Punch was another, and a still greater delight. I was never allowed to go out into the street to mingle with the little crowd which gathered under the stage, and as I was extremely near-sighted, the impression I received was vague. But when, by happy chance, the show stopped opposite our door, I saw enough of that ancient drama to be thrilled with terror and delight. I was much affected by the internal troubles of the Punch family;

I thought that with a little more tact on the part of Mrs. Punch and some restraint held over a temper, naturally violent, by Mr. Punch, a great deal of this sad misunderstanding might have been prevented.

The momentous close, when a figure of shapeless horror appears on the stage, and quells the hitherto undaunted Mr. Punch, was to me the bouquet of the entire performance. When Mr. Punch, losing his nerve, points to this shape and says in an awestruck, squeaking whisper, " Who's that ? Is it the butcher ? " and the stern answer comes, " No, Mr. Punch ! " And then, " Is it the baker ? " " No, Mr. Punch ! " " Who is it then ? " (this in a squeak trembling with emotion and terror) ; and then the full, loud reply, booming like a judgment-bell, " It is the Devil come to take you down to Hell," and the form of Punch, with kicking legs, sunken in epilepsy on the floor,—all this was solemn and exquisite to me beyond words. I was not amused—I was deeply moved and exhilarated, " purged," as the old phrase hath it, " with pity and terror."

Another joy, in a lighter key, was watching a fantastic old man who came slowly up the street, hung about with drums and flutes and kites and coloured balls, and bearing over his shoulders a great sack. Children and servant-girls used to bolt up out of areas, and chaffer with this gaudy person, who would presently trudge on, always repeating the same set of words—

Here's your toys
For girls and boys,
For bits of brass
And broken glass,

(these four lines being spoken in a breathless hurry)

A penny or a vial-bottèll. . . .

(this being drawled out in an endless wail).

I was not permitted to go forth and trade with this old person, but sometimes our servant-maid did; thereby making me feel that if I did not hold the rose of merchandise, I was very near it. My experiences with my cousins at Clifton had given me the habit of looking out into the world,—even though it was only into the pale world of our quiet street.

My Father and I were now great friends. I do not doubt that he felt his responsibility to fill as far as might be the gap which the death of my Mother had made in my existence. I spent a large portion of my time in his study, while he was writing or drawing, and though very little conversation passed between us, I think that each enjoyed the companionship of the other. There were two, and sometimes three aquaria in the room, tanks of sea-water, with glass sides, inside which all sorts of creatures crawled and swam ; these were sources of end-less pleasure to me, and at this time began to be laid upon me the occasional task of watching and afterwards reporting the habits of animals.

At other times, I dragged a folio volume of the " Penny Cyclopædia " up to the study with me, and sat there reading successive articles on such subjects as Parrots, Parthians, Passion-flowers, Passover and Pastry, without any invidious preferences, all information being equally welcome, and equally fugitive. That something of all this loose stream of knowledge clung to odd cells of the back of my brain seems to be shown by the fact that to this day, I occasionally find myself aware of some stray useless fact about peonies or pemmican or pepper, which I can only trace back to the " Penny Cyclopædia " of my infancy.

It will be asked what the attitude of my Father's mind was to me, and of mine to his, as regards religion, at this time, when we were thrown together alone so much. It is difficult to reply with exactitude. But so far as the former is concerned, I think that the extreme violence of the spiritual emotions to which my Father had been subjected, had now been followed by a certain reaction. He had not changed his views in any respect, and he was prepared to work out the results of them with greater zeal than ever, but just at present his religious nature, like his physical nature, was tired out with anxiety and sorrow. He accepted the supposition that I was entirely with him in all respects, so far, that is to say, as a being so rudimentary and feeble as a little child could be. My Mother, in her last hours, had dwelt on our unity in God ; we were drawn together, she said, elect from the world, in a

triplicity of faith and joy. She had constantly
repeated the words : " We shall be one family,
one song. One Song ! one Family ! " My
Father, I think, accepted this as a prophecy,
he felt no doubt of our triple unity ; my Mother
had now merely passed before us, through
a door, into a world of light, where we should
presently join her, where all things would
be radiant and blissful, but where we three
would, in some unknown way, be particularly
drawn together in a tie of inexpressible be-
atitude. He fretted at the delay ; he would
fain have taken me by the hand, and have
joined her in the realms of holiness and light,
at once, without this dreary dalliance with
earthly cares.

He held this confidence and vision steadily
before him, but nothing availed against the
melancholy of his natural state. He was
conscious of his dull and solitary condition,
and he saw, too, that it enveloped me. I
think his heart was, at this time, drawn
out towards me in an immense tenderness.
Sometimes, when the early twilight descended
upon us in the study, and he could no longer
peer with advantage into the depths of his
microscope, he would beckon me to him silently,
and fold me closely in his arms. I used to
turn my face up to his, patiently and wonder-
ingly, while the large, unwilling tears gathered
in the corners of his eyelids. My training
had given me a preternatural faculty of stillness,
and we would stay so, without a word or a

movement, until the darkness filled the room.
And then, with my little hand in his, we would
walk sedately downstairs, to the parlour, where
we would find that the lamp was lighted, and
that our melancholy vigil was ended. I do
not think that at any part of our lives my Father
and I were drawn so close to one another
as we were in that summer of 1857. Yet we
seldom spoke of what lay so warm and fragrant
between us, the flower-like thought of our
Departed.

The visit to my cousins had made one considerable change in me. Under the old solitary
discipline, my intelligence had grown at the
expense of my sentiment. I was innocent,
but inhuman. The long suffering and the
death of my Mother had awakened my heart,
had taught me what pain was, but had left
me savage and morose. I had still no idea
of the relations of human beings to one another ;
I had learned no word of that philosophy which
comes to the children of the poor in the struggle
of the street and to the children of the well-
to-do in the clash of the nursery. In other
words, I had no humanity ; I had been carefully shielded from the chance of " catching "
it, as though it were the most dangerous of
microbes. But now that I had enjoyed a little
of the common experience of childhood, a
great change had come upon me. Before I went
to Clifton, my mental life was all interior, a rack
of baseless dream upon dream. But, now, I
was eager to look out of window, to go out in

the streets ; I was taken with a curiosity about
human life. Even, from my vantage of the
window-pane, I watched boys and girls go by
with an interest which began to be almost
wistful.

Still I continued to have no young companions. But on summer evenings I used to
drag my Father out, taking the initiative myself, stamping in playful impatience at his
irresolution, fetching his hat and stick, and
waiting. We used to sally forth at last
together, hand in hand, descending the Caledonian Road, with all its shops, as far as
Mother Shipton, or else winding among the
semi-genteel squares and terraces westward by
Copenhagen Street, or, best of all, mounting to
the Regent's Canal, where we paused to lean
over the bridge and watch flotillas of ducks
steer under us, or little white dogs dash, im-
potently furious, from stem to stern of the
great, lazy barges painted in a crude vehemence
of vermilion and azure. These were happy
hours, when the spectre of Religion ceased to
overshadow us for a little while, when my
Father forgot the Apocalypse and dropped his
austere phraseology, and when our bass and
treble voices used to ring out together over
some foolish little jest or some mirthful recollection of his past experiences. Little soft
oases these, in the hard desert of our sandy
spiritual life at home.

There was an unbending, too, when we used
to sing together, in my case very tunelessly.

I had inherited a plentiful lack of musical
genius from my Mother, who had neither ear
nor voice, and who had said, in the course of
her last illness, "I shall sing His praise, *at
length,* in strains I never could master here
below." My Father, on the other hand, had
some knowledge of the principles of vocal
music, although not, I am afraid, much taste.
He had at least great fondness for singing
hymns, in the manner then popular with the
Evangelicals, very loudly, and so slowly that I
used to count how many words I could read
silently, between one syllable of the singing
and another. My lack of skill did not prevent
me from being zealous at these vocal exercises,
and my Father and I used to sing lustily together.
The Wesleys, Charlotte Elliott ("Just as I
am, without one plea"), and James Montgomery ("For ever with the Lord") represented his predilection in hymnology. I ac-
quiesced, although that would not have been
my independent choice. These represented the
devotional verse which made its direct appeal
to the evangelical mind, and served in those
"Puseyite" days to counteract the High Church
poetry founded on "The Christian Year." Of
that famous volume I never met with a copy
until I was grown up, and equally unknown
in our circle were the hymns of Newman, Faber
and Neale.

It was my Father's plan from the first to
keep me entirely ignorant of the poetry of
the High Church, which deeply offended his

Calvinism ; he thought that religious truth could be sucked in, like mother's milk, from hymns which were godly and sound, and yet correctly versified ; and I was therefore carefully trained in this direction from an early date. But my spirit had rebelled against some of these hymns, especially against those written —a mighty multitude—by Horatius Bonar ; naughtily refusing to read Bonar's " I heard the voice of Jesus say " to my Mother in our Pimlico lodgings. A secret hostility to this particular form of effusion was already, at the age of seven, beginning to define itself in my brain, side by side with an unctuous infantile conformity.

I find a difficulty in recalling the precise nature of the religious instruction which my Father gave me at this time. It was incessant, and it was founded on the close inspection of the Bible, particularly of the epistles of the New Testament. This summer, as my eighth year advanced, we read the " Epistle to the Hebrews," with very great deliberation, stopping every moment, that my Father might expound it, verse by verse. The extraordinary beauty of the language,—for instance, the matchless cadences and images of the first chapter,—made a certain impression upon my imagination, and were (I think) my earliest initiation into the magic of literature. I was incapable of defining what I felt, but I certainly had a grip in the throat, which was in its essence a purely æsthetic emotion, when

my Father read, in his pure, large, ringing
voice, such passages as " The heavens are
the works of Thy hands. They shall perish,
but Thou remainest, and they all shall wax old
as doth a garment, and as a vesture shalt Thou
fold them up, and they shall be changed ; but
Thou art the same, and Thy years shall not
fail." But the dialectic parts of the Epistle
puzzled and confused me. Such metaphysical
ideas as " laying again the foundation of repentance from dead works " and " crucifying
the Son of God afresh " were not successfully
brought down to the level of my understanding.

My Father's religious teaching to me was
almost exclusively doctrinal. He did not observe
the value of negative education, that is to
say, of leaving Nature alone to fill up the gaps
which it is her design to deal with at a later
and riper date. He did not, even, satisfy
himself with those moral injunctions which
should form the basis of infantile discipline.
He was in a tremendous hurry to push on my
spiritual growth, and he fed me with theological meat which it was impossible for me to
digest. Some glimmer of a suspicion that he
was sailing on the wrong tack must, I should
suppose, have broken in upon him when we
had reached the eighth and ninth chapters of
Hebrews, where, addressing readers who had
been brought up under the Jewish dispensa-
tion, and had the formalities of the Law of
Moses in their very blood, the apostle battles
with their dangerous conservatism. It is a very

noble piece of spiritual casuistry, but it is
signally unfitted for the comprehension of a
child.   Suddenly, by my flushing up with
anger and saying, " O how I do hate that Law,"
my Father perceived, and paused in amazement to perceive, that I took the Law to be a
person of malignant temper from whose cruel
bondage, and from whose intolerable tyranny
and unfairness, some excellent person was crying
out to be delivered.   I wished to hit Law with
my fist, for being so mean and unreasonable.

Upon this, of course, it was necessary to
reopen the whole line of exposition.   My Father,
without realising it, had been talking on his
own level, not on mine, and now he condescended
to me.   But without very great success.   The
melodious   language,   the   divine   forensic
audacities, the magnificent ebb and flow of
argument which make the " Epistle to the
Hebrews " such a miracle, were far and away
beyond my reach, and they only bewildered me.
Some evangelical children of my generation, I
understand, were brought up on a work called
" Line upon Line : Here a Little, and there a
Little."   My Father's ambition would not sub-
mit to anything suggested by such a title as
that, and he committed, from his own point
of view, a fatal mistake when he sought to
build spires and battlements without having been
at the pains to settle a foundation beneath them.

We were not always reading the " Epistle to
the Hebrews," however ; not always was my
flesh being made to creep by having it insisted

upon that " almost all things are by the Law
purged with blood, and without blood is no
remission of sin." In our lighter moods, we
turned to the " Book of Revelation," and
chased the phantom of Popery through its
fuliginous pages. My Father, I think, missed
my Mother's company almost more acutely in
his researches into prophecy than in anything
else. This had been their unceasing recreation,
and no third person could possibly follow the
curious path which they had hewn for themselves through this jungle of symbols. But,
more and more, my Father persuaded himself
that I, too, was initiated, and by degrees I
was made to share in all his speculations and
interpretations.

Hand in hand we investigated the number
of the Beast, which number is six hundred
three score and six. Hand in hand we
inspected the nations, to see whether they
had the mark of Babylon in their foreheads. Hand in hand we watched the spirits
of devils gathering the kings of the earth into
the place which is called in the Hebrew
tongue Armageddon. Our unity in these
excursions was so delightful, that my Father
was lulled in any suspicion he might have
formed that I did not quite understand what
it was all about. Nor could he have desired a
pupil more docile or more ardent than I was in
my flaming denunciations of the Papacy.

If there was one institution more than another
which, at this early stage of my history, I

loathed and feared, it was what we invariably
spoke of as "the so-called Church of Rome."
In later years, I have met with stout Protestants,
gallant "Down-with-the-Pope" men from
County Antrim, and ladies who see the hand of
the Jesuits in every public and private misfortune. It is the habit of a loose and indifferent age to consider this dwindling body
of enthusiasts with suspicion, and to regard
their attitude towards Rome as illiberal. But
my own feeling is that they are all too mild,
that their denunciations err on the side of the
anodyne. I have no longer the slightest wish
myself to denounce the Roman communion,
but, if it is to be done, I have an idea that the
latter-day Protestants do not know how to do
it. In Lord Chesterfield's phrase, these anti-
Pope men "don't understand their own silly business." They make concessions and allowances,
they put on gloves to touch the accursed thing.

Not thus did we approach the Scarlet Woman
in the 'fifties. We palliated nothing, we believed in no good intentions, we used (I myself
used, in my tender innocency) language of the
seventeenth century such as is now no longer
introduced into any species of controversy. As
a little boy, when I thought, with intense
vagueness, of the Pope, I used to shut my
eyes tight and clench my fists. We welcomed
any social disorder in any part of Italy, as
likely to be annoying to the Papacy. If there
was a custom-house officer stabbed in a fracas
at Sassari, we gave loud thanks that liberty

and light were breaking in upon Sardinia. If there was an unsuccessful attempt to murder the Grand Duke, we lifted up our voices to celebrate the faith and sufferings of the dear persecuted Tuscans, and the record of some apocryphal monstrosity in Naples would only reveal to us a glorious opening for Gospel energy. My Father celebrated the announcement in the newspapers of a considerable emigration from the Papal Dominions, by rejoicing at '' this outcrowding of many, throughout the harlot's domain, from her sins and her plagues.'';

No, the Protestant League may consider itself to be an earnest and active body, but I can never look upon its efforts as anything but lukewarm, standing, as I do, with the light of other days around me. As a child, whatever I might question, I never doubted the turpitude of Rome. I do not think I had formed any idea whatever of the character or pretensions or practices of the Catholic Church, or indeed of what it consisted, or its nature, but I regarded it with a vague terror as a wild beast, the only good point about it being that it was very old and was soon to die. When I turned to Jukes or Newton for further detail, I could not understand what they said. Perhaps, on the whole, there was no disadvantage in that.

It is possible that some one may have observed to my Father that the conditions of our life were unfavourable to our health, although I hardly think that he would have encouraged any such advice. As I look back upon this

far-away time, I am surprised at the absence
in it of any figures but our own. He and I
together, now in the study among the sea-
anemones and star-fishes ; now on the canal-
bridge, looking down at the ducks ; now at our
hard little meals, served up as those of a dreamy
widower are likely to be when one maid-of-all-
work provides them, now under the lamp at
the maps we both loved so much, this is what
I see :—no third presence is ever with us.
Whether it occurred to himself that such a
solitude *à deux* was excellent, in the long
run, for neither of us, or whether any chance
visitor or one of the " Saints," who used to see
me at the Room every Sunday morning, suggested that a female influence might put a little
rose-colour into my pasty cheeks, I know not.
All I am sure of is that one day, towards the close
of the summer, as I was gazing into the street,
I saw a four-wheeled cab stop outside our
door, and deposit, with several packages, a
strange lady, who was shown up into my
Father's study and was presently brought down
and introduced to me.

Miss Marks, as I shall take the liberty of
calling this person, was so long a part of my
life that I must pause to describe her. She
was tall, rather gaunt, with high cheek-bones ;
her teeth were prominent and very white ; her
eyes were china-blue, and were always absolutely
fixed, wide open, on the person she spoke
to ; her nose was inclined to be red at the
tip. She had a kind, hearty, sharp mode of

talking, but did not exercise it much, being on the whole taciturn. She was bustling and nervous, not particularly refined, not quite, I imagine, what is called "a lady." I supposed her, if I thought of the matter at all, to be very old, but perhaps she may have seen, when we knew her first, some forty-five summers. Miss Marks was an orphan, depending upon her work for her living; she would not, in these days of examinations, have come up to the necessary educational standards, but she had enjoyed experience in teaching, and was prepared to be a conscientious and careful governess, up to her lights. I was now informed by my Father that it was in this capacity that she would in future take her place in our household. I was not informed, what I gradually learned by observation, that she would also act in it as housekeeper.

Miss Marks was a somewhat grotesque personage, and might easily be painted as a kind of eccentric Dickens character, a mixture of Mrs. Pipchin and Miss Sally Brass. I will confess that when, in years to come, I read "Dombey and Son," certain features of Mrs. Pipchin did irresistibly remind me of my excellent past governess. I can imagine Miss Marks saying, but with a facetious intent, that children who sniffed would not go to heaven. But I was instantly ashamed of the parallel, because my gaunt old friend was a thoroughly good and honest woman, not intelligent and not graceful, but desirous in every way to do

her duty. Her duty to me she certainly did,
and I am afraid I hardly rewarded her with
the devotion she deserved. From the first, I
was indifferent to her wishes, and, as much as
was convenient, I ignored her existence. She
held no power over my attention, and if I
accepted her guidance along the path of instruction, it was because, odd as it may sound,
I really loved knowledge. I accepted her company without objection, and though there were
occasional outbreaks of tantrums on both sides,
we got on very well together for several years.
I did not, however, at any time surrender my
inward will to the wishes of Miss Marks.

In the circle of our life the religious element
took so preponderating a place, that it is impossible to avoid mentioning, what might otherwise seem unimportant, the theological views
of Miss Marks. How my Father had discovered
her, or from what field of educational enterprise
he plucked her in her prime, I never knew,
but she used to mention that my Father's
ministrations had "opened her eyes," from
which "scales" had fallen. She had accepted,
on their presentation to her, the entire gamut
of his principles. Miss Marks was accustomed,
while putting me to bed, to dwell darkly on
the incidents of her past, which had, I fear,
been an afflicted one. I believe I do her rather
limited intelligence no injury when I say that
it was prepared to swallow, at one mouthful,
whatever my Father presented to it, so delighted
was its way-worn possessor to find herself

in a comfortable, or, at least, an independent
position. She soon bowed, if there was indeed
any resistance from the first, very contentedly
in the House of Rimmon, learning to repeat,
with marked fluency, the customary formulas
and shibboleths. On my own religious development she had no great influence. Any such
guttering theological rushlight as Miss Marks
might dutifully exhibit faded for me in the blaze
of my Father's glaring beacon-lamp of faith.

Hardly was Miss Marks settled in the family,
than my Father left us on an expedition about
which my curiosity was exercised, but not
until later, satisfied. He had gone, as we
afterwards found, to South Devon, to a point
on the coast which he had known of old.
Here he had hired a horse, and had ridden
about until he saw a spot he liked, where a
villa was being built on speculation. Nothing
equals the courage of these recluse men ; my
Father got off his horse, and tied it to the gate,
and then he went in and bought the house on
a ninety-nine years' lease. I need hardly say
that he had made the matter a subject of the
most earnest prayer, and had entreated the Lord
for guidance. When he felt attracted to this
particular villa, he did not doubt that he was
directed to it in answer to his supplication,
and he wasted no time in further balancing or
inquiring. On my eighth birthday, with bag
and baggage complete, we all made the toilful
journey down into Devonshire, and I was a
town-child no longer.

CHAPTER V

A NEW element now entered into my life, a fresh rival arose to compete for me with my Father's dogmatic theology. This rival was the Sea. When Wordsworth was a little child, the presence of the mountains and the clouds lighted up his spirit with gleams that were like the flashing of a shield. He has described, in the marvellous pages of the "Prelude," the impact of nature upon the infant soul, but he has described it vaguely and faintly, with some "infirmity of love for days disowned by memory,"—I think because he was brought up in the midst of spectacular beauty, and could name no moment, mark no "here" or "now," when the wonder broke upon him. It was at the age of twice five summers, he thought, that he began to hold unconscious intercourse with nature, "drinking in a pure organic pleasure" from the floating mists and winding waters. Perhaps, in his anxiety to be truthful, and in the absence of any record, he put the date of this conscious rapture too late rather than too early. Certainly my own impregnation with the obscurely-defined but keenly-felt loveliness of the open sea dates from the first week of my ninth year.

The village, on the outskirts of which we had taken up our abode, was built parallel to

the cliff-line above the shore, but half a mile
inland. For a long time after the date I have
now reached, no other form of natural scenery
than the sea had any effect upon me at all.
The tors of the distant moor might be drawn
in deep blue against the pallor of our morning
or our evening sky, but I never looked at
them. It was the Sea, always the sea, nothing
but the sea. From our house, or from the
field at the back of our house, or from any
part of the village itself, there was no appearance to suggest that there could lie anything
in an easterly direction to break the infinitude
of red ploughed fields. But on that earliest
morning, how my heart remembers! we
hastened,—Miss Marks, the maid, and I
between them,—along a couple of high-walled
lanes, when suddenly, far below us, in an
immense arc of light, there stretched the
enormous plain of waters. We had but to
cross a step or two of downs, when the hollow
sides of the great limestone cove yawned at
our feet, descending, like a broken cup, down,
down to the moon of snow-white shingle and
the expanse of blue-green sea.

In these twentieth-century days, a careful
municipality has studded the down with rustic
seats and has shut its dangers out with railings,
has cut a winding carriage-drive round the
curves of the cove down to the shore, and has
planted sausage-laurels at intervals in clearings
made for that æsthetic purpose. When last I
saw the place, thus smartened and secured,

with its hair in curl-papers and its feet in
patent-leathers, I turned from it in anger and
disgust, and could almost have wept. I suppose that to those who knew it in no other
guise, it may still have beauty.   No parish
councils, beneficent and shrewd, can obscure
the lustre of the waters or compress the vastness
of the sky.   But what man could do to make
wild beauty ineffectual, tame and empty, has
amply been performed at Oddicombe.

Very different was it fifty years ago, in its
uncouth majesty.   No road, save the merest
goat-path, led down its concave wilderness, in
which loose furze-bushes and untrimmed
brambles wantoned into the likeness of trees,
each draped in audacious tissue of wild cle-
matis.   Through this fantastic maze the traveller
wound his way, led by little other clue than
by the instinct of descent.   For me, as a child,
it meant the labour of a long, an endless morning,
to descend to the snow-white pebbles, to sport
at the edge of the cold, sharp sea, and then
to climb up home again, slipping in the sticky
red mud, clutching at the smooth boughs
of the wild ash, toiling, toiling upwards into
flat land out of that hollow world of rocks.

On the first occasion, I recollect, our Cock-
ney housemaid, enthusiastic young creature
that she was, flung herself down upon her
knees, and drank of the salt waters. Miss
Marks, more instructed in phenomena, refrained, but I, although I was perfectly aware
what the taste would be, insisted on sipping a

few drops from the palm of my hand. This
was a slight recurrence of what I have called
my "natural magic" practices, which had
passed into the background of my mind, but
had not quite disappeared. I recollect that I
thought I might secure some power of walking
on the sea, if I drank of it—a perfectly irrational
movement of mind, like those of savages.

My great desire was to walk out over the
sea as far as I could, and then lie flat on it,
face downwards, and peer into the depths. I
was tormented with this ambition, and, like
many grown-up people, was so fully occupied
by these vain and ridiculous desires that I
neglected the actual natural pleasures around
me. The idea was not quite so demented as
it may seem, because we were in the habit
of singing, as well as reading, of those en-
raptured beings who spend their days in "fling-
ing down their golden crowns upon the jasper
sea." Why, I argued, should I not be able
to fling down my straw hat upon the tides
of Oddicombe? And, without question, a
majestic scene upon the Lake of Gennesaret
had also inflamed my fancy. Of all these
things, of course, I was careful to speak to no
one.

It was not with Miss Marks, however, but
with my Father, that I became accustomed to
make the laborious and exquisite journeys
down to the sea and back again. His work
as a naturalist eventually took him, laden with
implements, to the rock-pools on the shore, and

I was in attendance as an acolyte. But our earliest winter in South Devon was darkened for us both by disappointments, the cause of which lay, at the time, far out of my reach. In the spirit of my Father were then running, with furious velocity, two hostile streams of influence. I was standing, just now, thinking of these things, where the Cascine ends in the wooded point which is carved out sharply by the lion-coloured swirl of the Arno on the one side and by the pure flow of the Mugnone on the other. The rivers meet, and run parallel, but there comes a moment when the one or the other must conquer, and it is the yellow vehemence that drowns the purer tide.

So, through my Father's brain, in that year of scientific crisis, 1857, there rushed two kinds of thought, each absorbing, each convincing, yet totally irreconcilable. There is a peculiar agony in the paradox that truth has two forms, each of them indisputable, yet each antagonistic to the other. It was this discovery, that there were two theories of physical life, each of which was true, but the truth of each incompatible with the truth of the other, which shook the spirit of my Father with perturbation. It was not, really, a paradox, it was a fallacy, if he could only have known it, but he allowed the turbid volume of superstition to drown the delicate stream of reason. He took one step in the service of truth, and then he drew back in an agony, and accepted the servitude of error.

This was the great moment in the history
of thought when the theory of the mutability
of species was preparing to throw a flood of
light upon all departments of human speculation and action. It was becoming necessary to
stand emphatically in one army or the other.
Lyell was surrounding himself with disciples,
who were making strides in the direction of
discovery. Darwin had long been collecting
facts with regard to the variation of animals
and plants. Hooker and Wallace, Asa Gray
and even Agassiz, each in his own sphere, were
coming closer and closer to a perception of that
secret which was first to reveal itself clearly
to the patient and humble genius of Darwin.
In the year before, in 1856, Darwin, under
pressure from Lyell, had begun that modest
statement of the new revelation, that " abstract
of an essay," which developed so mightily into
" The Origin of Species." Wollaston's " Variation of Species " had just appeared, and had
been a nine days' wonder in the wilderness.

On the other side, the reactionaries, although
never dreaming of the fate which hung over
them, had not been idle. In 1857 the astounding question had for the first time been propounded with contumely, " What, then, did
we come from an orang-outang ? " The famous
" Vestiges of Creation " had been supplying a
sugar-and-water panacea for those who could
not escape from the trend of evidence, and who
yet clung to revelation. Owen was encouraging reaction by resisting, with all the strength

of his prestige, the theory of the mutability of species.

In this period of intellectual ferment, as when a great political revolution is being planned, many possible adherents were confidentially tested with hints and encouraged to reveal their bias in a whisper. It was the notion of Lyell, himself a great mover of men, that, before the doctrine of natural selection was given to a world which would be sure to lift up at it a howl of execration, a certain body-guard of sound and experienced naturalists, expert in the description of species, should be privately made aware of its tenour. Among those who were thus initiated, or approached with a view towards possible illumination, was my Father. He was spoken to by Hooker, and later on by Darwin, after meetings of the Royal Society in the summer of 1857.

My Father's attitude towards the theory of natural selection was critical in his career, and oddly enough, it exercised an immense influence on my own experience as a child. Let it be admitted at once, mournful as the admission is, that every instinct in his intelligence went out at first to greet the new light. It had hardly done so, when a recollection of the opening chapter of " Genesis " checked it at the outset. He consulted with Carpenter, a great investigator, but one who was fully as incapable as himself of remodelling his ideas with regard to the old, accepted hypotheses. They both determined, on various grounds, to have

nothing to do with the terrible theory, but to
hold steadily to the law of the fixity of species.
It was exactly at this juncture that we left
London, and the slight and occasional, but
always extremely salutary personal intercourse
with men of scientific leading which my Father
had enjoyed at the British Museum and at the
Royal Society came to an end. His next act
was to burn his ships, down to the last beam
and log out of which a raft could have been
made. By a strange act of wilfulness, he closed
the doors upon himself for ever.

My Father had never admired Sir Charles
Lyell.   I   think   that   the   famous   " Lord
Chancellor manner " of the geologist intimi-
dated him, and we undervalue the intelligence
of those whose conversation puts us at a disadvantage. For Darwin and Hooker, on the
other hand, he had a profound esteem, and I
know not whether this had anything to do
with the fact that he chose, for his impetuous
experiment in reaction, the field of geology,
rather than that of zoology or botany. Lyell
had been threatening to publish a book on the
geological history of Man, which was to be a
bomb-shell flung into the camp of the catas-
trophists. My Father, after long reflection,
prepared a theory of his own, which, as he
fondly hoped, would take the wind out of
Lyell's sails, and justify geology to godly readers
of " Genesis." It was, very briefly, that there
had been no gradual modification of the surface
of the earth, or slow development of organic

forms, but that when the catastrophic act of
creation took place, the world presented, instantly, the structural appearance of a planet
on which life had long existed.

The theory, coarsely enough, and to my
Father's great indignation, was defined by a
hasty press as being this—that God hid the
fossils in the rocks in order to tempt geologists
into infidelity. In truth, it was the logical and
inevitable conclusion of accepting, literally, the
doctrine of a sudden act of creation ; it emphasised the fact that any breach in the circular
course of nature could be conceived only on the
supposition that the object created bore false
witness to past processes, which had never
taken place. For instance, Adam would certainly possess hair and teeth and bones in
a condition which it must have taken many
years to accomplish, yet he was created full-
grown yesterday. He would certainly—though
Sir Thomas Browne denied it—display an
"omphalos," yet no umbilical cord had ever
attached him to a mother.

Never was a book cast upon the waters with
greater anticipations of success than was this
curious, this obstinate, this fanatical volume.
My Father lived in a fever of suspense, waiting
for the tremendous issue. This " Omphalos "
of his, he thought, was to bring all the turmoil
of scientific speculation to a close, fling geology
into the arms of Scripture, and make the lion
eat grass with the lamb. It was not surprising,
he admitted, that there had been experienced

an ever-increasing discord between the facts which geology brings to light and the direct statements of the early chapters of "Genesis." Nobody was to blame for that. My Father, and my Father alone, possessed the secret of the enigma ; he alone held the key which could smoothly open the lock of geological mystery. He offered it, with a glowing gesture, to atheists and Christians alike. This was to be the universal panacea ; this the system of intellectual therapeutics which could not but heal all the maladies of the age. But, alas ! atheists and Christians alike looked at it, and laughed, and threw it away.

In the course of that dismal winter, as the post began to bring in private letters, few and chilly, and public reviews, many and scornful, my Father looked in vain for the approval of the churches, and in vain for the acquiescence of the scientific societies, and in vain for the gratitude of those "thousands of thinking persons," which he had rashly assured himself of receiving. As his reconciliation of Scripture statements and geological deductions was welcomed nowhere ; as Darwin continued silent, and the youthful Huxley was scornful, and even Charles Kingsley, from whom my Father had expected the most instant appreciation, wrote that he could not " give up the painful and slow conclusion of five and twenty years' study of geology, and believe that God has written on the rocks one enormous and superfluous lie,"—as all this happened or failed to happen, a gloom,

cold and dismal, descended upon our morning
teacups. It was what the poets mean by an
" inspissated " gloom ; it thickened day by day,
as hope and self-confidence evaporated in thin
clouds of disappointment. My Father was not
prepared for such a fate. He had been the
spoiled darling of the public, the constant
favourite of the press, and now, like the dark
angels of old,

> so huge a rout
> Encumbered him with ruin.

He could not recover from amazement at
having offended everybody by an enterprise
which had been undertaken in the cause of
universal reconciliation.

During that grim season, my Father was no
lively companion, and circumstance after circumstance combined to drive him further from
humanity. He missed more than ever the sympathetic ear of my Mother ; there was present
to support him nothing of that artful, female
casuistry which insinuates into the wounded
consciousness of a man the conviction that,
after all, he is right and all the rest of the
world is wrong. My Father used to tramp in
solitude round and round the red ploughed
field which was going to be his lawn, or, shel-
tering himself from the thin Devonian rain,
pace up and down the still-naked verandah
where blossoming creepers were to be. And
I think that there was added to his chagrin
with all his fellow mortals a first tincture of
that heresy which was to attack him later on.

It was now that, I fancy, he began, in his depression, to be angry with God.   How much devotion had he given, how many sacrifices had he made, only to be left storming round this red morass with no one in all the world to care for him except one pale-faced child with its cheek pressed to the window !

After one or two brilliant excursions to the sea, winter, in its dampest, muddiest, most languid form, had fallen upon us and shut us in.   It was a dreary winter for the wifeless man and the motherless boy.   We had come into the house, in precipitate abandonment to that supposed answer to prayer, a great deal too soon.   In order to rake together the lump sum for buying it, my Father had denuded himself of almost everything, and our sticks of chairs and tables filled but two or three rooms. Half the little house, or " villa " as we called it, was not papered, two-thirds were not furnished.   The workmen were still finishing the outside when we arrived, and in that connection I recall a little incident which exhibits my Father's morbid delicacy of conscience. He was accustomed, in his brighter moments —and this was before the publication of his " Omphalos "—occasionally to sing loud Dorsetshire songs of his early days, in a strange, broad Wessex lingo that I loved.   One October afternoon he and I were sitting on the verandah, and my Father was singing ; just round the corner, out of sight, two carpenters were putting up the framework of a greenhouse.   In a pause, one of them said to his fellow : "He can zing a zong, zo well's another, though he be a minister." My Father, who was holding my hand loosely, clutched it, and looking up, I saw his eyes darken. He never sang a secular song again during the whole of his life.

Later in the year, and after his literary misfortune, his conscience became more troublesome than ever. I think he considered the failure of his attempt at the reconciliation of science with religion to have been intended by God as a punishment for something he had done or left undone. In those brooding tramps round and round the garden, his soul was on its knees searching the corners of his conscience for some sin of omission or commission, and one by one every pleasure, every recreation, every trifle scraped out of the dust of past experience, was magnified into a huge offence. He thought that the smallest evidence of levity, the least unbending to human instinct, might be seized by those around him as evidence of inconsistency, and might lead the weaker brethren into offence. The incident of the carpenters and the comic song is typical of a condition of mind which now possessed my Father, in which act after act became taboo, not because each was sinful in itself, but because it might lead others into sin.

I have the conviction that Miss Marks was now mightily afraid of my Father. Whenever she could, she withdrew to the room she called her "boudoir," a small, chilly apartment, sparsely furnished, looking over what was in process of becoming the vegetable garden. Very properly, that she might have some sanctuary, Miss Marks forbade me to enter this virginal bower, which, of course, became to me an object of harrowing curiosity. Through the key-hole I could see practically nothing ; one day I contrived to slip inside, and discovered that there was nothing to see but a plain bedstead and a toilet-table, void of all attraction. In this " boudoir," on winter afternoons, a fire would be lighted, and Miss Marks would withdraw to it, not seen by us any more between high-tea and the apocalyptic exercise known as " worship "—in less strenuous households much less austerely practised under the name of " family prayers." Left meanwhile to our own devices, my Father would mainly be reading, his book or paper held close up to the candle, while his lips and heavy eyebrows occasionally quivered and palpitated, with literary ardour, in a manner strangely exciting to me. Miss Marks, in a very high cap, and her large teeth shining, would occasionally appear in the doorway, desiring, with spurious geniality, to know how we were " getting on." But on these occasions neither of us replied to Miss Marks.

Sometimes, in the course of this winter, my Father and I had long cosy talks together over the fire. Our favourite subject was murders. I wonder whether little boys of eight, soon to

go up-stairs alone at night, often discuss violent
crime with a widower-papa ? The practice, I
cannot help thinking, is unusual ; it was, however, consecutive with us.   We tried other
secular subjects, but we were sure to come
round at last to " what do you suppose they
really did with the body ? " I was told, a
thrilled listener, the adventure of Mrs. Manning,
who killed a gentleman on the stairs and buried
him in quick-lime in the back-kitchen, and it
was at this time that I learned the useful
historical fact, which abides with me after half
a century, that Mrs. Manning was hanged
in black satin, which thereupon went wholly
out of fashion in England.   I also heard about
Burke and Hare, whose story nearly froze me
into stone with horror.

These were crimes which appear in the
chronicles. But who will tell me what " the
Carpet-bag Mystery " was, which my Father
and I discussed evening after evening ? I have
never come across a whisper of it since, and I
suspect it of having been a hoax. As I recall
the details, people in a boat, passing down the
Thames, saw a carpet-bag hung high in air,
on one of the projections of a pier of Waterloo
Bridge. Being with difficulty dragged down—
or perhaps up—this bag was found to be full
of human remains, dreadful butcher's business
of joints and fragments. Persons were missed,
were identified, were again denied—the whole
is a vapour in my memory which shifts as I try
to define it. But clear enough is the picture

I hold of myself, in a high chair, on the left-hand side of the sitting-room fire-place, the leaping flames reflected in the glass-case of tropical insects on the opposite wall, and my Father, leaning anxiously forward, with uplifted finger, emphasising to me the pros and cons of the horrible carpet-bag evidence.

I suppose that my interest in these discussions—and Heaven knows I was animated enough—amused and distracted my Father, whose idea of a suitable theme for childhood's ear now seems to me surprising. I soon found that these subjects were not welcome to everybody, for, starting the Carpet-bag Mystery one morning with Miss Marks, in the hope of delaying my arithmetic lesson, she fairly threw her apron over her ears, and told me, from that vantage, that if I did not desist at once, she should scream.

Occasionally we took winter walks together, my Father and I, down some lane that led to a sight of the sea, or over the rolling downs. We tried to recapture the charm of those delightful strolls in London, when we used to lean over the bridges and watch the ducks. But we could not recover this pleasure. My Father was deeply enwoven in the chain of his own thoughts, and would stalk on, without a word, buried in angry reverie. If he spoke to me, on these excursions, it was a pain to me to answer him. I could talk on easy terms with him indoors, seated in my high chair, with our heads on a level, but it was intolerably laborious

to look up into the firmament and converse
with a dark face against the sky. The actual
exercise of walking, too, was very exhausting to
me ; the bright red mud, to the strange colour
of which I could not for a long while get accustomed, becoming caked about my little shoes,
and wearying me extremely. I would grow
petulant and cross, contradict my Father, and
oppose his whims. These walks were distressing
to us both, yet he did not like to walk alone,
and he had no other friend. However, as the
winter advanced, they had to be abandoned, and
the habit of our taking a " constitutional "
together was never resumed.

I look back upon myself at this time as upon
a cantankerous, ill-tempered and unobliging
child. The only excuse I can offer is that I
really was not well. The change to Devonshire
had not suited me ; my health gave the excellent
Miss Marks some anxiety, but she was not ready
in resource. The dampness of the house was
terrible ; indoors and out, the atmosphere
seemed soaked in chilly vapours. Under my
bed-clothes at night I shook like a jelly, unable
to sleep for cold, though I was heaped with
coverings, while my skin was all puckered
with goose-flesh. I could eat nothing solid,
without suffering immediately from violent hiccough, so that much of my time was spent
lying prone on my back upon the hearth-
rug, awakening the echoes like a cuckoo.
Miss Marks, therefore, cut off all food but
milk-sop, a loathly bowl of which appeared at

every meal. In consequence the hiccough
lessened, but my strength declined with it. I
languished in a perpetual catarrh. I was roused
to a consciousness that I was not considered
well by the fact that my Father prayed publicly
at morning and evening " worship " that if
it was the Lord's will to take me to himself
there might be no doubt whatever about my
being a sealed child of God and an inheritor
of glory. I was partly disconcerted by, partly
vain of, this open advertisement of my ailments.

Of our dealings with the " Saints," a fresh
assortment of whom met us on our arrival in
Devonshire, I shall speak presently. My Father's
austerity of behaviour was, I think, perpetually
accentuated by his fear of doing anything to
offend the consciences of these persons, whom
he supposed, no doubt, to be more sensitive
than they really were. He was fond of saying
that " a very little stain upon the conscience
makes a wide breach in our communion with
God," and he counted possible errors of conduct by hundreds and by thousands. It was
in this winter that his attention was particularly
drawn to the festival of Christmas, which,
apparently, he had scarcely noticed in
London.

On the subject of all feasts of the Church he
held views of an almost grotesque peculiarity.
He looked upon each of them as nugatory
and worthless, but the keeping of Christmas
appeared to him by far the most hateful, and

nothing less than an act of idolatry. "The very word is Popish," he used to exclaim, "Christ's Mass!" pursing up his lips with the gesture of one who tastes assafœtida by accident. Then he would adduce the antiquity of the so-called feast, adapted from horrible heathen rites, and itself a soiled relic of the abominable Yule-Tide. He would denounce the horrors of Christmas until it almost made me blush to look at a holly-berry.

On Christmas Day of this year 1857 our villa saw a very unusual sight. My Father had given strictest charge that no difference whatever was to be made in our meals on that day ; the dinner was to be neither more copious than usual nor less so. He was obeyed, but the servants, secretly rebellious, made a small plum-pudding for themselves. (I discovered afterwards, with pain, that Miss Marks received a slice of it in her boudoir.) Early in the afternoon, the maids,—of whom we were now advanced to keeping two,— kindly remarked that "the poor dear child ought to have a bit, anyhow," and wheedled me into the kitchen, where I ate a slice of plum-pudding. Shortly I began to feel that pain inside which in my frail state was in- evitable, and my conscience smote me violently. At length I could bear my spiritual anguish no longer, and bursting into the study I called out : "Oh! Papa, Papa, I have eaten of flesh offered to idols!" It took some time, between my sobs, to explain what had hap-

pened. Then my Father sternly said : " Where
is the accursed thing ? " I explained that
as much as was left of it was still on the kitchen
table. He took me by the hand, and ran
with me into the midst of the startled servants,
seized what remained of the pudding, and
with the plate in one hand and me still tight
in the other, ran till we reached the dust-heap,
when he flung the idolatrous confectionery
on to the middle of the ashes, and then raked
it deep down into the mass. The suddenness,
the violence, the velocity of this extraordinary
act made an impression on my memory which
nothing will ever efface.

The key is lost by which I might unlock
the perverse malady from which my Father's
conscience seemed to suffer during the whole
of this melancholy winter. But I think that
a dislocation of his intellectual system had a
great deal to do with it. Up to this point in
his career, he had, as we have seen, nourished
the delusion that science and revelation could
be mutually justified, that some sort of
compromise was possible. With great and
ever greater distinctness, his investigations had
shown him that in all departments of organic
nature there are visible the evidences of slow
modification of forms, of the type developed
by the pressure and practice of æons. This
conviction had been borne in upon him until
it was positively irresistible. Where was his
place, then, as a sincere and accurate observer ?
Manifestly, it was with the pioneers of the

new truth, it was with Darwin, Wallace and Hooker.   But did not the second chapter of "Genesis" say that in six days the heavens and earth were finished, and the host of them, and that on the seventh day God ended his work which he had made?

Here was a dilemma! Geology certainly *seemed* to be true, but the Bible, which was God's word, *was* true. If the Bible said that all things in Heaven and Earth were created in six days, created in six days they were,—in six literal days of twenty-four hours each. The evidences of spontaneous variation of form, acting, over an immense space of time, upon ever-modifying organic structures, *seemed* overwhelming, but they must either be brought into line with the six-day labour of creation, or they must be rejected. I have already shown how my Father worked out the ingenious "Omphalos" theory in order to justify himself as a strictly scientific observer who was also a humble slave of revelation. But the old convention and the new rebellion would alike have none of his compromise.

To a mind so acute and at the same time so narrow as that of my Father—a mind which is all logical and positive without breadth, without suppleness and without imagination —to be subjected to a check of this kind is agony. It has not the relief of a smaller nature, which escapes from the dilemma by some foggy formula; nor the resolution of a larger nature to take to it wings and sur-

mount the obstacle.   My Father, although
half suffocated by the emotion of being lifted,
as it were, on the great biological wave, never
dreamed of letting go his clutch of the ancient
tradition, but hung there, strained and buffeted.
It is extraordinary that he—an "honest hod-
man of science," as Huxley once called him—
should not have been content to allow others,
whose horizons were wider than his could be,
to pursue those purely intellectual surveys for
which he had no species of aptitude.   As a
collector of facts and marshaller of observations,
he had not a rival in that age ; his very absence
of imagination aided him in this work.   But
he was more an attorney than a philosopher,
and he lacked that sublime humility which is
the crown of genius.   For, this obstinate persuasion that he alone knew the mind of God,
that he alone could interpret the designs of
the Creator, what did it result from if not from
a congenital lack of that highest modesty which
replies "I do not know" even to the questions
which Faith, with menacing finger, insists on
having most positively answered ?

CHAPTER VI

DURING the first year of our life in Devonshire, the ninth year of my age, my Father's existence, and therefore mine, was almost entirely divided between attending to the little community of " Saints " in the village and collecting, examining and describing marine creatures from the sea-shore. In the course of these twelve months, we had scarcely any social distractions of any kind, and I never once crossed the bounds of the parish. After the worst of the winter was over, my Father recovered much of his spirits and his power of work, and the earliest sunshine soothed and refreshed us both. I was still almost always with him, but we had now some curious companions.

The village, at the southern end of which our villa stood, was not pretty. It had no rural picturesqueness of any kind. The only pleasant feature of it, the handsome and ancient parish church, with its umbrageous churchyard, was then almost entirely concealed by a congeries of mean shops, which were ultimately, before the close of my childhood, removed. The village consisted of two parallel lines of contiguous houses, all whitewashed and most of them fronted by trifling shop-windows ; for half a mile this street ascended to the church, and then it descended for another half-mile,

ending suddenly in fields, the hedges of which
displayed, at intervals, the inevitable pollard
elm-tree. The walk through the village, which
we seemed to make incessantly, was very
wearisome to me. I dreaded the rudeness of
the children, and there was nothing in the
shops to amuse me. Walking on the inch
or two of broken pavement in front of the
houses was disagreeable and tiresome, and
the fœtor which breathed on close days from
the open doors and windows made me feel
faint. But this walk was obligatory, since the
"Public Room," as our little chapel was
called, lay at the further extremity of the dreary
street.

We attended this place of worship immediately on our arrival, and my Father, uninvited
but unresisted, immediately assumed the ad-
ministration of it. It was a square, empty
room, built, for I know not what purpose, over
a stable. Ammoniac odours used to rise through
the floor as we sat there at our long devotions.
Before our coming, a little flock of persons
met in the Room, a community of the indefinite
sort just then becoming frequent in the West
of England, pious rustics connected with no
other recognised body of Christians, and depending directly on the independent study of
the Bible. They were largely women, but
there was more than a sprinkling of men,
poor, simple and generally sickly. In later
days, under my Father's ministration, the body
increased and positively flourished. It came

to include retired professional men, an admiral, nay, even the brother of a peer. But in those earliest years the "brethren" and "sisters" were all of them ordinary peasants. They were jobbing gardeners and journeymen carpenters, masons and tailors, washerwomen and domestic servants. I wish that I could paint, in colours so vivid that my readers could perceive what their little society consisted of, this quaint collection of humble, conscientious, ignorant and gentle persons. In chronicle or fiction, I have never been fortunate enough to meet with anything which resembled them. The caricatures of enmity and worldly scorn are as crude, to my memory, as the unction of religious conventionality is featureless.

The origin of the meeting had been odd. A few years before we came, a crew of Cornish fishermen, quite unknown to the villagers, were driven by stress of weather into the haven under the cliff. They landed, and, instead of going to a public-house, they looked about for a room where they could hold a prayer-meeting. They were devout Wesleyans; they had come from the open sea, they were far from home, and they had been starved by lack of their customary religious privileges. As they stood about in the street before their meeting, they challenged the respectable girls who came out to stare at them, with the question, "Do you love the Lord Jesus, my maid?" Receiving dubious answers, they pressed the inhabitants to come in and pray with them, which several did. Ann Burmington, who long afterwards told me about it, was one of those girls, and she repeated that the fishermen said, "What a dreadful thing it will be, at the Last Day, when the Lord says, 'Come, ye blessed,' and says it not to you, and then, 'Depart, ye cursed,' and you maidens have to depart." They were finely-built young men, with black beards and shining eyes, and I do not question that some flash of sex unconsciously mingled with the curious episode, although their behaviour was in all respects discreet. It was, perhaps, not wholly a coincidence that almost all those particular girls remained unmarried to the end of their lives. After two or three days, the fishermen went off to sea again. They prayed and sailed away, and the girls, who had not even asked their names, never heard of them again. But several of the young women were definitely converted, and they formed the nucleus of our little gathering.

My Father preached, standing at a desk; or celebrated the communion in front of a deal table, with a white napkin spread over it. Sometimes the audience was so small, generally so unexhilarating, that he was discouraged, but he never flagged in energy and zeal. Only those who had given evidence of intelligent acceptance of the theory of simple faith in their atonement through the Blood of Jesus were admitted to the communion, or, as it was called, "the Breaking of Bread." It was made a very strong point that no one should

" break bread,"—unless for good reason shown
—until he or she had been baptized, that is to
say, totally immersed, in solemn conclave, by
the ministering brother. This rite used, in
our earliest days, to be performed, with picturesque simplicity, in the sea on the Oddicombe beach, but to this there were, even in
those quiet years, extreme objections. A jeer-
ing crowd could scarcely be avoided, and women,
in particular, shrank from the ordeal. This
used to be a practical difficulty, and my Father,
when communicants confessed that they had
not yet been baptized, would shake his head
and say gravely, "Ah! ah! you shun the
Cross of Christ!" But that baptism in the
sea on the open beach *was* a "cross," he
would not deny, and when we built our own
little chapel, a sort of font, planked over, was
arranged in the room itself.

Among these quiet, taciturn people, there
were several whom I recall with affection.
In this remote corner of Devonshire, on the
road nowhither, they had preserved much of
the air of that eighteenth century which the
elders among them perfectly remembered. There
was one old man, born before the French
Revolution, whose figure often recurs to me.
This was James Petherbridge, the Nestor of
our meeting, extremely tall and attenuated ;
he came on Sundays in a full, white smock-
frock, smartly embroidered down the front, and
when he settled himself to listen, he would
raise this smock like a skirt, and reveal a pair

of immensely long thin legs, cased in tight leggings, and ending in shoes with buckles. As the sacred message fell from my Father's lips the lantern jaws of Mr. Petherbridge slowly fell apart, while his knees sloped to so immense a distance from one another that it seemed as though they never could meet again. He had been pious all his life, and he would tell us, in some modest pride, that when he was a lad, the farmer's wife who was his mistress used to say, "I think our Jem is going to be a Methody, he do so hanker after godly discoursings." Mr. Petherbridge was accustomed to pray orally, at our prayer-meetings, in a funny old voice like wind in a hollow tree, and he seldom failed to express a hope that "the Lord would support Miss Lafroy"—who was the village schoolmistress, and one of our congregation,—"in her labour of teaching the young idea how to shoot." I, not understanding this literary allusion, long believed the school to be addicted to some species of pistol-practice.

The key of the Room was kept by Richard Moxhay, the mason, who was of a generation younger than Mr. Petherbridge, but yet "getting on in years." Moxhay, I cannot tell why, was always dressed in white corduroy, on which any stain of Devonshire scarlet mud was painfully conspicuous ; when he was smartened up, his appearance suggested that somebody had given him a coating of that rich Western whitewash which looks like

Devonshire cream. His locks were long and sparse, and as deadly black as his clothes were white. He was a modest, gentle man, with a wife even more meek and gracious than himself. They never, to my recollection, spoke unless they were spoken to, and their melancholy impassiveness used to vex my Father, who once, referring to the Moxhays, described them, sententiously but justly, as being "laborious, but it would be an exaggeration to say happy, Christians." Indeed, my memory pictures almost all the "saints" of that early time as sad and humble souls, lacking vitality, yet not complaining of anything definite. A quite surprising number of them, it is true, male and female, suffered from different forms of consumption, so that the Room rang in winter evenings with a discord of hacking coughs. But it seems to me that, when I was quite young, half the inhabitants of our rural district were affected with phthisis. No doubt, our peculiar religious community was more likely to attract the feeble members of a population, than to tempt the flush and the fair.

Miss Marks, patient pilgrim that she was, accepted this quaint society without a murmur, although I do not think it was much to her taste. But in a very short time it was sweetened to her by the formation of a devoted and romantic friendship for one of the "sisters," who was, indeed, if my childish recollection does not fail me, a very charming person. The consequence of this enthusiastic alliance was that I was carried into the bosom of the family to which Miss Marks' new friend belonged, and of these excellent people I must give what picture I can. Almost opposite the Room, therefore at the far end of the village, across one of the rare small gardens, (in which this first winter I discovered with rapture the magenta stars of a new flower, hepatica)—a shop-window displayed a thin row of plates and dishes, cups and saucers ; above it was painted the name of Burmington. This china-shop was the property of three orphan sisters, Ann, Mary Grace, and Bess, the latter lately married to a carpenter, who was " elder " at our meeting ; the other two, resolute old maids. Ann, whom I have already mentioned, had been one of the girls converted by the Cornish fishermen. She was about ten years older than Bess, and Mary Grace came half-way between them. Ann was a very worthy woman, but masterful and passionate, suffering from an ungovernable temper, which, at calmer moments she used to refer to, not without complacency, as " the sin which doth most easily beset me." Bess was insignificant, and vulgarised by domestic cares. But Mary Grace was a delightful creature.

The Burmingtons lived in what was almost the only old house surviving in the village. It was an extraordinary construction of two storeys, with vast rooms, and winding passages, and surprising changes of level. The sisters were poor, but very industrious, and never in anything like want ; they sold, as I have said, crockery, and they took in washing, and did a little fine needlework, and sold the produce of a great, vague garden at the back. In process of time, the elder sisters took a young woman, whose name was Drusilla Elliott, to live with them as servant and companion ; she was a converted person, worshipping with a kindred sect, the Bible Christians. I remember being much interested in hearing how Bess, before her marriage, became converted. Mary Grace, on account of her infirm health, slept alone in one room ; in another, of vast size, stood a family four-poster, where Ann slept with Drusilla Elliott, and another bed in the same room took Bess. The sisters and their friend had been constantly praying that Bess might "find peace," for she was still a stranger to salvation. One night, she suddenly called out, rather crossly, "What are you two whispering about ? Do go to sleep," to which Ann replied : "We are praying for you." "How do you know," answered Bess, "that I don't believe ? " And then she told them that, that very night, when she was sitting in the shop, she had closed with God's offer of redemption. Late in the night as it was, Ann and Drusilla could do no less than go in and waken Mary Grace, whom, however, they found awake, praying, she too, for the conversion of Bess. They told her the good news, and all four, kneeling in the darkness, gave thanks aloud to God for his infinite mercy.

It was Mary Grace Burmington who now became the romantic friend of Miss Marks, and a sort of second benevolence to me. She must have been under thirty years of age ; she was very small, and she was distressingly deformed in the spine, but she had an animated, almost a sparkling countenance. When we first arrived in the village, Mary Grace was only just recovering from a gastric fever which had taken her close to the grave. I remember hearing that the vicar, a stout and pompous man at whom we always glared defiance, went, in Mary Grace's supposed extremity, to the Burmingtons' shop-door, and shouted : " Peace be to this house," intending to offer his ministrations, but that Ann, who was in one of her tantrums, positively hounded him from the doorstep and down the garden, in her passionate nonconformity. Mary Grace, however, recovered, and soon became, not merely Miss Marks' inseparable friend, but my Father's spiritual factotum. He found it irksome to visit the " saints " from house to house, and Mary Grace Burmington gladly assumed this labour. She proved a most efficient coadjutor ; searched out, cherished and confirmed any of those, especially the young, who were attracted by my Father's preaching, and for several years was a great joy and comfort to us all. Even when her illness so increased that she could no longer rise from her bed, she was a centre of usefulness and cheerfulness from that retreat, where she " received," in a kind of rustic state, under a patchwork coverlid that was like a basket of flowers.

My Father, ever reflecting on what could be done to confirm my spiritual vocation, to pin me down, as it were, beyond any possibility of escape, bethought him that it would accustom me to what he called "pastoral work in the Lord's service," if I accompanied Mary Grace on her visits from house to house. If it is remembered that I was only eight and a half when this scheme was carried into practice, it will surprise no one to hear that it was not crowned with success. I disliked extremely this visitation of the poor. I felt shy, I had nothing to say, with difficulty could I understand their soft Devonian patois, and most of all—a signal perhaps of my neurotic condition—I dreaded and loathed the smells of their cottages. One had to run over the whole gamut of odours, some so faint that they embraced the nostril with a fairy kiss, others bluntly gross, of the "knock-you-down" order ; some sweet, with a dreadful sourness ; some bitter, with a smack of rancid hair-oil. There were fine manly smells of the pigsty and the open drain, and these prided themselves on being all they seemed to be ; but there were also feminine odours, masquerading as you knew not what, in which penny whiffs, vials of balm and opoponax, seemed to have become tainted, vaguely, with the residue of the slop-pail. It was not, I think, that the villagers were particularly dirty, but those were days before the invention of sanitary science, and my

poor young nose was morbidly, nay ridiculously
sensitive. I often came home from "visiting
the saints" absolutely incapable of eating the
milk-sop, with brown sugar strewn over it,
which was my evening meal.

There was one exception to my unwillingness
to join in the pastoral labours of Mary Grace.
When she announced, on a fine afternoon, that
we were going to Pavor and Barton, I was always
agog to start. These were two hamlets in our
parish, and, I should suppose, the original home
of its population. Pavor was, even then, de-
cayed almost to extinction, but Barton preserved
its desultory street of ancient, detached cottages.
Each, however poor, had a wild garden round it,
and, where the inhabitants possessed some pride
in their surroundings, the roses and the jasmines
and that distinguished creeper,—which one sees
nowhere at its best but in Devonshire cottage-
gardens,—the stately cotoniaster, made the whole
place a bower. Barton was in vivid contrast
to our own harsh, open, squalid village, with its
mean modern houses, its absence of all vegeta-
tion. The ancient thatched cottages of Barton were
shut in by moist hills, and canopied by ancient
trees; they were approached along a deep lane
which was all a wonder and a revelation to me
that spring, since, in the very words of Shelley:

There in the warm hedge grew lush eglantine,
  Green cow-bind and the moonlight-coloured may,
And cherry blossoms, and white cups, whose wine
  Was the bright dew yet drained not by the day;
And wild roses, and ivy serpentine
  With its dark buds and leaves, wandering astray.

Around and beyond Barton there lay fairy-land. All was mysterious, unexplored, rich with infinite possibilities. I should one day enter it, the sword of make-believe in my hand, the cap of courage on my head, " when you are a big boy," said the oracle of Mary Grace. For the present, we had to content ourselves with being an unadventurous couple—a little woman, bent half double, and a preternaturally sedate small boy—as we walked very slowly, side by side, conversing on terms of high familiarity, in which Biblical and colloquial phrases were quaintly jumbled, through the sticky red mud of the Pavor lanes with Barton as a bourne before us.

When we came home, my Father would sometimes ask me for particulars. Where had we been, whom had we found at home, what testimony had those visited been able to give of the Lord's goodness to them, what had Mary Grace replied in the way of exhortation, reproof or condolence ? These questions I hated at the time, but they were very useful to me, since they gave me the habit of concentrating my attention on what was going on in the course of our visits, in case I might be called upon to give a report. My Father was very kind in the matter ; he cultivated my powers of expression, he did not snub me when I failed to be intelligent. But I overheard Miss Marks and Mary Grace dis-cussing the whole question under the guise of referring to " you know whom, not a hundred miles hence," fancying that I could not recognise their little ostrich because its head was in a bag of metaphor. I understood perfectly, and gathered that they both of them thought this business of my going into undrained cottages injudicious. Accordingly, I was by degrees taken " visiting " only when Mary Grace was going into the country-hamlets, and then I was usually left outside, to skip among the flowers and stalk the butterflies.

I must not, however, underestimate the very prominent part taken all through this spring and summer of 1858 by the collection of specimens on the sea-shore. My Father had returned, the chagrin of his failure in theorising now being mitigated, to what was his real work in life, the practical study of animal forms in detail. He was not a biologist, in the true sense of the term. That luminous indication which Flaubert gives of what the action of the scientific mind should be, " affranchissant l'esprit et pesant les mondes, sans haine, sans peur, sans pitié, sans amour et sans Dieu," was opposed in every segment to the attitude of my Father, who, nevertheless, was a man of very high scientific attainment. But, again I repeat, he was not a philosopher ; he was incapable, by temperament and education, of forming broad generalisations and of escaping in a vast survey from the troublesome pettiness of detail. He saw everything through a lens, nothing in the immensity of nature. Certain senses were absent in him ; I think that, with all his justice, he had no conception of the importance of liberty ;

with all his intelligence, the boundaries of the
atmosphere in which his mind could think at
all were always close about him ; with all his
faith in the Word of God, he had no confidence
in the Divine Benevolence ; and with all his
passionate piety, he habitually mistook fear for
love.

It was down on the shore, tramping along
the pebbled terraces of the beach, clambering
over the great blocks of fallen conglomerate
which broke the white curve with rufous promontories that jutted into the sea, or, finally,
bending over those shallow tidal pools in the
limestone rocks which were our proper hunting-
ground,—it was in such circumstances as these
that my Father became most easy, most happy,
most human. That hard look across his brows,
which it wearied me to see, the look that came
from sleepless anxiety of conscience, faded away,
and left the dark countenance still always stern
indeed, but serene and unupbraiding. Those
pools were our mirrors, in which, reflected in
the dark hyaline and framed by the sleek and
shining fronds of oar-weed, there used to appear
the shapes of a middle-aged man and a funny
little boy, equally eager, and, I almost find the
presumption to say, equally well prepared for
business.

If any one goes down to those shores now,
if man or boy seeks to follow in our traces, let
him realise at once, before he takes the trouble
to roll up his sleeves, that his zeal will end in
labour lost. There is nothing, now, where in

our days there was so much. Then the rocks
between tide and tide were submarine gardens
of a beauty that seemed often to be fabulous,
and was positively delusive, since, if we delicately
lifted the weed-curtains of a windless pool,
though we might for a moment see its sides and
floor paven with living blossoms, ivory-white,
rosy-red, orange and amethyst, yet all that
panoply would melt away, furled into the hollow
rock, if we so much as dropped a pebble in to
disturb the magic dream.

Half a century ago, in many parts of the
coast of Devonshire and Cornwall, where the
limestone at the water's edge is wrought into
crevices and hollows, the tide-line was, like
Keats' Grecian vase, '' a still unravished bride
of quietness.'' These cups and basins were
always full, whether the tide was high or low,
and the only way in which they were affected
was that twice in the twenty-four hours they
were replenished by cold streams from the
great sea, and then twice were left brimming
to be vivified by the temperate movement of
the upper air. They were living flower-beds,
so exquisite in their perfection, that my Father,
in spite of his scientific requirements, used not
seldom to pause before he began to rifle them,
ejaculating that it was indeed a pity to disturb
such congregated beauty. The antiquity of these
rock-pools, and the infinite succession of the
soft and radiant forms, sea-anemones, sea-weeds,
shells, fishes, which had inhabited them, undisturbed since the creation of the world, used

to occupy my Father's fancy. We burst in, he used to say, where no one had ever thought of intruding before ; and if the Garden of Eden had been situate in Devonshire, Adam and Eve, stepping lightly down to bathe in the rainbow-coloured spray, would have seen the identical sights that we now saw,—the great prawns gliding like transparent launches, anthea waving in the twilight its thick white waxen tentacles, and the fronds of the dulse faintly streaming on the water, like huge red banners in some reverted atmosphere.

All this is long over, and done with. The ring of living beauty drawn about our shores was a very thin and fragile one. It had existed all those centuries solely in consequence of the indifference, the blissful ignorance of man. These rock-basins, fringed by corallines, filled with still water almost as pellucid as the upper air itself, thronged with beautiful sensitive forms of life,—they exist no longer, they are all profaned, and emptied, and vulgarised. An army of " collectors " has passed over them, and ravaged every corner of them. The fairy paradise has been violated, the exquisite product of centuries of natural selection has been crushed under the rough paw of well-meaning, idle-minded curiosity. That my Father, himself so reverent, so conservative, had by the popularity of his books acquired the direct responsibility for a calamity that he had never anticipated, became clear enough to himself before many years had passed, and cost him great chagrin.

No one will see again on the shore of England what I saw in my early childhood, the submarine vision of dark rocks, speckled and starred with an infinite variety of colour, and streamed over by silken flags of royal crimson and purple.

In reviving these impressions, I am unable to give any exact chronological sequence to them. These particular adventures began early in 1858, they reached their greatest intensity in the summer of 1859, and they did not altogether cease, so far as my Father was concerned, until nearly twenty years later. But it was while he was composing what, as I am told by scientific men of to-day, continues to be his most valuable contribution to knowledge, his "History of the British Sea-Anemones and Corals," that we worked together on the shore for a definite purpose, and the last instalment of that still-classic volume was ready for press by the close of 1859.

The way in which my Father worked, in his most desperate escapades, was to wade breast-high into one of the huge pools, and examine the worm-eaten surface of the rock above and below the brim. In such remote places—spots where I could never venture, being left, a slightly timorous Andromeda, chained to a safer level of the cliff—in these extreme basins, there used often to lurk a marvellous profusion of animal and vegetable forms. My Father would search for the roughest and most corroded points of rock, those offering the best refuge for a variety of creatures, and would then chisel off fragments as low down in the water as he could. These pieces of rock were instantly plunged in the salt water of jars which we had brought with us for the purpose. When as much had been collected as we could carry away—my Father always dragged about an immense square basket, the creak of whose handles I can still fancy that I hear—we turned to trudge up the long climb home. Then all our prizes were spread out, face upward, in shallow pans of clean sea-water.

In a few hours, when all dirt had subsided, and what living creatures we had brought seemed to have recovered their composure, my work began. My eyes were extremely keen and powerful, though they were vexatiously near-sighted. Of no use in examining objects at any distance, in investigating a minute surface my vision was trained to be invaluable. The shallow pan, with our spoils, would rest on a table near the window, and I, kneeling on a chair opposite the light, would lean over the surface till everything was within an inch or two of my eyes. Often I bent, in my zeal, so far forward that the water touched the tip of my nose and gave me a little icy shock. In this attitude—an idle spectator might have formed the impression that I was trying to wash my head and could not quite summon up resolution enough to plunge—in this odd pose I would remain for a long time, holding my breath, and examining with extreme care every atom of rock, every swirl of detritus. This was a task

which my Father could only perform by the
help of a lens, with which, of course, he took
care to supplement my examination. But that
my survey was of use, he has himself most
handsomely testified in his " Actinologia Britannica," where he expresses his debt to the " keen
and well-practised eye of my little son." Nor,
if boasting is not to be excluded, is it every
eminent biologist, every proud and masterful
F.R.S., who can lay his hand on his heart and
swear that, before reaching the age of ten years,
he had added, not merely a new species, but a
new genus to the British fauna. That, however, the author of these pages can do, who
on June 29, 1859, discovered a tiny atom,—
and ran in the greatest agitation to announce
the discovery of that object " as a form with
which he was unacquainted,"—which figures
since then on all lists of sea-anemones as
phellia murocincta, or the walled corklet. Alas !
that so fair a swallow should have made no
biological summer in after-life.

These delicious agitations by the edge of the
salt sea wave must have greatly improved my
health, which however was still looked upon as
fragile. I was loaded with coats and comforters,
and strolled out between Miss Marks and Mary
Grace Burmington, a muffled ball of flannel.
This alone was enough to give me a look of
delicacy, which the " saints," in their blunt
way, made no scruple of commenting upon to
my face. I was greatly impressed by a conversation held over my bed one evening by

the servants. Our cook, Susan, a person of
enormous size, and Kate, the tattling, tiresome
parlour-maid who waited upon us, on the
summer evening I speak of were standing—I
cannot tell why—on each side of my bed. I
shut my eyes, and lay quite still, in order to
escape conversing with them, and they spoke
to one another. " Ah, poor lamb," Kate said
trivially, " *he's* not long for this world ; going
home to Jesus, he is,—in a jiffy, I should say
by the look of 'un.'' But Susan answered :
" Not so. I dreamed about 'un, and I know for
sure that he is to be spared for missionary
service." " Missionary service ? " repeated
Kate, impressed. " Yes," Susan went on, with
solemn emphasis, " he'll bleed for his Lord in
heathen parts, that's what the future have in
store for *'im*.'' When they were gone, I beat
upon the coverlid with my fists, and I determined that whatever happened, I would not,
not, *not*, go out to preach the Gospel among
horrid, tropical niggers.

CHAPTER VII

IN the history of an infancy so cloistered and uniform as mine, such a real adventure as my being publicly and successfully kidnapped cannot be overlooked. There were several " innocents " in our village, harmless eccentrics who had more or less unquestionably crossed the barrier which divides the sane from the insane. They were not discouraged by public opinion ; indeed, several of them were favoured beings, suspected by my Father of exaggerating their mental density in order to escape having to work, like dogs, who, as we all know, could speak as well as we do, were they not afraid of being made to fetch and carry. Miss Mary Flaw was not one of these imbeciles. She was what the French call a *detraquée;* she had enjoyed a good intelligence and an active mind, but her wits had left the rails and were careering about the country. Miss Flaw was the daughter of a retired Baptist minister, and she lived, with I remember not what relations, in a little solitary house high up at Barton Cross, whither Mary Grace and I would sometimes struggle when our pastoral duties were over. In later years, when I met with those celebrated verses in which the philosopher expresses the hope

In the downhill of life, when I find I'm declining,
    May my lot no less fortunate be
Than a snug elbow-chair can afford for reclining,
    And a cot that o'erlooks the wide sea

my thoughts returned instinctively, and they still return, to the high abode of Miss Flaw. There was a porch at her door, both for shelter and shade, and it was covered with jasmine ; but the charm of the place was a summer-house close by, containing a table, encrusted with cowry-shells, and seats from which one saw the distant waters of the bay.   At the entrance to this grot there was always set a " snug elbow-chair," destined, I suppose, for the Rev. Mr. Flaw, or else left there in pious memory of him, since I cannot recollect whether he was alive or dead.

I delighted in these visits to Mary Flaw. She always received us with effusion, tripping forward to meet us, and leading us, each by a hand held high, with a dancing movement which I thought infinitely graceful, to the cowry-shell bower, where she would regale us with Devonshire cream and with small hard biscuits that were like pebbles.   The conversation of Mary Flaw was a great treat to me.   I enjoyed its irregularities, its waywardness ; it was like a tune that wandered into several keys.   As Mary Grace Burmington put it, one never knew what dear Mary Flaw would say next, and that she did not herself know added to the charm.   She had become crazed, poor thing, in consequence of a disappointment in love, but of course I did not know that, nor that she was crazed at all.   I thought her brilliant and original, and I liked her very much.   In the light of coming events, it would be affectation were I to pre-

tend that she did not feel a similar partiality
for me.

Miss Flaw was, from the first, devoted to
my Father's ministrations, and it was part of
our odd village indulgence that no one ever
dreamed of preventing her from coming to the
Room. On Sunday evenings the bulk of the
audience was arranged on forms, with backs
to them, set in the middle of the floor, with a
passage round them, while other forms were
placed against the walls. My Father preached
from a lectern, facing the audience. If darkness came on in the course of the service,
Richard Moxhay, glimmering in his cream-
white corduroys, used to go slowly round,
lighting groups of tallow candles by the help
of a box of lucifers. Mary Flaw always assumed
the place of honour, on the left extremity of
the front bench, immediately opposite my Father.
Miss Marks and Mary Grace, with me ensconced
and almost buried between them, occupied the
right of the same bench. While the lighting
proceeded, Miss Flaw used to direct it from her
seat, silently, by pointing out to Moxhay, who
took no notice, what groups of candles he should
light next. She did this just as the clown in
the circus directs the grooms how to move the
furniture, and Moxhay paid no more attention
to her than the grooms do to the clown. Miss
Flaw had another peculiarity : she silently
went through a service exactly similar to ours,
but much briefer. The course of our evening
service was this. My Father prayed, and we

all knelt down ; then he gave out a hymn.
and most of us stood up to sing ; then he
preached for about an hour, while we sat and
listened ; then a hymn again, then prayer and
the valediction.

Mary Flaw went through this ritual, but on
a smaller scale. We all knelt down together,
but when we rose from our knees, Miss Flaw
was already standing up, and was pretending,
without a sound, to sing a hymn ; in the midst
of our hymn, she sat down, opened her Bible,
found a text, and then leaned back, her eyes
fixed in space, listening to an imaginary sermon,
which our own real one soon caught up, and
coincided with for about three-quarters of an
hour. Then, while our sermon went peacefully
on, Miss Flaw would rise, and sing in silence
(if I am permitted to use such an expression)
her own visionary hymn ; then she would kneel
down and pray, then rise, collect her belongings,
and sweep, in fairy majesty, out of the chapel,
my Father still rounding his periods from the
pulpit. Nobody ever thought of preventing these
movements, or of checking the poor creature in
her innocent flightiness, until the evening of the
great event.

It was all my own fault. Mary Flaw had
finished her imaginary service earlier than usual.
She had stood up alone with her hymn-book
before her ; she had flung herself on her knees
alone, in the attitude of devotion ; she had
risen ; she had seated herself for a moment
to put on her gloves, and to collect her Bible,

her hymn-book and her pocket-handkerchief in her reticule. She was ready to start, and she looked around her with a pleasant air ; my Father, all undisturbed, booming away meanwhile over our heads. I know not why the manœuvres of Miss Flaw especially attracted me that evening, but I leaned out across Miss Marks and I caught Miss Flaw's eye. She nodded, I nodded ; and the amazing deed was done, I hardly know how. Miss Flaw, with incredible swiftness, flew along the line, plucked me by the coat-collar from between my paralysed protectresses, darted with me down the chapel and out into the dark, before any one had time to say " Jack Robinson."

My Father gazed from the pulpit and the stream of exhortation withered on his lips. No one in the body of the audience stirred ; no one but himself had clearly seen what had happened. Vague rows of " saints " with gaping countenances stared up at him, while he shouted, " Will nobody stop them ? " as we whisked out through the doorway. Forth into the moist night we went, and up the lampless village, where, a few minutes later, the swiftest of the congregation, with my Father at their head, found us sitting on the doorstep of the butcher's shop. My captor was now quite quiet, and made no objection to my quitting her,—" without a single kiss or a good-bye," as the poet says.

Although I had scarcely felt frightened at the time, doubtless my nerves were shaken by this escapade, and it may have had something to do with the recurrence of the distressing visions from which I had suffered as a very little child. These came back, with a force and expansion due to my increased maturity. I had hardly laid my head down on the pillow, than, as it seemed to me, I was taking part in a mad gallop through space. Some force, which had tight hold of me, so that I felt myself an atom in its grasp, was hurrying me on, over an endless slender bridge, under which on either side a loud torrent rushed at a vertiginous depth below. At first our helpless flight,—for I was bound hand and foot like Mazeppa,—proceeded in a straight line, but presently it began to curve, and we raced and roared along, in what gradually became a monstrous vortex, reverberant with noises, loud with light, while, as we proceeded, enormous concentric circles engulfed us, and wheeled above and about us. It seemed as if we,—I, that is, and the undefined force which carried me,—were pushing feverishly on towards a goal which our whole concentrated energies were bent on reaching, but which a frenzied despair in my heart told me we never could reach, yet the attainment of which alone could save us from destruction. Far away, in the pulsation of the great luminous whorls, I could just see that goal, a ruby-coloured point waxing and waning, and it bore, or to be exact it consisted of, the letters of the word CARMINE.

This agitating vision recurred night after

night, and filled me with inexpressible distress. The details of it altered very little, and I knew what I had to expect when I crept into bed. I knew that for a few minutes I should be battling with the chill of the linen sheets, and trying to keep awake, but that then, without a pause, I should slip into that terrible realm of storm and stress in which I was bound hand and foot, and sent galloping through infinity. Often have I wakened, with unutterable joy, to find my Father and Miss Marks, whom my screams had disturbed, standing one on each side of my bed. They could release me from my nightmare, which seldom assailed me twice a night, but how to preserve me from its original attack passed their understanding. My Father, in his tenderness, thought to exorcise the demon by prayer. He would appear in the bed-room, just as I was first slipping into bed, and he would kneel at my side. The light from a candle on the mantel-shelf streamed down upon his dark head of hair while his face was buried in the coverlid, from which a loud voice came up, a little muffled, begging that I might be preserved against all the evil spirits that walk in darkness and that the deep might not swallow me up.

This little ceremony gave a distraction to my thoughts, and may have been useful in that way. But it led to an unfortunate circumstance. My Father began to enjoy these orisons at my bed-side, and to prolong them. Perhaps they lasted a little too long, but I contrived to keep

awake through them, sometimes by a great
effort. On one unhappy night, however, I gave
even worse offence than slumber would have
given. My Father was praying aloud, in the
attitude I have described, and I was half sitting,
half lying in bed, with the clothes sloping from
my chin. Suddenly a rather large insect, dark
and flat, with more legs than a self-respecting
insect ought to need, appeared at the bottom of
the counterpane, and slowly advanced. I think
it was nothing worse than a beetle. It walked
successfully past my Father's sleek black ball
of a head, and climbed straight up at me,
nearer, nearer, till it seemed all a twinkle of
horns and joints. I bore it in silent fascination
till it almost tickled my chin, and then I
screamed " Papa ! Papa ! " My Father rose
in great dudgeon, removed the insect (what
were insects to him !) and then gave me a
tremendous lecture.

The sense of desperation which this incident
produced I shall not easily forget. Life seemed
really to be very harassing when to visions
within and beetles without there was joined the
consciousness of having grievously offended God
by an act of disrespect. It is difficult for me
to justify to myself the violent jobation which
my Father gave me in consequence of my
scream, except by attributing to him something
of the human weakness of vanity. I cannot help
thinking that he liked to hear himself speak to
God in the presence of an admiring listener.
He prayed with fervour and animation, in pure

Johnsonian English, and I hope I am not un-
dutiful if I add my impression that he was not
displeased with the sound of his own devotions.
My cry for help had needlessly, as he thought,
broken in upon this holy and seemly performance. "You, the child of a naturalist," he
remarked in awesome tones, " *you* to pretend
to feel terror at the advance of an insect ? " It
could but be a pretext, he declared, for avoid-
ing the testimony of faith in prayer. "If your
heart were fixed, if it panted after the Lord,
it would take more than the movements of a
beetle to make you disturb oral supplication
at His footstool. Beware I for God is a jealous
God and He consumes them in wrath who make
a noise like a dog."

My Father took at all times a singular pleasure
in repeating that " our God is a jealous God."
He liked the word, which I suppose he used in
an antiquated sense. He was accustomed to
tell the " saints " at the room,—in a very genial
manner, and smiling at them as he said it,—
" I am jealous over you, my beloved brothers
and sisters, with a godly jealousy." I know
that this was interpreted by some of the saints,—
for I heard Mary Grace say so to Miss Marks,—
as meaning that my Father was resentful because
some of them attended the service at the Wesleyan
chapel on Thursday evenings. But my Father
was utterly incapable of such littleness as this,
and when he talked of " jealousy " he meant
a lofty solicitude, a careful watchfulness. He
meant that their spiritual honour was a matter

of anxiety to him. No doubt when he used to tell me to remember that our God is a jealous God, he meant that my sins and shortcomings were not matters of indifference to the Divine Being. But I think, looking back, that it was very extraordinary for a man, so instructed and so intelligent as he, to dwell so much on the possible anger of the Lord, rather than on his pity and love. The theory of extreme Puritanism can surely offer no quainter example of its fallacy than this idea that the omnipotent Jehovah could be seriously offended, and could stoop to revenge, because a little, nervous child of nine had disturbed a prayer by being frightened at a beetle.

The fact that the word " Carmine " appeared as the goal of my visionary pursuits is not so inexplicable as it may seem. My Father was at this time producing numerous water-colour drawings of minute and even of microscopic forms of life. These he executed in the manner of miniature, with an amazing fidelity of form and with a brilliancy of colour which remains unfaded after fifty years. By far the most costly of his pigments was the intense crimson which is manufactured out of the very spirit and essence of cochineal. I had lately become a fervent imitator of his works of art, and I was allowed to use all of his colours, except one ; I was strictly forbidden to let a hair of my paint-brush touch the little broken mass of carmine which was all that he possessed. We believed, but I do not know whether this could be the fact, that carmine of this superlative quality was sold at a guinea a cake. "Carmine," therefore, became my shibboleth of self-indulgence ; it was a symbol of all that taste and art and wealth could combine to produce. I imagined, for instance, that at Belshazzar's feast, the loftiest épergne of gold, surrounded by flowers and jewels, carried the monarch's proudest possession, a cake of carmine. I knew of no object in the world of luxury more desirable than this, and its obsession in my waking hours is quite enough, I think, to account for "carmine" having been the torment of my dreams.

The little incident of the beetle displays my Father's mood at this period in its worst light. His severity was not very creditable, perhaps, to his good sense, but without a word of explanation it may seem even more unreasonable than it was. My Father might have been less stern to my lapses from high conduct, and my own mind at the same time less armoured against his arrows, if our relations had been those which exist in an ordinary religious family. He would have been more indulgent, and my own affections might nevertheless have been more easily alienated, if I had been treated by him as a commonplace child, standing as yet outside the pale of conscious Christianity. But he had formed the idea, and cultivated it assiduously, that I was an "âme d'élite," a being to whom the mysteries of salvation had been divinely revealed and by whom they had been accepted.

I was, to his partial fancy, one in whom the Holy Ghost had already performed a real and permanent work. Hence, I was inside the pale ; I had attained that inner position which divided, as we used to say, the Sheep from the Goats. Another little boy might be very well-behaved, but if he had not consciously " laid hold on Christ," his good deeds, so far, were absolutely useless. Whereas I might be a very naughty boy, and require much chastisement from God and man, but nothing—so my Father thought —could invalidate my election, and sooner or later, perhaps even after many stripes, I must inevitably be brought back to a state of grace.

The paradox between this unquestionable sanctification by faith and my equally unquestionable naughtiness, occupied my Father greatly at this time. He made it a frequent subject of intercession at family prayers, not caring to hide from the servants misdemeanours of mine, which he spread out with a melancholy unction before the Lord. He cultivated the belief that all my little ailments, all my aches and pains, were sent to correct my faults. He carried this persuasion very far, even putting this exhortation before, instead of after, an instant relief of my sufferings. If I burned my finger with a sulphur match, or pinched the end of my nose in the door (to mention but two sorrows that recur to my memory), my Father would solemnly ejaculate : " O may these afflictions be much sanctified to him ! " before offering any remedy for my pain. So that I almost longed, under

the pressure of these pangs, to be a godless
child, who had never known the privileges of
saving grace, since I argued that such a child
would be subjected to none of the sufferings
which seemed to assail my path.

What the ideas or conduct of " another
child " might be I had, however, at this time
no idea, for, strange as it may sound, I had
not, until my tenth year was far advanced,
made acquaintance with any such creature.
The " saints " had children, but I was not
called upon to cultivate their company, and I
had not the slightest wish to do so. But early
in 1859 I was allowed, at last, to associate with
a child of my own age. I do not recall that this
permission gave me any rapture ; I accepted it
philosophically, but without that delighted eagerness which I might have been expected to show.
My earliest companion, then, was a little boy of
almost exactly my own age. His name was
Benny, which no doubt was short for Benjamin.
His surname was Jeffries ; his mother—I think
he had no father—was a solemn and shadowy
lady of means who lived in a villa, which was
older and much larger than ours, on the opposite
side of the road. Going to " play with Benny "
involved a small public excursion, and this I
was now allowed to make by myself—an immense source of self-respect.

Everything in my little memories seems to
run askew ; obviously I ought to have been
extremely stirred and broadened by this earliest
association with a boy of my own age ! Yet

I cannot truly say that it was so. Benny's
mother possessed what seemed to me a vast
domain, with lawns winding among broad
shrubberies, and a kitchen-garden, with aged
fruit-trees in it. The ripeness of this place,
mossed and leafy, was gratifying to my senses,
on which the rawness of our own bald garden
jarred. There was an old brick wall between
the two divisions, upon which it was possible
for us to climb up, and from this we gained
Pisgah-views which were a prodigious pleasure.
But I had not the faintest idea how to "play";
I had never learned, had never heard of any
"games." I think Benny must have lacked
initiative almost as much as I did. We walked
about, and shook the bushes, and climbed along
the wall; I think that was almost all we ever
did do. And, sadly enough, I cannot recover a
phrase from Benny's lips, nor an action, nor a
gesture, although I remember quite clearly how
some grown-up people of that time looked, and
the very words they said.

For example, I recollect Miss Wilkes very
distinctly, since I studied her with great deliberation, and with a suspicious watchfulness
that was above my years. In Miss Wilkes a
type that had hitherto been absolutely unfamiliar to us obtruded upon our experience.
In our Eveless Eden, Woman, if not exactly
"hirsuta et horrida," had always been "of a
certain age." But Miss Wilkes was a comparatively young thing, and she advanced not
by any means unconscious of her charms. All

was feminine, all was impulsive, about Miss
Wilkes ; every gesture seemed eloquent with
girlish innocence and the playful dawn of life.
In actual years I fancy she was not so extremely
youthful, since she was the responsible and
trusted head-mistress of a large boarding-school
for girls, but in her heart the joy of life ran high.
Miss Wilkes had a small, round face, with melting
eyes, and when she lifted her head, her ringlets
seemed to vibrate and shiver like the bells of a
pagoda. She had a charming way of clasping
her hands, and holding them against her bodice,
while she said, " O, but—really now ? " in a
manner inexpressibly engaging. She was very
earnest, and she had a pleading way of calling
out : " O, but aren't you teasing me ? " which
would have brought a tiger fawning to her
crinoline.

After we had spent a full year without any
social distractions, it seems that our circle of
acquaintances had now begun to extend, in
spite of my Father's unwillingness to visit his
neighbours. He was a fortress that required
to be stormed, but there was considerable local
curiosity about him, so that by-and-by escalading
parties were formed, some of which were partly
successful. In the first place, Charles Kingsley
had never hesitated to come, from the beginning,
ever since our arrival. He had reason to visit
our neighbouring town rather frequently, and on
such occasions he always marched up and
attacked us. It was extraordinary how persistent he was, for my Father must have been a

very trying friend. I vividly recollect that a sort of cross-examination of would-be communicants was going on in our half-furnished drawing-room one week-day morning, when Mr. Kingsley was announced; my Father, in stentorian tones, replied: "Tell Mr. Kingsley that I am engaged in examining Scripture with certain of the Lord's children." And I, a little later, kneeling at the window, while the candidates were being dismissed with prayer, watched the author of "Hypatia" nervously careering about the garden, very restless and impatient, yet preferring this ignominy to the chance of losing my Father's company altogether. Kingsley, a daring spirit, used sometimes to drag us out trawling with him in Torbay, and although his hawk's beak and rattling voice frightened me a little, his was always a jolly presence that brought some refreshment to our seriousness.

But the other visitors who came in Kingsley's wake and without his excuse, how they disturbed us! We used to be seated, my Father at his microscope, I with my map or book, in the down-stairs room we called the study. There would be a hush around us in which you could hear a sea-anemone sigh. Then, abruptly, would come a ring at the front door; my Father would bend at me a corrugated brow, and murmur, under his breath, "What's that?" and then, at the sound of footsteps, would bolt into the verandah, and round the garden into the potting-shed. If it was no visitor more serious than the postman or the tax-gatherer, I used to go forth and coax the timid wanderer home. If it was a caller, above all a female caller, it was my privilege to prevaricate, remarking innocently that "Papa is out!"

Into a paradise so carefully guarded, I know not how that serpent Miss Wilkes could penetrate, but there she was. She "broke bread" with the Brethren at the adjacent town, from which she carried on strategical movements, which were, up to a certain point, highly successful. She professed herself deeply interested in microscopy, and desired that some of her young ladies should study it also. She came attended by an unimportant mamma, and by pupils to whom I had sometimes, very unwillingly, to show our "natural objects." They would invade us, and fill our quietness with chattering noise; I could bear none of them, and I was singularly drawn to Miss Marks by finding that she disliked them too.

By whatever arts she worked, Miss Wilkes certainly achieved a certain ascendency. When the knocks came at the front door, I was now instructed to see whether the visitor were not she, before my Father bolted to the potting-shed. She was an untiring listener, and my Father had a genius for instruction. Miss Wilkes was never weary of expressing what a revelation of the wonderful works of God in creation her acquaintance with us had been. She would gaze through the microscope at awful forms, and would persevere until the silver rim which marked the confines of the drop of water under inspection

would ripple inwards with a flash of light and
vanish, because the drop itself had evaporated.
"Well, I can only say, how marvellous are
Thy doings!" was a frequent ejaculation of
Miss Wilkes, and one that was very well received.
She learned the Latin names of many of the
species, and it seems quite pathetic to me, looking back, to realise how much trouble the poor
woman took. She "hung," as the expression
is, upon my Father's every word, and one
instance of this led to a certain revelation.

My Father, who had an extraordinary way
of saying anything that came up into his mind,
stated one day,—the fashions, I must suppose,
being under discussion,—that he thought white
the only becoming colour for a lady's stockings.
The stockings of Miss Wilkes had up to that
hour been of a deep violet, but she wore white
ones in future whenever she came to our house.
This delicacy would have been beyond my
unaided infant observation, but I heard Miss
Marks mention the matter, in terms which
they supposed to be secret, to her confidante,
and I verified it at the ankles of the lady. Miss
Marks continued by saying, in confidence, and
"quite as between you and me, dear Mary
Grace," that Miss Wilkes was a "minx." I
had the greatest curiosity about words, and
as this was a new one, I looked it up in our
large English Dictionary. But there the definition of the term was this :—"Minx : the
female of minnock ; a pert wanton." I was
as much in the dark as ever.

Whether she was the female of a minnock
(whatever that may be) or whether she was
only a very well-meaning schoolmistress desirous of enlivening a monotonous existence,
Miss Wilkes certainly took us out of ourselves
a good deal. Did my Father know what danger
he ran? It was the opinion of Miss Marks and
of Mary Grace that he did not, and in the back-
kitchen, a room which served those ladies as a
private oratory in the summer-time, much
prayer was offered up that his eyes might be
opened ere it was too late. But I am inclined to
think that they were open all the time, that, at
all events, they were what the French call
"entr'ouvert," that enough light for practical
purposes came sifted in through his eyelashes.
At a later time, being reminded of Miss Wilkes,
he said with a certain complaisance, " Ah, yes!
she proffered much entertainment during my
widowed years!" He used to go down to her
boarding-school, the garden of which had been
the scene of a murder, and was romantically
situated on the edge of a quarried cliff; he
always took me with him, and kept me at his
side all through these visits, notwithstanding
Miss Wilkes' solicitude that the fatigue and
excitement would be too much for the dear
child's strength, unless I rested a little on the
parlour sofa.

About this time, the question of my education
came up for discussion in the household, as
indeed it well might. Miss Marks had long
proved practically inadequate in this respect,

her slender acquirements evaporating, I suppose,
like the drops of water under the microscope,
while the field of her general duties became
wider. The subjects in which I took pleasure,
and upon which I possessed books, I sedulously
taught myself ; the other subjects, which formed
the vast majority, I did not learn at all. Like
Aurora Leigh,

> I brushed with extreme flounce
> The circle of the universe,

especially zoology, botany and astronomy, but
with the explicit exception of geology, which
my Father regarded as tending directly to the
encouragement of infidelity. I copied a great
quantity of maps, and read all the books of
travels that I could find. But I acquired no
mathematics, no languages, no history, so that
I was in danger of gross illiteracy in these
important departments.

My Father grudged the time, but he felt
it a duty to do something to fill up these de-
ficiencies, and we now started Latin, in a little
eighteenth-century reading-book, out of which
my Grandfather had been taught. It consisted
of strings of words, and of grim arrangements
of conjunction and declension, presented in a
manner appallingly unattractive. I used to be
set down in the study, under my Father's eye,
to learn a solid page of this compilation, while
he wrote or painted. The window would be
open in summer, and my seat was close to it.
Outside, a bee was shaking the clematis-blossom,

or a red-admiral butterfly was opening and
shutting his wings on the hot concrete of the
verandah, or a blackbird was racing across the
lawn. It was almost more than human nature
could bear to have to sit holding up to my
face the dreary little Latin book, with its sheep-
skin cover that smelt of mildewed paste.

But out of this strength there came an unexpected sudden sweetness. The exercise of
hearing me repeat my strings of nouns and
verbs had revived in my Father his memories
of the classics. In the old solitary years, a
long time ago, by the shores of Canadian rapids,
on the edge of West Indian swamps, his Virgil
had been an inestimable solace to him. To
extremely devout persons, there is something
objectionable in most of the great writers of
antiquity. Horace, Lucretius, Terence, Catullus,
Juvenal,—in each there is one quality or another
definitely repulsive to a reader who is determined
to know nothing but Christ and him crucified.
From time immemorial, however, it has been
recognised in the Christian church that this
objection does not apply to Virgil. He is the
most evangelical of the classics ; he is the one
who can be enjoyed with least to explain away
and least to excuse. One evening my Father
took down his Virgil from an upper shelf, and
his thoughts wandered away from surrounding
things ; he travelled in the past again. The
book was a Delphin edition of 1798, which
had followed him in all his wanderings ; there
was a great scratch on the sheep-skin cover that

a thorn had made in a forest of Alabama. And
then, in the twilight, as he shut the volume at
last, oblivious of my presence, he began to
murmur and to chant the adorable verses by
memory.

Tityre, tu patulae recubans sub tegmine fagi,

he warbled ; and I stopped my play, and listened
as if to a nightingale, till he reached

tu, Tityre, lentus in umbra
Formosam resonare doces Amaryllida silvas.

" O Papa, what is that ? " I could not prevent
myself from asking. He translated the verses,
he explained their meaning, but his exposition
gave me little interest. What to me was
beautiful Amaryllis ? She and her love-sick
Tityrus awakened no image whatever in my
mind.

But a miracle had been revealed to me,
the incalculable, the amazing beauty which
could exist in the sound of verses. My pro-
sodical instinct was awakened, quite suddenly
that dim evening, as my Father and I sat
alone in the breakfast-room after tea, serenely
accepting the hour, for once, with no idea of
exhortation or profit. Verse, "a breeze mid
blossoms playing," as Coleridge says, descended
from the roses as a moth might have done,
and the magic of it took hold of my heart for
ever. I persuaded my Father, who was a
little astonished at my insistence, to repeat

the lines over and over again. At last my
brain caught them, and as I walked in Benny's
garden, or as I hung over the tidal pools at
the edge of the sea, all my inner being used to
ring out with the sound of

Formosam resonare doces Amaryllida silvas.

CHAPTER VIII

IN the previous chapter I have dwelt on some
of the lighter conditions of our life at this time ;
I must now turn to it in a less frivolous aspect.
As my tenth year advanced, the development of
my character gave my Father, I will not say
anxiety, but matter for serious reflection. My
intelligence was now perceived to be taking a
sudden start ; visitors drew my Father's attention to the fact that I was " coming out so
much." I grew rapidly in stature, having been
a little shrimp of a thing up to that time, and I
no longer appeared much younger than my
years. Looking back, I do not think that there
was any sudden mental development, but that
the change was mainly a social one. I had
been reserved, timid and taciturn ; I had disliked the company of strangers. But with my
tenth year, I certainly unfolded, so far as to
become sociable and talkative, and perhaps I
struck those around me as grown " clever,"
because I said the things which I had previously
only thought. There was a change, no doubt,
yet I believe that it was mainly physical, rather
than mental. My excessive fragility—or apparent fragility, for I must have been always
wiry—decreased ; I slept better, and therefore
grew less nervous ; I ate better, and therefore
put on flesh. If I preserved a delicate look

—people still used to say in my presence,
" That dear child is not long for this world ! "
—it was in consequence of a sort of habit into
which my body had grown ; it was a trans-
parency which did not speak of what was in
store for me, but of what I had already passed
through.

The increased activity of my intellectual
system now showed itself in what I believe to
be a very healthy form, direct imitation. The
rage for what is called " originality " is pushed
to such a length in these days that even children
are not considered promising, unless they attempt
things preposterous and unparalleled. From, his
earliest hour, the ambitious person is told that
to make a road where none has walked before,
to do easily what it is impossible for others to
do at all, to create new forms of thought and
expression, are the only recipes for genius ; and
in trying to escape on all sides from every
resemblance to his predecessors, he adopts at
once an air of eccentricity and pretentiousness.
This continues to be the accepted view of
originality ; but, in spite of this conventional
opinion, I hold that the healthy sign of an
activity of mind in early youth is not to be
striving after unheard-of miracles, but to imitate
closely and carefully what is being said and done
in the vicinity. The child of a great sculptor
will hang about the studio, and will try to
hammer a head out of a waste piece of marble
with a nail ; it does not follow that he too will
be a sculptor. The child of a politician will sit

in committee with a row of empty chairs, and will harangue an imaginary senate from behind the curtains. I, the son of a man who looked through a microscope and painted what he saw there, would fain observe for myself, and paint my observations. It did not follow, alas! that I was built to be a miniature-painter or a savant, but the activity of a childish intelligence was shown by my desire to copy the results of such energy as I saw nearest at hand.

In the secular direction, this now took the form of my preparing little monographs on sea-side creatures, which were arranged, tabulated and divided as exactly as possible on the pattern of those which my Father was composing for his "Actinologia Britannica." I wrote these out upon sheets of paper of the same size as his printed page, and I adorned them with water-colour plates, meant to emulate his precise and exquisite illustrations. One or two of these ludicrous postiches are still preserved, and in glancing at them now I wonder, not at any skill that they possess, but at the perseverance and the patience, the evidence of close and persistent labour. I was not set to these tasks by my Father, who, in fact, did not much approve of them. He was touched, too, with the "originality" heresy, and exhorted me not to copy him, but to go out into the garden or the shore and describe something new, in a new way. That was quite impossible; I possessed no initiative. But I can now well understand why my Father, very indulgently and good-tem-

peredly, deprecated these exercises of mine.
They took up, and, as he might well think,
wasted, an enormous quantity of time ; and
they were, moreover, parodies, rather than
imitations, of his writings, for I invented new
species, with sapphire spots and crimson tentacles
and amber bands, which were close enough to
his real species to be disconcerting. He came
from conscientiously shepherding the flocks of
ocean, and I do not wonder that my ring-straked,
speckled and spotted varieties put him out of
countenance. If I had not been so innocent
and solemn, he might have fancied I was mocking
him.

These extraordinary excursions into science,
falsely so called, occupied a large part of my
time. There was a little spare room at the
back of our house, dedicated to lumber and to
empty portmanteaux. There was a table in it
already, and I added a stool ; this cheerless
apartment now became my study. I spent so
many hours here, in solitude and without
making a sound, that my Father's curiosity, if
not his suspicion, was occasionally roused, and
he would make a sudden raid on me. I was
always discovered, doubled up over the table,
with my pen and ink, or else my box of colours
and tumbler of turbid water by my hand,
working away like a Chinese student shut up
in his matriculating box.

It might have been done for a wager, if
anything so sinful had ever been dreamed of
in our pious household. The apparatus was

F*

slow and laboured.   In order to keep my uncouth handwriting in bounds, I was obliged to
rule not lines only, but borders to my pages.
The subject did not lend itself to any flow of
language, and I was obliged incessantly to
borrow sentences, word for word, from my
Father's published books.   Discouraged by every
one around me, daunted by the laborious effort
needful to carry out the scheme, it seems odd
to me now that I persisted in so strange and
wearisome an employment, but it became an
absorbing passion, and was indulged in to the
neglect of other lessons and other pleasures.

My Father, as the spring advanced, used to
come up to the Box-room, as my retreat was
called, and hunt me out into the sunshine.
But I soon crept back to my mania.   It gave
him much trouble, and Miss Marks, who thought
it sheer idleness, was vociferous in objection.
She would gladly have torn up all my writings
and paintings, and have set me to a useful
task.   My Father, with his strong natural individualism, could not take this view.   He was
interested in this strange freak of mine, and he
could not wholly condemn it.   But he must
have thought it a little crazy, and it is evident to
me now that it led to the revolution in domestic
polity by which he began to encourage my
acquaintance with other young people as much
as he had previously discouraged it.   He saw
that I could not be allowed to spend my whole
time in a little stuffy room making solemn and
ridiculous imitations of Papers read before the

Linnæan Society. He was grieved, moreover,
at the badness of my pictures, for I had no native
skill ; and he tried to teach me his own system
of miniature-painting as applied to natural
history. I was forced, in deep depression of
spirits, to turn from my grotesque monographs,
and paint under my Father's eye, and from a
finished drawing of his, a gorgeous tropic bird
in flight. Aided by my habit of imitation, I did
at length produce something which might have
shown promise, if it had not been wrung from
me, touch by touch, pigment by pigment, under
the orders of a task-master.

All this had its absurd side, but I seem to
perceive that it had also its value. It is, surely,
a mistake to look too near at hand for the
benefits of education. What is actually taught
in early childhood is often that part of training
which makes least impression on the character,
and is of the least permanent importance. My
labours failed to make me a zoologist, and the
multitude of my designs and my descriptions
have left me helplessly ignorant of the anatomy
of a sea-anemone. Yet I cannot look upon the
mental discipline as useless. It taught me to
concentrate my attention, to define the nature
of distinctions, to see accurately, and to name
what I saw. Moreover, it gave me the habit of
going on with any piece of work I had in hand,
not flagging because the interest or picturesqueness of the theme had declined, but pushing
forth towards a definite goal, well foreseen and
limited beforehand. For almost any intellectual

employment in later life, it seems to me that this discipline was valuable. I am, however, not the less conscious how ludicrous was the mode in which, in my tenth year, I obtained it.

My spiritual condition occupied my Father's thoughts very insistently at this time. Closing, as he did, most of the doors of worldly pleasure and energy upon his conscience, he had continued to pursue his scientific investigations without any sense of sin. Most fortunate it was, that the collecting of marine animals in the tidal pools, and the description of them in pages which were addressed to the wide scientific public, at no time occurred to him as in any way inconsistent with his holy calling. His conscience was so delicate, and often so morbid in its delicacy, that if that had occurred to him, he would certainly have abandoned his investigations, and have been left without an employment. But happily he justified his investigation by regarding it as a glorification of God's created works. In the introduction to his " Actinologia Britannica," written at the time which I have now reached in this narrative, he sent forth his labours with a phrase which I should think unparalleled in connection with a learned and technical biological treatise. He stated concerning that book, that he published it " as one more tribute humbly offered to the glory of the Triune God, who is wonderful in counsel, and excellent in working." Scientific investigation sincerely carried out in that spirit became a kind of week-day interpretation of the current creed of Sundays.

The development of my faculties, of which I have spoken, extended to the religious sphere no less than to the secular. Here also, as I look back, I see that I was extremely imitative. I expanded in the warmth of my Father's fervour, and, on the whole, in a manner that was satisfactory to him. He observed the richer hold that I was now taking on life ; he saw my faculties branching in many directions, and he became very anxious to secure my maintenance in grace. In earlier years, certain sides of my character had offered a sort of passive resistance to his ideas. I had let what I did not care to welcome pass over my mind in the curious density that children adopt in order to avoid receiving impressions—blankly, dumbly, achieving by stupidity what they cannot achieve by argument. I think that I had frequently done this ; that he had been brought up against a dead wall ; although on other sides of my nature I had been responsive and docile. But now, in my tenth year, the imitative faculty got the upper hand, and nothing seemed so attractive as to be what I was expected to be. If there was a doubt now, it lay in the other direction ; it seemed hardly normal that so young a child should appear so receptive and so apt.

My Father believed himself justified, at this juncture, in making a tremendous effort. He wished to secure me finally, exhaustively, before

the age of puberty could dawn, before my soul
was fettered with the love of carnal things.
He thought that if I could now be identified
with the " saints," and could stand on exactly
their footing, a habit of conformity would be
secured. I should meet the paganising ten-
dencies of advancing years with security if I
could be forearmed with all the weapons of a
sanctified life. He wished me, in short, to be
received into the community of the Brethren
on the terms of an adult. There were difficulties
in the way of carrying out this scheme, and
they were urged upon him, more or less courageously, by the elders of the church. But he
overbore them. What the difficulties were, and
what were the arguments which he used to
sweep those difficulties away, I must now
explain, for in this lay the centre of our future
relations as father and son.

In dealing with the peasants around him,
among whom he was engaged in an active
propaganda, my Father always insisted on the
necessity of conversion. There must be a new
birth and being, a fresh creation in God. This
crisis he was accustomed to regard as manifesting
itself in a sudden and definite upheaval. There
might have been prolonged practical piety, deep
and true contrition for sin, but these, although
the natural and suitable prologue to conversion,
were not conversion itself. People hung on at
the confines of regeneration, often for a very
long time ; my Father dealt earnestly with
them, the elders ministered to them, with ex-

planation, exhortation and prayer. Such persons
were in a gracious state, but they were not in
a state of grace. If they should suddenly die,
they would pass away in an unconverted condition, and all that could be said in their favour
was a vague expression of hope that they would
benefit from God's uncovenanted mercies.

But on some day, at some hour and minute,
if life was spared to them, the way of salvation
would be revealed to these persons in such an
aspect that they would be enabled instan-
taneously to accept it. They would take it
consciously, as one takes a gift from the hand
that offers it. This act of taking was the process
of conversion, and the person who so accepted
was a child of God now, although a single
minute ago he had been a child of wrath. The
very root of human nature had to be changed,
and, in the majority of cases, this change was
sudden, patent, palpable.

I have just said, " in the majority of cases,"
because my Father admitted the possibility of
exceptions. The formula was, " If any man
hath not the Spirit of Christ, he is none of
his." As a rule, no one could possess the
Spirit of Christ, without a conscious and full
abandonment of the soul, and this, however
carefully led up to, and prepared for with tears
and renunciations, was not, could not, be made,
except at a set moment of time. Faith, in
an esoteric and almost symbolic sense, was
necessary, and could not be a result of argument,
but was a state of heart. In these opinions my

Father departed in no wise from the strict evangelical doctrine of the Protestant churches, but he held it in a mode and with a severity peculiar to himself. Now, it is plain that this state of heart, this voluntary deed of acceptance, presupposed a full and rational consciousness of the relations of things. It might be clearly achieved by a person of humble cultivation, but only by one who was fully capable of independent thought, in other words by a more or less adult person. The man or woman claiming the privileges of conversion must be able to understand and to grasp what his religious education was aiming at.

It is extraordinary what trouble it often gave my Father to know whether he was justified in admitting to the communion people of very limited powers of expression. A harmless, humble labouring man would come with a request to be allowed to "break bread." It was only by the use of strong leading questions that he could be induced to mention Christ as the ground of his trust at all. I recollect an elderly agricultural labourer being closeted for a long time with my Father, who came out at last, in a sort of dazed condition, and replied to our inquiries,—with a shrug of his shoulders as he said it,—" I was obliged to put the Name and Blood and Work of Jesus into his very mouth. It is true that he assented cordially at last, but I confess I was grievously daunted by the poor intelligence ! "

But there was, or there might be, another

class of persons, whom early training, separation
from the world, and the care of godly parents
had so early familiarised with the acceptable
calling of Christ that their conversion had
occurred, unperceived and therefore unrecorded,
at an extraordinarily early age. It would be
in vain to look for a repetition of the phenomenon in those cases. The heavenly fire must
not be expected to descend a second time ; the
lips are touched with the burning coal once,
and once only. If, accordingly, these pre-
cociously selected spirits are to be excluded
because no new birth is observed in them at
a mature age, they must continue outside in
the cold, since the phenomenon cannot be
repeated. When, therefore, there is not possible
any further doubt of their being in possession
of salvation, longer delay is useless, and worse
than useless. The fact of conversion, though
not recorded nor even recollected, must be
accepted on the evidence of confession of faith,
and as soon as the intelligence is evidently
developed, the person not merely may, but
should be accepted into communion, although
still immature in body, although in years still
even a child. This my Father believed to be my
case, and in this rare class did he fondly persuade
himself to station me.

As I have said, the congregation,—although
docile and timid, and little able, as units, to
hold their own against their minister,—behind
his back were faintly hostile to this plan. None
of their own children had ever been so much

as suggested for membership, and each of
themselves, in ripe years, had been subjected
to severe cross-examination. I think it was
rather a bitter pill for some of them to swallow
that a pert little boy of ten should be admitted,
as a grown-up person, to all the hard-won privileges of their order. Mary Grace Burmington
came back from her visits to the cottagers,
reporting disaffection here and there, grumb-
lings in the rank and file. But quite as many,
especially of the women, enthusiastically supported my Father's wish, gloried aloud in the
manifestations of my early piety, and professed
to see in it something of miraculous promise.
The expression " another Infant Samuel " was
widely used. I became quite a subject of
contention. A war of the sexes threatened to
break out over me ; I was a disturbing element
at cottage breakfasts. I was mentioned at
public prayer-meetings, not indeed by name,
but, in the extraordinary allusive way customary in our devotions, as " one amongst us of
tender years " or as " a sapling in the Lord's
vineyard."

To all this my Father put a stop in his own
high-handed fashion. After the morning meeting, one Sunday in the autumn of 1859, he
desired the attention of the saints to a personal
matter which was, perhaps, not unfamiliar to
them by rumour. That was, he explained, the
question of the admission of his beloved little
son to the communion of saints in the breaking
of bread. He allowed—and I sat there in

evidence, palely smiling at the audience, my
feet scarcely touching the ground—that I was
not what is styled adult ; I was not, he frankly
admitted, a grown-up person. But I was adult
in a knowledge of the Lord ; I possessed an
insight into the plan of salvation which many a
hoary head might envy for its fulness, its clearness, its conformity with Scripture doctrine.
This was a palpable hit at more than one
stumbler and fumbler after the truth, and several
hoary heads were bowed.

My Father then went on to explain very
fully the position which I have already attempted
to define. He admitted the absence in my
case of a sudden, apparent act of conversion
resulting upon conviction of sin. But he stated
the grounds of his belief that I had, in still
earlier infancy, been converted, and he declared
that if so, I ought no longer to be excluded from
the privileges of communion. He said, moreover, that he was willing on this occasion to
waive his own privilege as a minister, and that
he would rather call on Brother Fawkes and
Brother Bere, the leading elders, to examine the
candidate in his stead. This was a master-
stroke, for Brothers Fawkes and Bere had been
suspected of leading the disaffection, and this
threw all the burden of responsibility on them.
The meeting broke up in great amiability, and
my Father and I went home together in the very
highest of spirits. I, indeed, in my pride,
crossed the verge of indiscretion by saying :
" When I have been admitted to fellowship,

Papa, shall I be allowed to call you ' beloved Brother ' ? " My Father was too well pleased with the morning's work to be critical. He laughed, and answered : " That, my Love, though strictly correct, would hardly, I fear, be thought judicious ! "

It was suggested that my tenth birthday, which followed this public announcement by a few days, would be a capital occasion for me to go through the ordeal. Accordingly, after dark (for our new lamp was lighted for the first time in honour of the event), I withdrew alone into our drawing-room, which had just, at length, been furnished, and which looked, I thought, very smart. Hither came to me, first Brother Fawkes, by himself ; then Brother Bere, by himself ; and then both together, so that you may say, if you are pedantically inclined, that I underwent three successive interviews. My Father, out of sight some-where, was, of course, playing the part of stage manager.

I felt not at all shy, but so highly strung that my whole nature seemed to throb with excitement. My first examiner, on the other hand, was extremely confused. Fawkes, who was a builder in a small business of his own, was short and fat ; his complexion, which wore a deeper and more uniform rose-colour than usual, I observed to be starred with dew-drops of nervous emotion, which he wiped away at intervals with a large bandana hand-kerchief. He was so long in coming to the point, that I was obliged to lead him to it myself, and I sat up on the sofa in the full lamplight, and testified my faith in the atonement with a fluency that surprised myself. Before I had done, Fawkes, a middle-aged man with the reputation of being a very stiff employer of labour, was weeping like a child.

Bere, the carpenter, a long, thin and dry man, with a curiously immobile eye, did not fall so easily a prey to my fascinations. He put me through my paces very sharply, for he had something of the temper of an attorney mingled with his religiousness. However, I was equal to him, and he, too, though he held his own head higher, was not less impressed than Fawkes had been, by the surroundings of the occasion. Neither of them had ever been in our drawing-room since it was furnished, and I thought that each of them noticed how smart the wall-paper was. Indeed, I believe I drew their attention to it. After the two solitary examinations were over, the elders came in again, as I have said, and they prayed for a long time. We all three knelt at the sofa, I between them. But by this time, to my great exaltation of spirits there had succeeded an equally dismal depression. It was my turn now to weep, and I dimly remember my Father coming into the room, and my being carried up to bed, in a state of collapse and fatigue, by the silent and kindly Miss Marks.

On the following Sunday morning, I was the principal subject which occupied an unusually

crowded meeting. My Father, looking whiter
and yet darker than usual, called upon Brother
Fawkes and Brother Bere to state to the
assembled saints what their experiences had
been in connection with their visits to '' one ''
who desired to be admitted to the breaking of
bread. It was tremendously exciting to me to
hear myself spoken of with this impersonal
publicity, and I had no fear of the result.

Events showed that I had no need of fear.
Fawkes and Bere were sometimes accused of a
rivalry, which indeed broke out a few years
later, and gave my Father much anxiety and
pain. But on this occasion their unanimity
was wonderful. Each strove to exceed the other
in the tributes which they paid to my piety. My
answers had been so full and clear, my humility
(save the mark !)had been so sweet, my acquaintance with Scripture so amazing, my testimony
to all the leading principles of salvation so
distinct and exhaustive, that they could only
say that they had felt confounded, and yet
deeply cheered and led far along their own
heavenly path, by hearing such accents fall from
the lips of a babe and a suckling. I did not
like being described as a suckling, but every
lot has its crumpled rose-leaf, and in all other
respects the report of the elders was a triumph.
My Father then clenched the whole matter by
rising and announcing that I had expressed an
independent desire to confess the Lord by the
act of public baptism, immediately after which
I should be admitted to communion '' as an

adult." Emotion ran so high at this, that a large portion of the congregation insisted on walking with us back to our garden-gate, to the stupefaction of the rest of the villagers.

My public baptism was the central event of my whole childhood. Everything, since the earliest dawn of consciousness, seemed to have been leading up to it. Everything, afterwards, seemed to be leading down and away from it. The practice of immersing communicants on the sea-beach at Oddicombe had now been completely abandoned, but we possessed as yet no tank for a baptismal purpose in our own Room. The Room in the adjoining town, however, was really quite a large chapel, and it was amply provided with the needful conveniences. It was our practice, therefore, at this time, to claim the hospitality of our neighbours. Baptisms were made an occasion for friendly relations between the two congregations, and led to pleasant social intercourse. I believe that the ministers and elders of the two meetings arranged to combine their forces at these times, and to baptize communicants from both congregations.

The minister of the town meeting was Mr. S., a very handsome old gentleman, of venerable and powerful appearance. He had snowy hair and a long white beard, but from under shaggy eyebrows there blazed out great black eyes which warned the beholder that the snow was an ornament and not a sign of decrepitude. The eve of my baptism at length drew near ;

it was fixed for October 12, almost exactly three weeks after my tenth birthday. I was dressed in old clothes, and a suit of smarter things was packed up in a carpet-bag. After night-fall, this carpet-bag, accompanied by my Father, myself, Miss Marks and Mary Grace, was put in a four-wheeled cab, and driven, a long way in the dark, to the chapel of our friends. There we were received, in a blaze of lights, with a pressure of hands, with a murmur of voices, with ejaculations and even with tears, and were conducted, amid unspeakable emotion, to places of honour in the front row of the congregation.

The scene was one which would have been impressive, not merely to such hermits as we were, but even to worldly persons accustomed to life and to its curious and variegated experiences. To me it was dazzling beyond words, inexpressibly exciting, an initiation to every kind of publicity and glory. There were many candidates, but the rest of them,—mere grown-up men and women,—gave thanks aloud that it was their privilege to follow where I led. I was the acknowledged hero of the hour. Those were days when newspaper enterprise was scarcely in its infancy, and the event owed nothing to journalistic effort. In spite of that, the news of this remarkable ceremony, the immersion of a little boy of ten years old '' as an adult,'' had spread far and wide through the county in the course of three weeks. The chapel of our hosts was, as I have said, very large ; it was commonly too large for their needs, but on this night it was crowded to the ceiling, and the crowd had come—as every soft murmurer assured me—to see *me*.

There were people there who had travelled from Exeter, from Dartmouth, from Totnes, to witness so extraordinary a ceremony. There was one old woman of eighty-five who had come, my neighbours whispered to me, all the way from Moreton-Hampstead, on purpose to see me baptized. I looked at her crumpled countenance with amazement, for there was no curiosity, no interest visible in it. She sat there perfectly listless, looking at nothing, but chewing between her toothless gums what appeared to be a jujube.

In the centre of the chapel-floor a number of planks had been taken up, and revealed a pool which might have been supposed to be a small swimming-bath. We gazed down into this dark square of mysterious waters, from the tepid surface of which faint swirls of vapour rose. The whole congregation was arranged, tier above tier, about the four straight sides of this pool ; every person was able to see what happened in it without any unseemly struggling or standing on forms. Mr. S. now rose, an impressive hieratic figure, commanding attention and imploring perfect silence. He held a small book in his hand, and he was preparing to give out the number of a hymn, when an astounding incident took place.

There was a great splash, and a tall young

woman was perceived to be in the baptismal
pool, her arms waving above her head, and
her figure held upright in the water by the
inflation of the air underneath her crinoline,
which was blown out like a bladder, as in
some extravagant old fashion-plate. Whether
her feet touched the bottom of the font I cannot
say, but I suppose they did so. An indescribable
turmoil of shrieks and cries followed on this
extraordinary apparition. A great many people
excitedly called upon other people to be calm,
and an instance was given of the remark of
James Smith that

> He who, in quest of quiet, " Silence ! " hoots
> Is apt to make the hubbub he imputes.

The young woman, in a more or less fainting
condition, was presently removed from the
water, and taken into the sort of tent which
was prepared for candidates. It was found
that she herself had wished to be a candidate
and had earnestly desired to be baptized, but
that this had been forbidden by her parents.
On the supposition that she fell in by accident,
a pious coincidence was detected in this affair ;
the Lord had pre-ordained that she should be
baptized in spite of all opposition. But my
Father, in his shrewd way, doubted. He pointed
out to us, next morning, that, in the first place,
she had not, in any sense, been baptized, as her
head had not been immersed ; and that, in the
second place, she must have deliberately jumped
in, since, had she stumbled and fallen forward,

her hands and face would have struck the water, whereas they remained quite dry. She belonged, however, to the neighbour congregation, and we had no responsibility to pursue the inquiry any further.

Decorum being again secured, Mr. S., with unimpaired dignity, proposed to the congregation a hymn, which was long enough to occupy them during the preparations for the actual baptism. He then retired to the vestry, and I (for I was to be the first to testify) was led by Miss Marks and Mary Grace into the species of tent of which I have just spoken. Its pale sides seemed to shake with the jubilant singing of the saints outside, while part of my clothing was removed and I was prepared for immersion. A sudden cessation of the hymn warned us that the Minister was now ready, and we emerged into the glare of lights and faces to find Mr. S. already standing in the water up to his knees. Feeling as small as one of our microscopical specimens, almost infinitesimally tiny as I descended into his Titanic arms, I was handed down the steps to him. He was dressed in a kind of long surplice, underneath which—as I could not, even in that moment, help observing —the air gathered in long bubbles which he strove to flatten out. The end of his noble beard he had tucked away ; his shirt-sleeves were turned up at the wrist.

The entire congregation was now silent, so silent that the uncertain splashing of my feet as I descended seemed to deafen me. Mr. S.,

a little embarrassed by my short stature, succeeded at length in securing me with one palm
on my chest and the other between my shoulders.
He said, slowly, in a loud, sonorous voice that
seemed to enter my brain and empty it, "I
baptize thee, my Brother, in the name of the
Father and of the Son and of the Holy Ghost!"
Having intoned this formula, he then gently
flung me backwards until I was wholly under
the water, and then—as he brought me up again,
and tenderly steadied my feet on the steps of
the font, and delivered me, dripping and splutter-
ing, into the anxious hands of the women, who
hurried me to the tent—the whole assembly
broke forth in a thunder of song, a pæan of
praise to God for this manifestation of his
marvellous goodness and mercy. So great was
the enthusiasm, that it could hardly be restrained
so as to allow the other candidates, the humdrum
adults who followed in my wet and glorious
footsteps, to undergo a ritual about which, in
their case, no one in the congregation pretended
to be able to take even the most languid
interest.

My Father's happiness during the next few
weeks it is now pathetic to me to look back
upon. His sternness melted into a universal
complaisance. He laughed and smiled, he paid
to my opinions the tribute of the gravest consideration, he indulged—utterly unlike his wont
—in shy and furtive caresses. I could express
no wish that he did not attempt to fulfil, and
the only warning which he cared to give me

was one, very gently expressed, against spiritual
pride.

This was certainly required, for I was puffed
out with a sense of my own holiness. I was
religiously confidential with my Father, con-
descending with Miss Marks (who I think had
given up trying to make it all out), haughty
with the servants, and insufferably patronising
with those young companions of my own age
with whom I was now beginning to associate.

I would fain close this remarkable episode
on a key of solemnity, but alas! if I am to be
loyal to the truth, I must record that some of
the other little boys presently complained to
Mary Grace that I put out my tongue at them
in mockery, during the service in the Room, to
remind them that I now broke bread as one of
the Saints and that they did not.

CHAPTER IX

THE result of my being admitted into the communion of the " Saints " was that, as soon as the nine days' wonder of the thing passed by, my position became, if anything, more harassing and pressed than ever. It is true that freedom was permitted to me in certain directions ; I was allowed to act a little more on my own responsibility, and was not so incessantly informed what " the Lord's will " might be in this matter and in that, because it was now conceived that, in such dilemmas, I could command private intelligence of my own. But there was no relaxation of our rigid manner of life, and I think I now began, by comparing it with the habits of others, to perceive how very strict it was.

The main difference in my lot as a communicant from that of a mere dweller in the tents of righteousness was that I was expected to respond with instant fervour to every appeal of conscience. When I did not do this, my position was almost worse than it had been before, because of the livelier nature of the responsibility which weighed upon me. My little faults of conduct, too, assumed shapes of terrible importance, since they proceeded from one so signally enlightened. My Father was never tired of reminding me that, now that I

was a professing Christian, I must remember,
in everything I did, that I was an example to
others. He used to draw dreadful pictures of
supposititious little boys who were secretly
watching me from afar, and whose whole
career, in time and in eternity, might be disas-
trously affected if I did not keep my lamp
burning.

The year which followed upon my baptism
did not open very happily at the Room. Considerable changes had now taken place in the
community. My Father's impressive services,
a certain prestige in his preaching, the mere
fact that so vigorous a person was at the head
of affairs, had induced a large increase in the
attendance. By this time, if my memory does
not fail me as to dates, we had left the dismal
loft over the stables, and had built ourselves a
perfectly plain, but commodious and well-
arranged chapel in the centre of the village.
This greatly added to the prosperity of the
meeting. Everything had combined to make
our services popular, and had attracted to us a
new element of younger people. Numbers of
youthful masons and carpenters, shop-girls and
domestic servants, found the Room a pleasant
trysting-place, and were more or less super-
ficially induced to accept salvation as it was
offered to them in my Father's searching
addresses. My Father was very shrewd in dealing with mere curiosity or idle motive, and
sharply packed off any youths who simply came
to make eyes at the girls, or any " maids "

whose only object was to display their new
bonnet-strings. But he was powerless against a
temporary sincerity, the simulacrum of a true
change of heart. I have often heard him say,—
of some young fellow who had attended our
services with fervour for a little while, and
then had turned cold and left us,—"and I
thought that the Holy Ghost had wrought
in him!" Such disappointments grievously
depress an evangelist.

Religious bodies are liable to strange and
unaccountable fluctuations. At the beginning
of the third year since our arrival, the congregation seemed to be in a very prosperous state,
as regards attendance, conversions and other
outward signs of activity. Yet it was quite
soon after this that my Father began to be
harassed by all sorts of troubles, and the spring
of 1860 was a critical moment in the history
of the community. Although he loved to take
a very high tone about the Saints, and involved
them sometimes in a cloud of laudatory metaphysics, the truth was that they were nothing
more than peasants of a somewhat primitive
type, not well instructed in the rules of conduct
and liable to exactly the same weaknesses as
invade the rural character in every country and
latitude. That they were exhorted to behave as
"children of light," and that the majority of
them sincerely desired to do credit to their high
calling, could not prevent their being beset by
the sins which had affected their forebears for
generations past.

The addition of so many young persons of each sex to the communion led to an entirely new class of embarrassment. Now there arose endless difficulties about "engagements," about youthful brethren who "went out walking" with even more youthful sisters. Glancing over my Father's notes, I observe the ceaseless repetition of cases in which So-and-So is "courting" Such-an-one, followed by the melancholy record that he has "deserted" her. In my Father's stern language, "desertion" would very often mean no more than that the amatory pair had blamelessly changed their minds ; but in some cases it meant more and worse than this. It was a very great distress to him that sometimes the young men and women who showed the most lively interest in Scripture, and who had apparently accepted the way of salvation with the fullest intelligence, were precisely those who seemed to struggle with least success against a temptation to unchastity. He put this down to the concentrated malignity of Satan, who directed his most poisoned darts against the fairest of the flock.

In addition to these troubles, there came recriminations, mutual charges of drunkenness in private, all sorts of petty jealousy and scandal. There were frequent definite acts of "backsliding" on the part of members, who had in consequence to be "put away." No one of these cases might be in itself extremely serious, but when many of them came together they seemed to indicate that the church was in an

G

unhealthy condition. The particulars of many
of these scandals were concealed from me,
but I was an adroit little pitcher, and had
cultivated the art of seeming to be interested in
something else, a book or a flower, while my
elders were talking confidentially. As a rule,
while I would fain have acquired more details,
I was fairly well-informed about the errors of
the Saints, although I was often quaintly ignorant of the real nature of those errors.

Not infrequently, persons who had fallen into
sin repented of it under my Father's penetrating
ministrations. They were apt in their penitence
to use strange symbolic expressions. I remember Mrs. Pewings, our washerwoman, who had
been accused of intemperance and had been
suspended from communion, reappearing with
a face that shone with soap and sanctification,
and saying to me, " Oh ! blessed Child, you're
wonderin' to zee old Pewings here again, but
He have rolled away my mountain ! " For
once, I was absolutely at a loss, but she meant
that the Lord had removed the load of her sins,
and restored her to a state of grace.

It was in consequence of these backslidings,
which had become alarmingly frequent, that
early in 1860 my Father determined on proclaiming a solemn fast. He delivered one
Sunday what seemed to me an awe-inspiring
address, calling upon us all closely to examine
our consciences, and reminding us of the appalling fate of the church of Laodicea. He said
that it was not enough to have made a satis-

factory confession of faith, nor even to have
sealed that confession in baptism, if we did not
live up to our protestations. Salvation, he told
us, must indeed precede holiness of life, yet both
are essential. It was a dark and rainy winter
morning when he made this terrible address,
which frightened the congregation extremely.
When the marrow was congealed within our
bones, and when the bowed heads before him,
and the faintly audible sobs of the women in
the background, told him that his lesson had
gone home, he pronounced the keeping of a
day in the following week as a fast of contrition.
" Those of you who have to pursue your daily
occupations will pursue them, but sustained
only by the bread of affliction and by the water
of affliction."

His influence over these gentle peasant
people was certainly remarkable, for no effort
was made to resist his exhortation. It was
his customary plan to stay a little while, after
the morning meeting was over, and in a very
affable fashion to shake hands with the saints.
But on this occasion he stalked forth without
a word, holding my hand tight until we had
swept out into the street.

How the rest of the congregation kept this
fast I do not know. But it was a dreadful
day for us. I was awakened in the pitchy
night to go off with my Father to the Room,
where a scanty gathering held a penitential
prayer-meeting. We came home, as dawn
was breaking, and in process of time sat down

to breakfast, which consisted—at that dismal hour—of slices of dry bread and a tumbler of cold water each. During the morning, I was not allowed to paint, or write, or withdraw to my study in the box-room. We sat, in a state of depression not to be described, in the breakfast-room, reading books of a devotional character, with occasional wailing of some very doleful hymn. Our midday dinner came at last ; the meal was strictly confined, as before, to dry slices of the loaf and a tumbler of water.

The afternoon would have been spent as the morning was, and so my Father spent it. But Miss Marks, seeing my white cheeks and the dark rings round my eyes, besought leave to take me out for a walk. This was permitted, with a pledge that I should be given no species of refreshment. Although I told Miss Marks, in the course of the walk, that I was feeling '' so leer '' (our Devonshire phrase for hungry), she dared not break her word. Our last meal was of the former character, and the day ended by our trapesing through the wet to another prayer-meeting, whence I returned in a state bordering on collapse. and was put to bed without further nourishment. There was no great hardship in all this, I daresay, but it was certainly rigorous. My Father took pains to see that what he had said about the bread and water of affliction was carried out in the bosom of his own family, and by no one more unflinchingly than by himself.

My attitude to other people's souls when

I was out of my Father's sight was now a constant anxiety to me. In our tattling world of small things he had extraordinary opportunities of learning how I behaved when I was away from home ; I did not realise this, and I used to think his acquaintance with my deeds and words savoured almost of wizardry. He was accustomed to urge upon me the necessity of " speaking for Jesus in season and out of season," and he so worked upon my feelings that I would start forth like St. Teresa, wild for the Moors and martyrdom. But any actual impact with persons marvellously cooled my zeal, and I should hardly ever have " spoken " at all if it had not been for that unfortunate phrase " out of season." It really seemed that one must talk of nothing else, since if an occasion was not in season it was out of season ; there was no alternative, no close time for souls.

My Father was very generous. He used to magnify any little effort that I made, with stammering tongue, to sanctify a visit ; and people, I now see, were accustomed to give me a friendly lead in this direction, so that they might please him by reporting that I had " testified " in the Lord's service. The whole thing, however, was artificial, and was part of my Father's restless inability to let well alone. It was not in harshness or in ill-nature that he worried me so much ; on the contrary, it was all part of his too-anxious love. He was in a hurry to see me become a shining light, everything that he had himself desired to be, yet with none of his shortcomings.

It was about this time that he harrowed my whole soul into painful agitation by a phrase that he let fall, without, I believe, attaching any particular importance to it at the time. He was occupied, as he so often was, in polishing and burnishing my faith, and he was led to speak of the day when I should ascend the pulpit to preach my first sermon. "Oh! if I may be there, out of sight, and hear the gospel message proclaimed from your lips, then I shall say, ' My poor work is done. Oh! Lord Jesus, receive my spirit.' " I cannot express the dismay which this aspiration gave me, the horror with which I anticipated such a *nunc dimittis*. I felt like a small and solitary bird, caught and hung out hopelessly and endlessly in a great glittering cage. The clearness of the personal image affected me as all the texts and prayers and predictions had failed to do. I saw myself imprisoned for ever in the religious system which had caught me and would whirl my helpless spirit as in the concentric wheels of my nightly vision. I did not struggle against it, because I believed that it was inevitable, and that there was no other way of making peace with the terrible and ever-watchful " God who is a jealous God." But I looked forward to my fate without zeal and without exhilaration, and the fear of the Lord altogether swallowed up and cancelled any notion of the love of Him.

I should do myself an injustice, however, if

I described my attitude to faith at this time as
wanting in candour.   I did very earnestly desire
to follow where my Father led.   That passion
for imitation, which I have already discussed,
was strongly developed at this time, and it induced me to repeat the language of pious books
in godly ejaculations which greatly edified my
grown-up companions, and were, so far as I can
judge, perfectly sincere.   I wished extremely to
be good and holy, and I had no doubt in my mind
of the absolute infallibility of my Father as a
guide in heavenly things.   But I am perfectly
sure that there never was a moment in which
my heart truly responded, with native ardour,
to the words which flowed so readily, in such a
stream of unction, from my anointed lips.   I
cannot recall anything but an intellectual surrender ; there was never joy in the act of resignation, never the mystic's rapture at feeling his
phantom self, his own threadbare soul, suffused,
thrilled through, robed again in glory by a fire
which burns up everything personal and individual about him.

Through thick and thin I clung to a hard nut
of individuality, deep down in my childish
nature.   To the pressure from without, I resigned everything else, my thoughts, my words,
my anticipations, my assurances, but there was
something which I never resigned, my innate
and persistent self.   Meek as I seemed, and
gently respondent, I was always conscious of
that innermost quality which I had learned to
recognise in my earlier days in Islington, that

existence of two in the depths who could speak to one another in inviolable secrecy.

" This a natural man may discourse of, and that very knowingly, and give a kind of natural credit to it, as to a history that may be true ; but firmly to believe that there is divine truth in all these things, and to have a persuasion of it stronger than of the very thing we see with our eyes ; such an assent as this is the peculiar work of the Spirit of God, and is certainly saving faith.'' This passage is not to be found in the writings of any extravagant Plymouth Brother, but in one of the most solid classics of the Church, in Archbishop Leighton's " Commentary on the First Epistle of Peter.'' I quote it because it defines, more exactly than words of my own could hope to do, the difference which already existed, and in secrecy began forthwith to be more and more acutely accentuated, between my Father and myself. He did indeed possess this saving faith, which could move mountains of evidence, and suffer no diminution under the action of failure or disappointment. I, on the other hand—as I began to feel dimly then, and see luminously now—had only acquired the habit of giving what the Archbishop means by " a kind of natural credit " to the doctrine so persistently impressed upon my conscience. From its very nature this could not but be molten in the dews and exhaled in the sunshine of life and thought and experience.

My Father, by an indulgent act for the caprice

of which I cannot wholly account, presently let
in a flood of imaginative light which was certainly hostile to my heavenly calling.   My instinctive interest in geography has already been
mentioned.   This was the one branch of knowledge in which I needed no instruction, geographical information seeming to soak into the cells
of my brain without an effort.   At the age of
eleven, I knew a great deal more of maps, and of
the mutual relation of localities all over the globe,
than most grown-up people do.   It was almost a
mechanical acquirement.   I was now greatly
taken with the geography of the West Indies,
of every part of which I had made MS. maps.
There was something powerfully attractive to
my fancy in the great chain of the Antilles,
lying on the sea like an open bracelet, with its
big jewels and little jewels strung on an invisible thread.   I liked to shut my eyes and
see it all, in a mental panorama, stretched from
Cape Sant' Antonio to the Serpent's Mouth.
Several of these lovely islands, these emeralds
and amethysts set on the Caribbean Sea, my
Father had known well in his youth, and I was
importunate in questioning him about them.
One day, as I multiplied inquiries, he rose in his
impetuous way, and climbing to the top of a
bookcase, brought down a thick volume and
presented it to me.   " You'll find all about the
Antilles there," he said, and left me with " Tom
Cringle's Log " in my possession.

The embargo laid upon every species of fiction
by my Mother's powerful scruple had never been

raised, although she had been dead four years.
As I have said in an earlier chapter, this was a
point on which I believe that my Father had
never entirely agreed with her. He had, however, yielded to her prejudice, and no work of
romance, no fictitious story, had ever come in
my way. It is remarkable that among our
books, which amounted to many hundreds, I
had never discovered a single work of fiction
until my Father himself revealed the existence
of Michael Scott's wild masterpiece. So little
did I understand what was allowable in the
way of literary invention that I began the story
without a doubt that it was true, and I think it
was my Father himself who, in answer to an
inquiry, explained to me that it was " all made
up." He advised me to read the descriptions
of the sea, and of the mountains of Jamaica,
and " skip " the pages which gave imaginary
adventures and conversations. But I did not
take his counsel ; these latter were the flower of
the book to me. I had never read, never dreamed
of anything like them, and they filled my whole
horizon with glory and with joy.

I suppose that when my Father was a younger
man, and less pietistic, he had read " Tom
Cringle's Log " with pleasure, because it re-
called familiar scenes to him. Much was explained by the fact that the frontispiece of this
edition was a delicate line-engraving of Blew-
fields, the great lonely house in a garden of
Jamaican all-spice where for eighteen months
he had worked as a naturalist. He could not

look at this print without recalling exquisite
memories and airs that blew from a terrestrial
paradise. But Michael Scott's noisy amorous
novel of adventure was an extraordinary book
to put in the hands of a child who had never
been allowed to glance at the mildest and most
febrifugal story-book.

It was like giving a glass of brandy neat to
some one who had never been weaned from a
milk diet. I have not read "Tom Cringle's
Log" from that day to this, and I think that
I should be unwilling now to break the charm
of memory, which may be largely illusion.
But I remember a great deal of the plot and
not a little of the language, and, while I am
sure it is enchantingly spirited, I am quite as
sure that the persons it describes were far from
being unspotted by the world. The scenes at
night in the streets of Spanish Town surpassed
not merely my experience, but, thank goodness,
my imagination. The nautical personages used,
in their conversations, what is called "a class
of language," and there ran, if I am not mis-
taken, a glow and gust of life through the
romance from beginning to end which was
nothing if it was not resolutely pagan.

There were certain scenes and images in
"Tom Cringle's Log" which made not merely
a lasting impression upon my mind, but tinged
my outlook upon life. The long adventures,
fightings and escapes, sudden storms without,
and mutinies within, drawn forth as they were,
surely with great skill, upon the fiery blue of

the boundless tropical ocean, produced on my
inner mind a sort of glimmering hope, very
vaguely felt at first, slowly developing, long
stationary and faint, but always tending towards
a belief that I should escape at last from the
narrowness of the life we led at home, from this
bondage to the Law and the Prophets.

I must not define too clearly, nor endeavour
too formally to insist on the blind movements
of a childish mind. But of this I am quite sure,
that the reading and re-reading of " Tom
Cringle's Log " did more than anything else, in
this critical eleventh year of my life, to give
fortitude to my individuality, which was in
great danger—as I now see—of succumbing to
the pressure my Father brought to bear upon it
from all sides. My soul was shut up, like Fatima,
in a tower to which no external influences could
come, and it might really have been starved to
death, or have lost the power of recovery and
rebound, if my captor, by some freak not yet
perfectly accounted for, had not gratuitously
opened a little window in it and added a powerful
telescope. The daring chapters of Michael
Scott's picaresque romance of the tropics were
that telescope and that window.

In the spring of this year, I began to walk
about the village and even proceed for considerable distances into the country by myself,
and after reading " Tom Cringle's Log " those
expeditions were accompanied by a constant
hope of meeting with some adventures. I did
not court events, however, except in fancy, for

I was very shy of real people, and would break off some gallant dream of prowess on the high seas to bolt into a field and hide behind the hedge, while a couple of labouring men went by. Sometimes, however, the wave of a great purpose would bear me on, as when once, but certainly at an earlier date than I have now reached, hearing the dangers of a persistent drought much dwelt upon, I carried my small red watering-pot, full of water, up to the top of the village, and then all the way down Petittor Lane, and discharged its contents in a cornfield, hoping by this act to improve the prospects of the harvest. A more eventful excursion must be described, because of the moral impression it left indelibly upon me.

I have described the sequestered and beautiful hamlet of Barton, to which I was so often taken visiting by Mary Grace Burmington. At Barton there lived a couple who were objects of peculiar interest to me, because of the rather odd fact that having come, out of pure curiosity, to see me baptized, they had been then and there deeply convinced of their spiritual danger. These were John Brooks, an Irish quarryman, and his wife, Ann Brooks. These people had not merely been hitherto unconverted, but they had openly treated the Brethren with anger and contempt. They came, indeed, to my baptism to mock, but they went away impressed.

Next morning, when Mrs. Brooks was at the wash-tub, as she told us, Hell opened at her feet, and the Devil came out holding a long scroll on which the list of her sins was written. She was so much excited, that the emotion brought about a miscarriage and she was seriously ill. Meanwhile, her husband, who had been equally moved at the baptism, was also converted, and as soon as she was well enough, they were baptized together, and then " broke bread " with us. The case of the Brookses was much talked about, and was attributed, in a distant sense, to me ; that is to say, if I had not been an object of public curiosity, the Brookses might have remained in the bond of iniquity. I, therefore, took a very particular interest in them, and as I presently heard that they were extremely poor, I was filled with a fervent longing to minister to their necessities.

Somebody had lately given me a present of money, and I begged little sums here and there until I reached the very considerable figure of seven shillings and sixpence. With these coins safe in a little linen bag, I started one Sunday afternoon, without saying anything to any one, and I arrived at the Brookses' cottage in Barton. John Brooks was a heavy dirty man, with a pock-marked face and two left legs ; his broad and red face carried small side-whiskers in the manner of that day, but was otherwise shaved. When I reached the cottage, husband and wife were at home, doing nothing at all in the approved Sunday style. I was received by them with some surprise, but I quickly explained my mission, and produced my linen bag. To my disgust, all John Brooks said was, '' I know'd the Lord would provide," and after emptying my little bag into the palm of an enormous hand, he swept the contents into his trousers pocket, and slapped his leg. He said not one single word of thanks or appreciation, and I was absolutely cut to the heart.

I think that in the course of a long life I have never experienced a bitterer disappointment. The woman, who was quicker, and more sensitive, doubtless saw my embarrassment, but the form of comfort which she chose was even more wounding to my pride. " Never mind, little master," she said, " you shall come and see me feed the pigs." But there is a limit to endurance, and with a sense of having been cruelly torn by the tooth of ingratitude, I fled from the threshold of the Brookses, never to return.

At tea that afternoon, I was very much downcast, and under cross-examination from Miss Marks, all my little story came out. My Father, who had been floating away in a meditation, as he very often did, caught a word that interested him and descended to consciousness. I had to tell my tale over again, this time very sadly, and with a fear that I should be reprimanded. But on the contrary, both my Father and Miss Marks were attentive and most sympathetic, and I was much comforted. " We must remember they are the Lord's children," said my Father. " Even the Lord can't make a silk purse out of a sow's ear," said Miss Marks, who was considerably ruffled. " Alas! alas! " replied my Father, waving his hand with a

deprecating gesture. "The dear child!" said
Miss Marks, bristling with indignation, and
patting my hand across the tea-table. "The
Lord will reward your zealous loving care of his
poor, even if they have neither the grace nor the
knowledge to thank you," said my Father, and
rested his brown eyes meltingly upon me.
"Brutes!" said Miss Marks, thinking of John
and Ann Brooks. "Oh no! no!" replied my
Father, "but hewers of wood and drawers of
water! We must bear with the limited intelligence." All this was an emollient to my
wounds, and I became consoled. But the springs
of benevolence were dried up within me, and to
this day I have never entirely recovered from the
shock of John Brooks's coarse leer and his
"I know'd the Lord would provide." The infant plant of philanthropy was burned in my
bosom as if by quick-lime.

In the course of the summer, a young schoolmaster called on my Father to announce to
him that he had just opened a day-school for
the sons of gentlemen in our vicinity, and he
begged for the favour of a visit. My Father
returned his call; he lived in one of the small
white villas, buried in laurels, which gave a discreet animation to our neighbourhood. Mr. M.
was frank and modest, deferential to my Father's
opinions and yet capable of defending his own.
His school and he produced an excellent impression, and in August I began to be one of his
pupils. The school was very informal; it was
held in the two principal dwelling-rooms on the

ground-floor of the villa, and I do not remember
that Mr. M. had any help from an usher.

There were perhaps twenty boys in the school
at most, and often fewer. I made the excursion
between home and school four times a day ; if
I walked fast, the transit might take five minutes,
and, as there were several objects of interest in
the way, it might be spread over an hour. In
fine weather the going to and from school was
very delightful, and small as the scope of it
was, it could be varied almost indefinitely. I
would sometimes meet with a schoolfellow proceeding in the same direction, and my Father,
observing us over the wall one morning, was
amused to notice that I always progressed by
dancing along the curbstone sideways, my face
turned inwards and my arms beating against
my legs, conversing loudly all the time. This
was a case of pure heredity, for so he used to go
to his school, forty years before, along the streets
of Poole.

One day when fortunately I was alone, I was
accosted by an old gentleman, dressed as a dis-
senting minister. He was pleased with my
replies, and he presently made it a habit to be
taking his constitutional when I was likely to
be on the high road. We became great friends,
and he took me at last to his house, a very modest
place, where to my great amazement, there hung
in the dining-room, two large portraits, one of a
man, the other of a woman, in extravagant
fancy-dress. My old friend told me that the
former was a picture of himself as he had ap-

peared, "long ago, in my unconverted days, on the stage."

I was so ignorant as not to have the slightest conception of what was meant by the stage, and he explained to me that he had been an actor and a poet, before the Lord had opened his eyes to better things. I knew nothing about actors, but poets were already the objects of my veneration. My friend was the first poet I had ever seen. He was no less a person than James Sheridan Knowles, the famous author of "Virginius" and "The Hunchback," who had become a Baptist minister in his old age. When, at home, I mentioned this acquaintance, it awakened no interest. I believe that my Father had never heard, or never noticed, the name of one who had been by far the most eminent English playwright of that age.

It was from Sheridan Knowles' lips that I first heard fall the name of Shakespeare. He was surprised, I fancy, to find me so curiously advanced in some branches of knowledge, and so utterly ignorant of others. He could hardly credit that the names of Hamlet and Falstaff and Prospero meant nothing to a little boy who knew so much theology and geography as I did. Mr. Knowles suggested that I should ask my schoolmaster to read some of the plays of Shakespeare with the boys, and he proposed "The Merchant of Venice" as particularly well-suited for this purpose. I repeated what my aged friend (Mr. Sheridan Knowles must have been nearly eighty at that time) had said, and Mr. M. accepted

the idea with promptitude. (All my memories
of this my earliest schoolmaster present him
to me as intelligent, amiable and quick, although I think not very soundly prepared for his
profession.)

Accordingly, it was announced that the reading of Shakespeare would be one of our lessons,
and on the following afternoon we began "The
Merchant of Venice." There was one large
volume, and it was handed about the class ;
I was permitted to read the part of Bassanio, and
I set forth, with ecstatic pipe, how

> In Belmont is a lady richly left,
> And she is fair, and fairer than that word !

Mr. M. must have had some fondness for the
stage himself ; his pleasure in the Shakespeare
scenes was obvious, and nothing else that he
taught me made so much impression on me as
what he said about a proper emphasis in reading aloud. I was in the seventh heaven of delight, but alas ! we had only reached the second
act of the play, when the readings mysteriously
stopped. I never knew the cause, but I suspect that it was at my Father's desire. He
prided himself on never having read a page of
Shakespeare, and on never having entered a
theatre but once. I think I must have spoken
at home about the readings, and that he must
have given the schoolmaster a hint to return to
the ordinary school curriculum.

The fact that I was "a believer," as it was
our custom to call one who had been admitted

to the arcana of our religion, and that therefore,
in all commerce with "unbelievers," it was my
duty to be "testifying for my Lord, in season
and out of season,"—this prevented my forming
any intimate friendships at my first school. I
shrank from the toilsome and embarrassing act
of button-holing a schoolfellow as he rushed
out of class, and of pressing upon him the probably unintelligible question "Have you found
Jesus?" It was simpler to avoid him, to slip
like a lizard through the laurels and emerge into
solitude.

The boys had a way of plunging out into the
road in front of the school-villa when afternoon school was over; it was a pleasant rural
road lined with high hedges and shadowed by
elm-trees. Here, especially towards the summer
twilight, they used to linger and play vague
games, swooping and whirling in the declining
sunshine, and I was glad to join these bat-like
sports. But my company, though not avoided,
was not greatly sought for. I think that something of my curious history was known, and that
I was, not unkindly but instinctively, avoided,
as an animal of a different species, not allied
to the herd. The conventionality of little boys
is constant; the colour of their traditions is
uniform. At the same time, although I made
no friends, I found no enemies. In class, except
in my extraordinary aptitude for geography,
which was looked upon as incomprehensible and
almost uncanny, I was rather behind than in
front of the others. I, therefore, awakened no

jealousies, and, intent on my own dreams, I think my little shadowy presence escaped the notice of most of my schoolfellows.

By the side of the road I have mentioned, between the school and my home, there was a large horse-pond. The hedge folded round three sides of it, while ancient pollard elms bent over it, and chequered with their foliage in it the reflection of the sky. The roadside edge of this pond was my favourite station ; it consisted of a hard clay which could be moulded into fairly tenacious forms. Here I created a maritime empire—islands, a seaboard with harbours, light-houses, fortifications. My geographical imita-tiveness had its full swing. Sometimes, while I was creating, a cart would be driven roughly into the pond, and a horse would drink deep of my ocean, his hooves trampling my archipelagoes and shattering my ports with what was worse than a typhoon. But I immediately set to work, as soon as the cart was gone and the mud had settled, to tidy up my coast-line again and to scoop out anew my harbours.

My pleasure in this sport was endless, and what I was able to see, in my mind's eye, was not the edge of a morass of mud, but a splendid line of coast, and gulfs of the type of Tor Bay. I do not recollect a sharper double humiliation than when old Sam Lamble, the blacksmith, who was one of the " saints," being asked by my Father whether he had met me, replied " Yes, I zeed 'un up-long, making mud pies in the ro-ad ! " What a position for one who had

been received into communion " as an adult " !
What a blot on the scutcheon of a would-be
Columbus !   " Mud-pies," indeed !

Yet I had an appreciator. One afternoon,
as I was busy on my geographical operations,
a good-looking middle-aged lady, with a soft
pink cheek and a sparkling hazel eye, paused
and asked me if my name was not what it was.
I had seen her before ; a stranger to our parts,
with a voice without a trace in it of the Devonshire drawl.   I knew, dimly, that she came
sometimes to the meeting, that she was lodging at Upton with some friends of ours who
accepted paying guests in an old house that
was simply a basket of roses.   She was Miss
Brightwen, and I now conversed with her for
the first time.

Her interest in my harbours and islands was
marked ; she did not smile ; she asked questions
about my peninsulas which were intelligent and
pertinent.   I was even persuaded at last to
leave my creations and to walk with her towards
the village.   I was pleased with her voice, her
refinement, her dress, which was more delicate,
and her manners, which were more easy, than
what I was accustomed to.   We had some very
pleasant conversation, and when we parted I
had the satisfaction of feeling that our intercourse had been both agreeable to me and instructive to her.   I told her that I should be
glad to tell her more on a future occasion ; she
thanked me very gravely, and then she laughed
a little.   I confess I did not see that there was

anything to laugh at. We parted on warm terms of mutual esteem, but I little thought that this sympathetic Quakerish lady was to become my mother.

CHAPTER X

I SLEPT in a little bed in a corner of the room, and my Father in the ancestral four-poster nearer to the door. Very early one bright September morning at the close of my eleventh year, my Father called me over to him. I climbed up, and was snugly wrapped in the coverlid ; and then we held a momentous conversation. It began abruptly by his asking me whether I should like to have a new mamma. I was never a sentimentalist, and I therefore answered, cannily, that that would depend on who she was. He parried this, and announced that, any way, a new mamma was coming ; I was sure to like her. Still in a non-committal mood, I asked : " Will she go with me to the back of the lime-kiln ? " This question caused my Father a great bewilderment. I had to explain that the ambition of my life was to go up behind the lime-kiln on the top of the hill that hung over Barton, a spot which was forbidden ground, being locally held one of extreme danger. " Oh ! I daresay she will," my Father then said, " but you must guess who she is." I guessed one or two of the less comely of the female " saints," and, this embarrassing my Father,—since the second I mentioned was a married woman who kept a sweet-shop in the village,—he cut my inquiries short by saying, "It is Miss Brightwen."

So far so good, and I was well pleased. But unfortunately I remembered that it was my duty to testify "in season and out of season." I therefore asked, with much earnestness, " But, Papa, is she one of the Lord's children ? " He replied, with gravity, that she was. " Has she taken up her cross in baptism ? " I went on, for this was my own strong point as a believer. My Father looked a little shame-faced, and replied : " Well, she has not as yet seen the necessity of that, but we must pray that the Lord may make her way clear before her. You see, she has been brought up, hitherto, in the so-called Church of England."

Our positions were now curiously changed. It seemed as if it were I who was the jealous monitor, and my Father the deprecating penitent. I sat up in the coverlid, and I shook a finger at him. " Papa," I said, " don't tell me that she's a pedobaptist ? " I had lately acquired that valuable word, and I seized this remarkable opportunity of using it. It affected my Father painfully, but he repeated his assurance that if we united our prayers, and set the Scripture plan plainly before Miss Brightwen, there could be no doubt that she would see her way to accepting the doctrine of adult baptism. And he said we must judge not, lest we ourselves be judged. I had just enough tact to let that pass, but I was quite aware that our whole system was one of judging, and that we had no intention whatever of being judged ourselves. Yet even at the age of eleven one sees that on certain occasions to press home the truth is not convenient.

Just before Christmas, on a piercing night of frost, my Father brought to us his bride. The smartening up of the house, the new furniture, the removal of my own possessions to a private bed-room, the wedding-gifts of the " saints," all these things paled in interest before the fact that Miss Marks had made a " scene," in the course of the afternoon. I was dancing about the drawing-room, and was saying : " Oh ! I am so glad my new Mamma is coming," when Miss Marks called out, in an unnatural voice, " Oh ! you cruel child." I stopped in amazement and stared at her, whereupon she threw prudence to the winds, and moaned : " I once thought I should be your dear mamma." I was simply stupefied, and I expressed my horror in terms that were clear and strong. Thereupon Miss Marks had a wild fit of hysterics, while I looked on, wholly unsympathetic and still deeply affronted. She was right ; I was cruel, alas ! but then, what a silly woman she had been ! The consequence was that she withdrew in a moist and quivering condition to her boudoir, where she had locked herself in when I, all smiles and caresses, was welcoming the bride and bridegroom on the doorstep as politely as if I had been a valued old family retainer.

My stepmother immediately became a great

ally of mine. She was never a tower of strength
to me, but at least she was always a lodge in
my garden of cucumbers. She was a very well-
meaning pious lady, but she was not a fanatic,
and her mind did not naturally revel in spiritual
aspirations. Almost her only social fault was
that she was sometimes a little fretful ; this
was the way in which her bruised individuality
asserted itself. But she was affectionate, serene,
and above all refined. Her refinement was
extraordinarily pleasant to my nerves, on which
much else in our surroundings jarred.

How life may have jarred, poor insulated
lady, on her during her first experience of our
life at the Room, I know not, but I think she
was a philosopher. She had, with surprising
rashness, and in opposition to the wishes of
every member of her own family, taken her cake,
and now she recognised that she must eat it, to
the last crumb. Over her wishes and prejudices
my Father exercised a constant, cheerful and
quiet pressure. He was never unkind or abrupt,
but he went on adding avoirdupois until her
will gave way under the sheer weight. Even
to public immersion, which, as was natural in
a shy and sensitive lady of advancing years, she
regarded with a horror which was long insurmountable,—even to baptism she yielded, and
my Father had the joy to announce to the Saints
one Sunday morning at the breaking of bread
that " my beloved wife has been able at length
to see the Lord's Will in the matter of baptism,
and will testify to the faith which is in her on

Thursday evening next." No wonder my stepmother was sometimes fretful.

On the physical side, I owe her an endless
debt of gratitude. Her relations, who objected
strongly to her marriage, had told her, among
other pleasant prophecies, that " the first thing
you will have to do will be to bury that poor
child." Under the old-world sway of Miss
Marks, I had slept beneath a load of blankets,
had never gone out save weighted with great
coat and comforter, and had been protected
from fresh air as if from a pestilence. With
real courage my stepmother reversed all this.
My bed-room window stood wide open all night
long, wraps were done away with, or exchanged
for flannel garments next the skin, and I was
urged to be out and about as much as possible.

All the quidnuncs among the " saints " shook
their heads ; Mary Grace Burmington, a little
embittered by the downfall of her Marks, made
a solemn remonstrance to my Father, who,
however, allowed my stepmother to carry out
her excellent plan. My health responded rapidly
to this change of régime, but increase of health
did not bring increase of spirituality. My
Father, fully occupied with moulding the will
and inflaming the piety of my stepmother, left
me now, to a degree not precedented, in undisturbed possession of my own devices. I did not
lose my faith, but many other things took a
prominent place in my mind.

It will, I suppose, be admitted that there is
no greater proof of complete religious sincerity

than fervour in private prayer. If an individual, alone by the side of his bed, prolongs his intercessions, lingers wrestling with his divine Companion, and will not leave off until he has what he believes to be evidence of a reply to his entreaties—then, no matter what the character of his public protestations, or what the frailty of his actions, it is absolutely certain that he believes in what he professes.

My Father prayed in private in what I may almost call a spirit of violence. He entreated for spiritual guidance with nothing less than importunity. It might be said that he stormed the citadels of God's grace, refusing to be baffled, urging his intercessions without mercy upon a Deity who sometimes struck me as inattentive to his prayers or wearied by them. My Father's acts of supplication, as I used to witness them at night, when I was supposed to be asleep, were accompanied by stretchings out of the hands, by crackings of the joints of the fingers, by deep breathings, by murmurous sounds which seemed just breaking out of silence, like Virgil's bees out of the hive, "magnis clamoribus." My Father fortified his religious life by prayer as an athlete does his physical life by lung-gymnastics and vigorous rubbings.

It was a trouble to my conscience that I could not emulate this fervour. The poverty of my prayers had now long been a source of distress to me, but I could not discover how to enrich them. My Father used to warn us very solemnly against "lip-service," by which

he meant singing hymns of experience and
joining in ministrations in which our hearts
took no vital or personal part. This was an
outward act, the tendency of which I could well
appreciate, but there was a " lip-service " even
more deadly than that, against which it never
occurred to him to warn me. It assailed me
when I had come alone by my bedside, and had
blown out the candle, and had sunken on my
knees in my night-gown. Then it was that my
deadness made itself felt, in the mechanical
address I put up, the emptiness of my language,
the absence of all real unction.

I never could contrive to ask God for spiritual
gifts in the same voice and spirit in which I
could ask a human being for objects which I
knew he could give me and which I earnestly
desired to possess. That sense of the reality
of intercession was for ever denied me, and it
was, I now see, the stigma of my want of faith.
But at the time, of course, I suspected nothing
of the kind, and I tried to keep up my zeal by a
desperate mental flogging, as if my soul had been
a peg-top.

In nothing did I gain from the advent of my
stepmother more than in the encouragement
she gave to my friendships with a group of boys
of my own age, of whom I had now lately formed
the acquaintance. These friendships she not
merely tolerated, but fostered ; it was even due
to her kind arrangements that they took a certain
set form, that our excursions started from this
house or from that on regular days. I hardly

know by what stages I ceased to be a lonely little creature of mock-monographs and mud-pies, and became a member of a sort of club of eight or ten active boys. The long summer holidays of 1861 were set in an enchanting brightness.

Looking back, I cannot see a cloud on the terrestrial horizon—I see nothing but a blaze of sunshine ; descents of slippery grass to moons of snow-white shingle, cold to the bare flesh ; red promontories running out into a sea that was like sapphire ; and our happy clan climbing, bathing, boating, lounging, chattering, all the hot day through. Once more I have to record the fact, which I think is not without interest, that precisely as my life ceases to be solitary, it ceases to be distinct. I have no difficulty in recalling, with the minuteness of a photograph, scenes in which my Father and I were the sole actors within the four walls of a room, but of the glorious life among wild boys on the margin of the sea I have nothing but vague and broken impressions, delicious and illusive.

It was a remarkable proof of my Father's temporary lapse into indulgence that he made no effort to thwart my intimacy with these my new companions. He was in an unusually humane mood himself. His marriage was one proof of it ; another was the composition at this time of the most picturesque, easy and graceful of all his writings, " The Romance of Natural History," even now a sort of classic. Everything combined to make him believe that the blessing of the Lord was upon him, and to clothe the darkness of the world with at least a mist of rose-colour. I do not recollect that ever at this time he bethought him, when I started in the morning for a long day with my friends on the edge of the sea, to remind me that I must speak to them, in season and out of season, of the Blood of Jesus. And I, young coward that I was, let sleeping dogmas lie.

My companions were not all of them the sons of saints in our communion ; their parents belonged to that professional class which we were only now beginning to attract to our services. They were brought up in religious, but not in fanatical, families, and I was the only "converted" one among them. Mrs. Paget, of whom I shall have presently to speak, characteristically said that it grieved her to see "one lamb among so many kids." But "kid" is a word of varied significance, and the symbol did not seem to us effectively applied. As a matter of fact, we made what I still feel was an excellent tacit compromise. My young companions never jeered at me for being "in communion with the saints," and I, on my part, never urged the Atonement upon them. I began, in fact, more and more to keep my own religion for use on Sundays.

It will, I hope, have been observed that among the very curious grown-up people into whose company I was thrown, although many were frail and some were foolish, none, so far as I can

discern, were hypocritical. I am not one of
those who believe that hypocrisy is a vice that
grows on every bush. Of course, in religious
more than in any other matters, there is a perpetual contradiction between our thoughts and
our deeds which is inevitable to our social order,
and is bound to lead to " cette tromperie mutu-
elle " of which Pascal speaks. But I have often
wondered, while admiring the splendid portrait
of Tartufe, whether such a monster ever, or
at least often, has walked the stage of life ;
whether Molière observed, or only invented
him.

To adopt a scheme of religious pretension,
with no belief whatever in its being true, merely
for sensuous advantage, openly acknowledging
to one's inner self the brazen system of deceit,—
such a course may, and doubtless has been, trod-
den, yet surely much less frequently than cynics
love to suggest. But at the juncture which I
have now reached in my narrative, I had the
advantage of knowing a person who was branded
before the whole world, and punished by the law
of his country, as a felonious hypocrite. My
Father himself could only sigh and admit the
charge. And yet—I doubt.

About half-way between our village and the
town there lay a comfortable villa inhabited by
a retired solicitor, or perhaps attorney, whom I
shall name Mr. Dormant. We often called at
his half-way house, and, although he was a
member of the town-meeting, he not unfre-
quently came up to us for " the breaking of

H

bread.'' Mr. Dormant was a solid, pink man, of a cosy habit. He had beautiful white hair, a very soft voice, and a welcoming, wheedling manner ; he was extremely fluent and zealous in using the pious phraseology of the sect. My Father had never been very much attracted to him, but the man professed, and I think felt, an overwhelming admiration for my Father. Mr. Dormant was not very well off, and in the previous year he had persuaded an aged gentleman of wealth to come and board with him. When, in the course of the winter, this gentleman died, much surprise was felt at the report that he had left almost his entire fortune, which was not inconsiderable, to Mr. Dormant.

Much surprise—for the old gentleman had a son to whom he had always been warmly attached, who was far away, I think in South America, practising a perfectly respectable profession of which his father entirely approved. My own Father always preserved a delicacy and a sense of honour about money which could not have been more sensitive if he had been an ungodly man, and I am very much pleased to remember that when the legacy was first spoken of, he regretted that Mr. Dormant should have allowed the old gentleman to make this will. If he knew the intention, my Father said, it would have shown a more proper sense of his responsibility if he had dissuaded the testator from so unbecoming a disposition. That was long before any legal question arose ; and now

Mr. Dormant came into his fortune, and began to make handsome gifts to missionary societies, and to his own meeting in the town. If I do not mistake, he gave, unsolicited, a sum to our building fund, which my Father afterwards returned. But in process of time we heard that the son had come come back from the Antipodes, and was making investigations. Before we knew where we were, the news burst upon us, like a bomb-shell, that Mr. Dormant had been arrested on a criminal charge and was now in gaol at Exeter.

Sympathy was at first much extended amongst us to the prisoner. But it was lessened when we understood that the old gentleman had been " converted " while under Dormant's roof, and had given the fact that his son was " an unbeliever " as a reason for disinheriting him. All doubt was set aside when it was divulged, under pressure, by the nurse who attended on the old gentleman, herself one of the " saints," that Dormant had traced the signature to the will by drawing the fingers of the testator over the document when he was already and finally comatose.

My Father, setting aside by a strong effort of will the repugnance which he felt, visited the prisoner in gaol before this final evidence had been extracted. When he returned he said that Dormant appeared to be enjoying a perfect confidence of heart, and had expressed a sense of his joy and peace in the Lord ; my Father regretted that he had not been able to persuade him to admit any error, even of judgment. But the prisoner's attitude in the dock, when the facts were proved, and not by him denied, was still more extraordinary. He could be induced to exhibit no species of remorse, and, to the obvious anger of the judge himself, stated that he had only done his duty as a Christian, in preventing this wealth from coming into the hands of an ungodly man, who would have spent it in the service of the flesh and of the devil. Sternly reprimanded by the judge, he made the final statement that at that very moment he was conscious of his Lord's presence, in the dock at his side, whispering to him " Well done, thou good and faithful servant ! " In this frame of conscience, and with a glowing countenance, he was hurried away to penal servitude.

This was a very painful incident, and it is easy to see how compromising, how cruel, it was in its effect upon our communion ; what occasion it gave to our enemies to blaspheme. No one, in either meeting, could or would raise a voice to defend Mr. Dormant. We had to bow our heads when we met our enemies in the gate. The blow fell more heavily on the meeting of which he had been a prominent and communicating member, but it fell on us too, and my Father felt it severely. For many years he would never mention the man's name, and he refused all discussion of the incident.

Yet I was never sure and I am not sure now, that the wretched being was a hypocrite. There

are as many vulgar fanatics as there are distinguished ones, and I am not convinced that
Dormant, coarse and narrow as he was, may
not have sincerely believed that it was better
for the money to be used in religious propaganda
than in the pleasures of the world, of which he
doubtless formed a very vague idea. On this
affair I meditated much, and it awakened in
my mind, for the first time, a doubt whether our
exclusive system of ethics was an entirely salutary one, if it could lead the conscience of a believer to tolerate such acts as these, acts which
my Father himself had denounced as dishonour-
able and disgraceful.

My stepmother brought with her a little
library of such books as we had not previously
seen, but which yet were known to all the world
except us. Prominent among these was a set
of the poems of Walter Scott, and in his un-
wonted geniality and provisional spirit of compromise, my Father must do no less than read
these works aloud to my stepmother in the
quiet spring evenings. This was a sort of after-
math of courtship, a tribute of song to his bride,
very sentimental and pretty. She would sit,
sedately, at her work-box, while he, facing her,
poured forth the verses at her like a blackbird.
I was not considered in this arrangement, which
was wholly matrimonial, but I was present, and
the exercise made more impression upon me
than it did upon either of the principal agents.

My Father read the verse admirably, with a
full,—some people (but not I) might say with

a too full—perception of the metre as well as of
the rhythm, rolling out the rhymes, and glory-
ing in the proper names. He began, and it
was a happy choice, with " The Lady of the
Lake." It gave me singular pleasure to hear
his large voice do justice to "Duncrannon"
and "Cambus-Kenneth," and wake the echoes
with "Roderigh Vich Alphine dhu, ho! ieroe!"
I almost gasped with excitement, while a shudder
floated down my backbone, when we came to :

> A sharp and shrieking echo gave,
> Coir-Uriskin, thy goblin cave !
> And the grey pass where birches wave,
> On Beala-nam-bo,

a passage which seemed to me to achieve the
ideal of sublime romance. My thoughts were
occupied all day long with the adventures of
Fitzjames and the denizens of Ellen's Isle. It
became an obsession, and when I was asked
whether I remembered the name of the cottage
where the minister of the Bible Christians
lodged, I answered, dreamily, "Yes,—Beala-
nam-bo."

Seeing me so much fascinated, thrown indeed
into a temporary frenzy, by the epic poetry of
Sir Walter Scott, my stepmother asked my
Father whether I might not start reading the
Waverley Novels. But he refused to permit this,
on the ground that those tales gave false and
disturbing pictures of life, and would lead away
my attention from heavenly things. I do not
fully apprehend what distinction he drew be-

tween the poems, which he permitted, and the
novels, which he refused. But I suppose he
regarded a work in verse as more artificial,
and therefore less likely to make a realistic
impression, than one in prose. There is something quaint in the conscientious scruple which
allows " The Lord of the Isles " and excludes
" Rob Roy."

But stranger still, and amounting almost to
a whim, was his sudden decision that, although
I might not touch the novels of Scott, I was
free to read those of Dickens. I recollect that
my stepmother showed some surprise at this,
and that my Father explained to her that
Dickens " exposes the passion of love in a ridiculous light." She did not seem to follow this
recommendation, which indeed tends to the
ultra-subtle, but she procured for me a copy
of " Pickwick," by which I was instantly and
gloriously enslaved. My shouts of laughing
at the richer passages were almost scandalous,
and led to my being reproved for disturbing
my Father while engaged, in an upper room,
in the study of God's Word. I must have
expended months on the perusal of " Pickwick,"
for I used to rush through a chapter, and then
read it over again very slowly, word for word,
and then shut my eyes to realise the figures and
the action.

I suppose no child will ever again enjoy that
rapture of unresisting humorous appreciation
of " Pickwick." I felt myself to be in the company of a gentleman so extremely funny that

I began to laugh before he began to speak ; no
sooner did he remark " the sky was dark and
gloomy, the air was damp and raw," than I was
in fits of hilarity. My retirement in our sequestered corner of life made me, perhaps, even
in this matter, somewhat old-fashioned, and
possibly I was the latest of the generation who
accepted Mr. Pickwick with an unquestioning
and hysterical abandonment. Certainly few
young people now seem sensitive, as I was, and
as thousands before me had been, to the quality
of his fascination.

It was curious that living in a household
where a certain delicate art of painting was
diligently cultivated, I had yet never seen a
real picture, and was scarcely familiar with
the design of one in engraving. My stepmother, however, brought a flavour of the fine
arts with her ; a kind of æsthetic odour, like
that of lavender, clung to her as she moved.
She had known authentic artists in her youth ;
she had watched Old Crome painting, and had
taken a course of drawing-lessons from no less
a person than Cotman. She painted small
water-colour landscapes herself, with a delicate
economy of means and a graceful Norwich
convention ; her sketch-books were filled with
abbeys gently washed in, river-banks in sepia
by which the elect might be dimly reminded
of "Liber Studiorum," and woodland scenes over
which the ghost of Creswick had faintly breathed.
It was not exciting art, but it was, so far as it
went, in its lady-like reserve, the real thing.

Our sea-anemones, our tropic birds, our bits
of spongy rock frilled and sprayed with corallines, had been very conscientious and skilful,
but, essentially, so far as art was concerned, the
wrong thing.

Thus I began to acquire, without understanding the value of it, some conception of the elegant
phases of early English water-colour painting,
and there was one singular piece of a marble
well brimming with water, and a greyish-blue
sky over it, and dark-green poplars, shaped like
wet brooms, menacing the middle distance,
which Cotman himself had painted ; and this
seemed beautiful and curious to me in its dim,
flat frame, when it was hoisted to a place on
our drawing-room wall.

But still I had never seen a subject-picture,
although my stepmother used to talk of the joys
of the Royal Academy, and it was therefore
with a considerable sense of excitement that I
went, with my Father, to examine Mr. Holman
Hunt's *Finding of Christ in the Temple* which at
this time was announced to be on public show
at our neighbouring town.   We paid our shillings
and ascended with others to an upper room,
bare of every disturbing object, in which a
strong top-light raked the large and uncom-
promising picture.   We looked at it for some
time in silence, and then my Father pointed out
to me various details, such as the phylacteries
and the mitres, and the robes which distinguished
the high priest.

Some of the other visitors, as I recollect,

H*

expressed astonishment and dislike of what they
called the " Preraphaelite " treatment, but we
were not affected by that. Indeed, if anything,
the exact, minute and hard execution of Mr.
Hunt was in sympathy with the methods we
ourselves were in the habit of using when we
painted butterflies and seaweeds, placing perfectly pure pigments side by side, without any
nonsense about chiaroscuro. This large, bright,
comprehensive picture made a very deep impression upon me, not exactly as a work of art,
but as a brilliant natural specimen. I was
pleased to have seen it, as I was pleased to have
seen the comet, and the whale which was brought
to our front door on a truck. It was a prominent addition to my experience.

The slender expansions of my interest which
were now budding hither and thither do not
seem to have alarmed my Father at all. His
views were short ; if I appeared to be contented and obedient, if I responded pleasantly
when he appealed to me, he was not concerned
to discover the source of my cheerfulness. He
put it down to my happy sense of joy in Christ,
a reflection of the sunshine of grace beaming
upon me through no intervening clouds of sin or
doubt. The " saints " were, as a rule, very easy
to comprehend ; their emotions lay upon the
surface. If they were gay, it was because they
had no burden on their consciences, while, if
they were depressed, the symptom might be de-
pended upon as showing that their consciences
were troubling them, and if they were indif-

ferent and cold, it was certain that they were
losing their faith and becoming hostile to godliness. It was almost a mechanical matter with
these simple souls. But, although I was so
much younger, I was more complex and more
crafty than the peasant " saints." My Father,
not a very subtle psychologist, applied to me
the same formulas which served him well at
the chapel, but in my case the results were
less uniformly successful.

The excitement of school-life and the en-
largement of my circle of interests, combined
to make Sunday, by contrast, a very tedious
occasion. The absence of every species of
recreation on the Lord's Day grew to be a burden
which might scarcely be borne. I have said
that my freedom during the week had now
become considerable ; if I was at home punctually at meal-times, the rest of my leisure was
not challenged. But this liberty, which in the
summer holidays came to surpass that of " fishes
that tipple in the deep," was put into more and
more painful contrast with the unbroken servitude of Sunday.

My Father objected very strongly to the
expression Sabbath-day, as it is commonly used
by Presbyterians and others. He said, quite
justly, that it was an inaccurate modern inno-
vation, that Sabbath was Saturday, the Seventh
day of the week, not the first, a Jewish festival
and not a Christian commemoration. Yet his
exaggerated view with regard to the observance
of the First Day, namely, that it must be ex-

clusively occupied with public and private exercises of divine worship, was based much more
upon a Jewish than upon a Christian law. In
fact, I do not remember that my Father ever
produced a definite argument from the New
Testament in support of his excessive passivity
on the Lord's Day. He followed the early
Puritan practice, except that he did not extend
his observance, as I believe the old Puritans
did, from sunset on Saturday to sunset on
Sunday.

The observance of the Lord's Day has already
become universally so lax that I think there may
be some value in preserving an accurate record
of how our Sundays were spent five and forty
years ago. We came down to breakfast at
the usual time. My Father prayed briefly before
we began the meal ; after it, the bell was rung,
and, before the breakfast was cleared away,
we had a lengthy service of exposition and
prayer with the servants. If the weather was
fine, we then walked about the garden, doing
nothing, for about half an hour. We then sat,
each in a separate room, with our Bibles open
and some commentary on the text beside us,
and prepared our minds for the morning service. A little before 11 a.m. we sallied forth,
carrying our Bibles and hymn-books, and went
through the morning-service of two hours at
the Room ; this was the central event of
Sunday.

We then came back to dinner,—curiously
enough to a hot dinner, always, with a joint,

vegetables and puddings, so that the cook at
least must have been busily at work,—and after
it my Father and my stepmother took a nap,
each in a different room, while I slipped out
into the garden for a little while, but never
venturing further afield. In the middle of the
afternoon, my stepmother and I proceeded up
the village to Sunday School, where I was early
promoted to the tuition of a few very little boys.
We returned in time for tea, immediately after
which we all marched forth, again armed, as
in the morning, with Bibles and hymn-books,
and we went through the evening-service, at
which my Father preached. The hour was now
already past my week-day bedtime, but we
had another service to attend, the Believers'
Prayer Meeting, which commonly occupied forty
minutes more. Then we used to creep home,
I often so tired that the weariness was like
physical pain, and I was permitted, without
further "worship," to slip upstairs to bed.

What made these Sundays, the observance
of which was absolutely uniform, so peculiarly
trying was that I was not permitted the indulgence of any secular respite. I might not open
a scientific book, nor make a drawing, nor
examine a specimen. I was not allowed to go
into the road, except to proceed with my parents
to the Room, nor to discuss worldly subjects at
meals, nor to enter the little chamber where I
kept my treasures. I was hotly and tightly
dressed in black, all day long, as though ready
at any moment to attend a funeral with decorum.

Sometimes, towards evening, I used to feel the monotony and weariness of my position to be almost unendurable, but at this time I was meek, and I bowed to what I supposed to be the order of the universe.

CHAPTER XI

AS my mental horizon widened, my Father followed the direction of my spiritual eyes with some bewilderment, and knew not at what I gazed. Nor could I have put into words, nor can I even now define, the visions which held my vague and timid attention. As a child develops, those who regard it with tenderness or impatience are seldom even approximately correct in their analysis of its intellectual movements, largely because, if there is anything to record, it defies adult definition. One curious freak of mentality I must now mention, because it took a considerable part in the enfranchisement of my mind, or rather in the formation of my thinking habits. But neither my Father nor my stepmother knew what to make of it, and to tell the truth I hardly know what to make of it myself.

Among the books which my new mother had brought with her were certain editions of the poets, an odd assortment. Campbell was there, and Burns, and Keats, and the " Tales " of Byron. Each of these might have been expected to appeal to me ; but my emotion was too young, and I did not listen to them yet. Their imperative voices called me later. By the side of these romantic classics stood a small, thick volume, bound in black morocco, and comprising four reprinted works of the eighteenth century, gloomy, funereal poems of an order as wholly out of date as are the crossbones and ruffled cherubim on the gravestones in a country churchyard. The four—and in this order, as I never shall forget—were " The Last Day " of Dr. Young, Blair's " Grave," " Death " by Bishop Beilby Porteus, and " The Deity " of Samuel Boyse. These lugubrious effusions, all in blank verse or in the heroic couplet, represented, in its most redundant form, the artistic theology of the middle of the eighteenth century. They were steeped in such vengeful and hortatory sentiments as passed for elegant piety in the reign of George II.

How I came to open this solemn volume is explained by the oppressive exclusiveness of our Sundays. On the afternoon of the Lord's Day, as I have already explained, I might neither walk, nor talk, nor explore our scientific library, nor indulge in furious feats of water-colour painting. The Plymouth-Brother theology which alone was open to me produced, at length, and particularly on hot afternoons, a faint physical nausea, a kind of secret headache. But, hitting one day upon the doleful book of verses, and observing its religious character, I asked " May I read that ? " and after a brief, astonished glance at the contents, I received " O certainly—if you can ! "

The lawn sloped directly from a verandah at our drawing-room window, and it contained two immense elm-trees, which had originally formed part of the hedge of a meadow. In our

trim and polished garden they then remained—
they were soon afterwards cut down—rude and
obtuse, with something primeval about them,
something autochthonous ; they were like two
peasant ancestors surviving in a family that had
advanced to gentility.   They rose each out of
a steep turfed hillock, and the root of one of
them was long my favourite summer reading-
desk ; for I could lie stretched on the lawn,
with my head and shoulders supported by the
elm-tree hillock, and the book in a fissure of the
rough turf.   Thither then I escaped with my grave-
yard poets, and who shall explain the rapture
with which I followed their austere morality ?

Whether I really read consecutively in my
black-bound volume I can no longer be sure,
but it became a companion whose society I
valued, and at worst it was a thousand times
more congenial to me than Jukes' "On the
Pentateuch" or than a perfectly excruciating
work ambiguously styled "The Javelin of
Phineas," which lay smouldering in a dull red
cover on the drawing-room table.   I dipped
my bucket here and there into my poets, and
I brought up strange things.   I brought up
out of the depths of "The Last Day" the
following ejaculation of a soul roused by the
trump of resurrection :—

> Father of mercies ! Why from silent earth
> Didst thou awake, and curse me into birth ?
> Tear me from quiet, ravish me from night,
> And make a thankless present of thy light ?
> Push into being a reverse of thee,
> And animate a clod with misery ?

I read these lines with a shiver of excitement, and in a sense I suppose little intended by the sanctimonious rector of Welwyn. I also read in the same piece the surprising description of how

> Now charnels rattle, scattered limbs, and all
> The various bones, obsequious to the call,
> Self-mov'd, advance—the neck perhaps to meet
> The distant head, the distant legs the feet,

but rejected it as not wholly supported by the testimony of Scripture. I think that the rhetoric and vigorous advance of Young's verse were pleasant to me. Beilby Porteus I discarded from the first as impenetrable. In " The Deity," —I knew nothing then of the life of its extravagant and preposterous author,—I took a kind of persistent, penitential pleasure, but it was Blair's " Grave " that really delighted me, and I frightened myself with its melodious doleful images in earnest.

About this time there was a great flow of tea-table hospitality in the village, and my friends and their friends used to be asked out, by respective parents and by more than one amiable spinster, to faint little entertainments where those sang who were ambitious to sing, and where all played post and forfeits after a rich tea. My Father was constantly exercised in mind as to whether I should or should not accept these glittering invitations. There hovered before him a painful sense of danger in resigning the soul to pleasures which savoured

of " the world." These, though apparently
innocent in themselves, might give an appetite
for yet more subversive dissipations.

I remember, on one occasion,—when the
Browns, a family of Baptists who kept a large
haberdashery shop in the neighbouring town,
asked for the pleasure of my company " to tea
and games," and carried complacency so far
as to offer to send that local vehicle, " the
midge," to fetch me and bring me back,—my
Father's conscience was so painfully perplexed,
that he desired me to come up with him to the
now-deserted " boudoir " of the departed
Marks, that we might " lay the matter before
the Lord." We did so, kneeling side by side,
with our backs to the window and our foreheads
pressed upon the horsehair cover of the small,
coffin-like sofa. My Father prayed aloud, with
great fervour, that it might be revealed to me,
by the voice of God, whether it was or was not
the Lord's will that I should attend the Browns'
party. My Father's attitude seemed to me to
be hardly fair, since he did not scruple to remind
the Deity of various objections to a life of
pleasure and of the snakes that lie hidden in
the grass of evening parties. It would have
been more scrupulous, I thought, to give no sort
of hint of the kind of answer he desired and
expected.

It will be justly said that my life was made
up of very trifling things, since I have to confess that this incident of the Browns' invitation
was one of its landmarks. As I knelt, feeling

very small, by the immense bulk of my Father,
there gushed through my veins like a wine the
determination to rebel. Never before, in all
these years of my vocation, had I felt my resistance take precisely this definite form. We
rose presently from the sofa, my forehead and
the backs of my hands still chafed by the tex-
ture of the horsehair, and we faced one another
in the dreary light. My Father, perfectly confident in the success of what had really been a
sort of incantation, asked me in a loud wheedling voice, "Well, and what is the answer
which our Lord vouchsafes?" I said nothing,
and so my Father, more sharply, continued,
"We have asked Him to direct you to a true
knowledge of His will. We have desired Him
to let you know whether it is, or is not, in
accordance with His wishes that you should
accept this invitation from the Browns." He
positively beamed down at me; he had no
doubt of the reply. He was already, I believe,
planning some little treat to make up to me
for the material deprivation. But my answer
came, in the high-piping accents of despair :
"The Lord says I may go to the Browns."
My Father gazed at me in speechless horror.
He was caught in his own trap, and though he
was certain that the Lord had said nothing of
the kind, there was no road open for him but
just sheer retreat. Yet surely it was an error
in tactics to slam the door.

It was at this party at the Browns—to which
I duly went, although in sore disgrace—that my

charnel poets played me a mean trick. It was
proposed that " our young friends " should give
their elders the treat of repeating any pretty
pieces that they knew by heart. Accordingly
a little girl recited " Casabianca," and another
little girl " We are Seven," and various children
were induced to repeat hymns, " some rather
long," as Calverley says, but all very mild and
innocuously evangelical. I was then asked by
Mrs. Brown's maiden sister, a gushing lady in
corkscrew curls, who led the revels, whether I
also would not indulge them " by repeating
some sweet stanzas." No one more ready
than I. Without a moment's hesitation, I stood
forth, and in a loud voice I began one of my
favourite passages from Blair's " Grave " :—

If death were nothing, and nought after death —
If when men died at once they ceased to be,—
Returning to the barren Womb of Nothing
Whence first they sprung, then might the debauchee . . .

" Thank you, dear, that will do nicely ! " interrupted the lady with the curls. " But that's
only the beginning of it," I cried. " Yes,
dear, but that will quite do ! We won't ask
you to repeat any more of it," and I withdrew
to the borders of the company in bewilderment. Nor did the Browns or their visitors
ever learn what it was the debauchee might
have said or done in more favourable circumstances.

The growing eagerness which I displayed for
the society of selected schoolfellows and for

such gentle dissipations as were within my
reach exercised my Father greatly. His fancy
rushed forward with the pace of a steam-engine,
and saw me the life and soul of a gambling club,
or flaunting it at the Mabille. He had no confidence in the action of moderating powers, and
he was fond of repeating that the downward
path is easy. If one fretted to be bathing with
one's companions on the shingle, and preferred
this exercise to the study of God's Word, it was
a symbol of a terrible decline, the angle of which
would grow steeper and steeper, till one plunged
into perdition. He was, himself, timid and re-
clusive, and he shrank from all avoidable companionship with others, except on the footing
of a master and teacher. My stepmother and
I, who neither taught nor ruled, yearned for a
looser chain and lighter relationships. With
regard to myself, my Father about this time
hit on a plan from which he hoped much, but
from which little resulted. He looked to George
to supply what my temperament seemed to
require of congenial juvenile companionship.

If I have not mentioned " George " until
now, it is not that he was a new acquaintance.
When we first came down into the country,
our sympathy had been called forth by an
accident to a little boy, who was knocked over
by a horse, and whose thigh was broken. Somebody (I suppose Mary Grace, since my Father
could rarely bring himself to pay these public
visits) went to see the child in the infirmary,
and accidentally discovered that he was exactly

the same age that I was.   This, and the fact
that he was a meditative and sober little boy,
attracted us all still further to George, who
became converted under one of my Father's
sermons.   He attended my public baptism, and
was so much moved by this ceremony that he
passionately desired to be baptized also, and was
in fact so immersed, a few months later, slightly
to my chagrin, since I thereupon ceased to be
the only infant prodigy in communion.   When
we were both in our thirteenth year, George
became an outdoor servant to us, and did odd
jobs under the gardener.   My Father, finding
him, as he said, " docile, obedient and engaging,"
petted George a good deal, and taught him a
little botany.   He called George, by a curious
contortion of thought, my " spiritual foster-
brother," and anticipated for him, I think, a
career, like mine, in the Ministry.

Our garden suffered from an incursion of
slugs, which laid the verbenas in the dust, and
shore off the carnations as it with pairs of scissors.
To cope with this plague we invested in a drake
and a duck, who were christened Philemon and
Baucis.   Every night large cabbage-leaves, containing the lees of beer, were spread about the
flower-beds as traps, and at dawn these had
become green parlours crammed with intoxi-
cated slugs.   One of George's earliest morning
duties was to free Philemon and Baucis from
their coop, and, armed with a small wand, to
guide their footsteps to the feast in one cabbage-
leaf after another.   My Father used to watch

this performance from an upper window, and, in moments of high facetiousness, he was wont to parody the poet Gray :

How jocund doth George drive his team afield !

This is all, or almost all, that I remember about George's occupations, but he was singularly blameless.

My Father's plan now was that I should form a close intimacy with George, as a boy of my own age, of my own faith, of my own future. My stepmother, still in bondage to the social conventions, was passionately troubled at this, and urged the barrier of class-differences. My Father replied that such an intimacy would keep me " lowly," and that from so good a boy as George I could learn nothing undesirable. " He will encourage him not to wipe his boots when he comes into the house," said my stepmother, and my Father sighed to think how narrow is the horizon of Woman's view of heavenly things.

In this caprice, if I may call it so, I think that my Father had before him the fine republican example of " Sandford and Merton," some parts of which book he admired extremely. Accordingly George and I were sent out to take walks together, and as we started, my Father, with an air of great benevolence, would suggest some passage of Scripture, or " some aspect of God's bountiful scheme in creation, on which you may profitably meditate together." George and I never pursued the discussion of the text with which my Father started us for more than a minute or two ; then we fell into silence, or investigated current scenes and rustic topics.

As is natural among the children of the poor, George was precocious where I was infantile, and undeveloped where I was elaborate. Our minds could hardly find a point at which to touch. He gave me, however, under cross-examination, interesting hints about rural matters, and I liked him, although I felt his company to be insipid. Sometimes he carried my books by my side to the larger and more distant school which I now attended, but I was always in a fever of dread lest my schoolfellows should see him, and should accuse me of having to be "brought" to school. To explain to them that the companionship of this wholesome and rather blunt young peasant was part of my spiritual discipline would have been all beyond my powers.

It was soon after this that my stepmother made her one vain effort to break through the stillness of our lives. My Father's energy seemed to decline, to become more fitful, to take unseasonable directions. My mother instinctively felt that his peculiarities were growing upon him ; he would scarcely stir from his microscope, except to go to the chapel, and he was visible to fewer and fewer visitors. She had taken a pleasure in his literary eminence, and she was aware that this, too, would slip from him ; that, so persistently kept out of sight, he must soon be out of mind. I know not how she gathered courage for her tremendous effort, but she took me, I recollect, into her counsels. We were to unite to oblige my Father to start to his feet and face the world. Alas! we might as well have attempted to rouse the summit of Yes Tor into volcanic action. To my mother's arguments, my Father—with that baffling smile of his—replied : " I esteem the reproach of Christ greater riches than the treasures of Egypt ! " and that this answer was indirect made it none the less conclusive. My mother wished him to give lectures, to go to London, to read papers before the Royal Society, to enter into controversy with foreign *savants*, to conduct classes of out-door zoology at fashionable watering-places. I held my breath with admiration as she poured forth her scheme, so daring, so brilliant, so sure to cover our great man with glory. He listened to her with an ambiguous smile, and shook his head at us, and resumed the reading of his Bible.

At the date of which I write these pages, the arts of illustration are so universally diffused that it is difficult to realise the darkness in which a remote English village was plunged half a century ago. No opportunity was offered to us dwellers in remote places of realising the outward appearances of unfamiliar persons, scenes or things. Although ours was perhaps the most cultivated household in the parish, I had never seen so much as a representation of a work of sculpture till I was thirteen. My mother then received from her earlier home certain volumes, among which was a gaudy gift-book of some kind, containing a few steel engravings of statues.

These attracted me violently, and here for the first time I gazed on Apollo with his proud gesture, Venus in her undulations, the kirtled shape of Diana, and Jupiter voluminously bearded. Very little information, and that to me not intelligible, was given in the text, but these were said to be figures of the old Greek gods. I asked my Father to tell me about these " old Greek gods." His answer was direct and disconcerting. He said—how I recollect the place and time, early in the morning, as I stood beside the window in our garish breakfast-room—he said that the so-called gods of the Greeks were the shadows cast by the vices of the heathen, and reflected their infamous lives ; " it was for such things as these that God poured down brimstone and fire on the Cities of the Plain, and there is nothing in the legends of these gods, or rather devils, that it is not better for a Christian not to know." His face blazed white with Puritan fury as he said this— I see him now in my mind's eye, in his violent emotion. You might have thought that he had himself escaped with horror from some Hellenic hippodrome.

My Father's prestige was by this time considerably lessened in my mind, and though I loved and admired him, I had now long ceased to hold him infallible. I did not accept his condemnation of the Greeks, although I bowed to it. In private I returned to examine my steel engravings of the statues, and I reflected that they were too beautiful to be so wicked as my Father thought they were. The dangerous and pagan notion that beauty palliates evil budded in my mind, without any external suggestion, and by this reflection alone I was still further sundered from the faith in which I had been trained. I gathered very diligently all I could pick up about the Greek gods and their statues ; it was not much, it was indeed ludicrously little and false, but it was a germ. And at this æsthetic juncture I was drawn into what was really rather an extraordinary circle of incidents.

Among the "Saints" in our village there lived a shoemaker and his wife, who had one daughter, Susan Flood. She was a flighty, excited young creature, and lately, during the passage of some itinerary revivalists, she had been "converted" in the noisiest way, with sobs, gasps and gurglings. When this crisis passed, she came with her parents to our meetings, and was received quietly enough to the breaking of bread. But about the time I speak of, Susan Flood went up to London to pay a visit to an unconverted uncle and aunt. It was first whispered amongst us, and then openly stated, that these relatives had taken her to the Crystal Palace, where, in passing through the Sculpture Gallery, Susan's sense of decency had been so grievously affronted, that she had smashed the naked figures with the handle of

her parasol, before her horrified companions
could stop her. She had, in fact, run amok
among the statuary, and had, to the intense
chagrin of her uncle and aunt, very worthy
persons, been arrested and brought before a
magistrate, who dismissed her with a warning
to her relations that she had better be sent home
to Devonshire and "looked after." Susan
Flood's return to us, however, was a triumph;
she had no sense of having acted injudiciously
or unbecomingly; she was ready to recount to
every one, in vague and veiled language, how
she had been able to testify for the Lord "in
the very temple of Belial," for so she poetically
described the Crystal Palace. She was, of course,
in a state of unbridled hysteria, but such physical
explanations were not encouraged amongst us,
and the case of Susan Flood awakened a great
deal of sympathy.

There was held a meeting of the elders in
our drawing-room to discuss it, and I contrived
to be present, though out of observation. My
Father, while he recognised the purity of Susan
Flood's zeal, questioned its wisdom. He noted
that the statuary was not her property, but
that of the Crystal Palace. Of the other communicants, none, I think, had the very slightest
notion what the objects were that Susan had
smashed, or tried to smash, and frankly maintained that they thought her conduct magnificent. As for me, I had gathered by persistent
inquiry enough information to know that what
her sacrilegious parasol had attacked were bodies

of my mysterious friends, the Greek gods, and if all the rest of the village applauded iconoclastic Susan, I at least would be ardent on the other side.

But I was conscious that there was nobody in the world to whom I could go for sympathy. If I had ever read "Hellas" I should have murmured

> Apollo, Pan and Love,
> And even Olympian Jove,
> Grew weak, when killing Susan glared on them.

On the day in question, I was unable to endure the drawing-room meeting to its close, but, clutching my volume of the Funereal Poets, I made a dash for the garden. In the midst of a mass of laurels, a clearing had been hollowed out, where ferns were grown and a garden-seat was placed. There was no regular path to this asylum ; one dived under the snake-like boughs of the laurel and came up again in absolute seclusion.

Into this haunt I now fled to meditate about the savage godliness of that vandal, Susan Flood. So extremely ignorant was I that I supposed her to have destroyed the originals of the statues, marble and unique. I knew nothing about plaster casts, and I thought the damage (it is possible that there had really been no damage whatever) was of an irreparable character. I sank into the seat, with the great wall of laurels whispering around me, and I burst into tears. There was something, surely, quaint

and pathetic in the figure of a little Plymouth
Brother sitting in that advanced year of grace,
weeping bitterly for indignities done to Hermes
and to Aphrodite. Then I opened my book
for consolation, and I read a great block of
pompous verse out of "The Deity," in the
midst of which exercise, yielding to the soft-
ness of the hot and aromatic air, I fell fast
asleep.

Among those who applauded the zeal of
Susan Flood's parasol, the Pagets were prominent. These were a retired Baptist minister and his wife, from Exmouth, who had lately
settled amongst us, and joined in the breaking
of bread. Mr. Paget was a fat old man, whose
round pale face was clean-shaven, and who
carried a full crop of loose white hair above it ;
his large lips were always moving, whether he
spoke or not. He resembled, as I now perceive,
the portraits of S. T. Coleridge in age, but with
all the intellect left out of them. He lived in a
sort of trance of solemn religious despondency.
He had thrown up his cure of souls, because he
became convinced that he had committed the
Sin against the Holy Ghost. His wife was
younger than he, very small, very tight, very
active, with black eyes like pin-pricks at the
base of an extremely high and narrow forehead,
bordered with glossy ringlets. He was very
cross to her, and it was murmured that " dear
Mrs. Paget had often had to pass through the
waters of affliction." They were very poor, but
rigidly genteel, and she was careful, so far as

she could, to conceal from the world the caprices of her poor lunatic husband.

In our circle, it was never for a moment admitted that Mr. Paget was a lunatic. It was said that he had gravely sinned, and was under the Lord's displeasure ; prayers were abundantly offered up that he might be led back into the pathway of light, and that the Smiling Face might be drawn forth for him from behind the Frowning Providence. When the man had an epileptic seizure in the High Street, he was not taken to a hospital, but we repeated to one another, with shaken heads, that Satan, that crookèd Serpent, had been unloosed for a season. Mr. Paget was fond of talking, in private and in public, of his dreadful spiritual condition and he would drop his voice while he spoke of having committed the Unpardonable Sin, with a sort of shuddering exultation, such as people sometimes feel in the possession of a very unusual disease.

It might be thought that the position held in any community by persons so afflicted and eccentric as the Pagets would be very precarious. But it was not so with us ; on the contrary, they took a prominent place at once. Mr. Paget, in spite of his spiritual bankruptcy, was only too anxious to help my Father in his ministrations, and used to beg to be allowed to pray and exhort. In the latter case he took the tone of a wounded veteran, who, though fallen on the bloody field himself, could still encourage younger warriors to march forward to victory.

Everybody longed to know what the exact nature had been of that sin against the Holy Ghost which had deprived Mr. Paget of every glimmer of hope for time or for eternity. It was whispered that even my Father himself was not precisely acquainted with the character of it.

This mysterious disability clothed Mr. Paget for us with a kind of romance. We watched him as the women watched Dante in Verona, whispering :

> Behold him, how Hell's reek
> Has crisped his hair and singed his cheek !

His person lacked, it is true, something of the dignity of Dante's, for it was his caprice to walk up and down the High Street at noonday with one of those cascades of coloured paper which were known as " ornaments for your fireplace " slung over the back and another over the front of his body. These he manufactured for sale, and he adopted the quaint practice of wearing the exuberant objects as a means for their advertisement.

Mrs. Paget had been accustomed to rule in the little ministry from which Mr. Paget's celebrated Sin had banished them, and she was inclined to clutch at the sceptre now. She was the only person I ever met with who was not afraid of the displeasure of my Father. She would fix her viper-coloured eyes on his, and say with a kind of gimlet firmness, " I hardly think that is the true interpretation, Brother

I

G.'', or, '' But let us turn to Colossians, and
see what the Holy Ghost says there upon this
matter.'' She fascinated my Father, who was
not accustomed to this kind of interruption,
and as she was not to be softened by any flattery
(such as :—'' Marvellous indeed, Sister, is your
acquaintance with the means of grace ! '') she
became almost a terror to him.

She abused her powers by taking great liberties,
which culminated in her drawing his attention
to the fact that my poor stepmother displayed
'' an overweening love of dress.'' The accusa-
tion was perfectly false ; my stepmother was,
if rather richly, always plainly dressed, in the
sober Quaker mode ; almost her only ornament was a large carnelian brooch, set in
flowered flat gold. To this the envenomed Paget
drew my Father's attention as '' likely to lead
' the little ones of the flock ' into temptation.''
My poor Father felt it his duty, thus directly
admonished, to speak to my mother. '' Do you
not think, my Love, that you should, as one who
sets an example to others, discard the wearing
of that gaudy brooch ? '' '' One must fasten one's
collar with something, I suppose ? '' '' Well,
but how does Sister Paget fasten her collar ? ''
'' Sister Paget,'' replied my Mother, stung at
last into rejoinder, '' fastens her collar with a
pin,—and that is a thing which I would rather
die than do ! ''

Nor did I escape the attentions of this zealous
reformer. Mrs. Paget was good enough to
take a great interest in me, and she was not

satisfied with the way in which I was being
brought up. Her presence seemed to pervade
the village, and I could neither come in nor
go out without seeing her hard bonnet and her
pursed-up lips. She would hasten to report to
my Father that she saw me laughing and talking
" with a lot of unconverted boys," these being
the companions with whom I had full permission
to bathe and boat. She urged my Father to
complete my holy vocation by some definite step,
by which he would dedicate me completely to
the Lord's service. Further schooling she
thought needless, and merely likely to foster
intellectual pride. Mr. Paget, she remarked,
had troubled very little in his youth about
worldly knowledge, and yet how blessed he had
been in the conversion of souls until he had
incurred the displeasure of the Holy Ghost !

I do not know exactly what she wanted my
Father to do with me ; perhaps she did not
know herself ; she was meddlesome, ignorant
and fanatical, and she liked to fancy that she
was exercising influence. But the wonderful,
the inexplicable thing is that my Father,—who,
with all his limitations, was so distinguished
and high-minded,—should listen to her for a
moment, and still more wonderful is it that he
really allowed her, grim vixen that she was, to
disturb his plans and retard his purposes. I
think the explanation lay in the perfectly logical
position she took up. My Father found himself
brought face to face at last, not with a disciple,
but with a trained expert in his own peculiar

scheme of religion. At every point she was armed with arguments the source of which he knew and the validity of which he recognised. He trembled before Mrs. Paget as a man in a dream may tremble before a parody of his own central self, and he could not blame her without laying himself open somewhere to censure.

But my stepmother's instincts were more primitive and her actions less wire-drawn than my Father's. She disliked Mrs. Paget as much as one earnest believer can bring herself to dislike a sister in the Lord. My stepmother had quietly devoted herself to what she thought the best way of bringing me up, and she did not propose now to be thwarted by the wife of a lunatic Baptist. At this time I was a mixture of childishness and priggishness, of curious knowledge and dense ignorance. Certain portions of my intellect were growing with unwholesome activity, while others were stunted, or had never stirred at all. I was like a plant on which a pot has been placed, with the effect that the centre is crushed and arrested, while shoots are straggling up to the light on all sides. My Father himself was aware of this, and in a spasmodic way he wished to regulate my thoughts. But all he did was to try to straighten the shoots, without removing the pot which kept them resolutely down.

It was my stepmother who decided that I was now old enough to go to boarding-school, and my Father, having discovered that an elderly couple of Plymouth Brethren kept an " academy

for young gentlemen '' in a neighbouring sea-
port town,—in the prospectus of which the
knowledge and love of the Lord were mentioned
as occupying the attention of the head-master
and his assistants far more closely than any
mere considerations of worldly tuition,—was
persuaded to entrust me to its care. He stipulated, however, that I should always come home
from Saturday night to Monday morning, not,
as he said, that I might receive any carnal indulgence, but that there might be no cessation
of my communion as a believer with the Saints
in our village on Sundays. To this school,
therefore, I presently departed, gawky and home-
sick, and the rift between my soul and that of
my Father widened a little more.

CHAPTER XII

LITTLE boys from quiet, pious households, commonly found, in those days, a chasm yawning at the feet of their inexperience when they arrived at Boarding-school. But the fact that I still slept at home on Saturday and Sunday nights preserved me, I fancy, from many surprises. There was a crisis, but it was broad and slow for me. On the other hand, for my Father I am inclined to think that it was definite and sharp. Permission for me to desert the parental hearth, even for five days in certain weeks, was tantamount, in his mind, to admitting that the great scheme, so long caressed, so passionately fostered, must in its primitive bigness be now dropped.

The Great Scheme (I cannot resist giving it the mortuary honour of capital letters) had been, as my readers know, that I should be exclusively and consecutively dedicated through the whole of my life, to the manifest and uninterrupted and uncompromised " service of the Lord.'' That had been the aspiration of my Mother, and at her death she had bequeathed that desire to my Father, like a dream of the Promised Land. In their ecstasy, my parents had taken me, as Elkanah and Hannah had long ago taken Samuel, from their mountain-home of Ramathaim-Zophim down to sacrifice to the

Lord of Hosts in Shiloh. They had girt me
about with a linen ephod, and had hoped to leave
me there; " as long as he liveth," they had
said, " he shall be lent unto the Lord."

Doubtless in the course of these fourteen
years it had occasionally flashed upon my
Father, as he overheard some speech of mine, or
detected some idiosyncrasy, that I was not one
of those whose temperament points them out
as ultimately fitted for an austere life of religion. What he hoped, however, was that
when the little roughnesses of childhood were
rubbed away, there would pass a deep mel-
lowness over my soul. He had a touching
way of condoning my faults of conduct, directly
after reproving them, and he would softly dep-
recate my frailty, saying, in a tone of harrowing tenderness, " Are you not the child of many
prayers? " He continued to think that prayer,
such passionate importunate prayer as his, must
prevail. Faith could move mountains; should
it not be able to mould the little ductile heart
of a child, since he was sure that his own faith
was unfaltering? He had yearned and waited
for a son who should be totally without human
audacities, who should be humble, pure, not
troubled by worldly agitations, a son whose
life should be cleansed and straightened from
above, *in custodiendo sermones Dei*; in whom
everything should be sacrificed except the one
thing needful to salvation.

How such a marvel of lowly piety was to
earn a living had never, I think, occurred to

him. My Father was singularly indifferent about money. Perhaps his notion was that, totally devoid of ambitions as I was to be, I should quietly become adult, and continue his ministrations among the poor of the Christian flock. He had some dim dream, I think, of there being just enough for us all without my having to take up any business or trade. I believe it was immediately after my first term at boarding-school, that I was a silent but indignant witness of a conversation between my Father and Mr. Thomas Brightwen, my stepmother's brother, who was a banker in one of the Eastern Counties.

This question, "What is he to be?" in a worldly sense, was being discussed, and I am sure that it was for the first time, at all events in my presence. Mr. Brightwen, I fancy, had been worked upon by my stepmother, whose affection for me was always on the increase, to suggest, or faintly to stir the air in the neighbourhood of suggesting, a query about my future. He was childless and so was she, and I think a kind impulse led them to "feel the way," as it is called. I believe he said that the banking business, wisely and honourably conducted, sometimes led, as we know that it is apt to lead, to affluence. To my horror, my Father, with rising emphasis, replied that "if there were offered to his belovèd child what is called 'an opening' that would lead to an income of £10,000 a year, and that would divert his thoughts and interest from the Lord's work he would reject it on his child's behalf." Mr.

Brightwen, a precise and polished gentleman who evidently never made an exaggerated statement in his life, was, I think, faintly scandalised ; he soon left us, and I do not recollect his paying us a second visit.

For my silent part, I felt very much like Gehazi, and I would fain have followed after the banker if I had dared to do so, into the night. I would have excused to him the ardour of my Elisha, and I would have reminded him of the sons of the prophets—" Give me, I pray thee," I would have said, " a talent of silver and two changes of garments." It seemed to me very hard that my Father should dispose of my possibilities of wealth in so summary a fashion, but the fact that I did resent it, and regretted what I supposed to be my " chance," shows how far apart we had already swung. My Father, I am convinced, thought that he gave words to my inward instincts when he repudiated the very mild and inconclusive benevolence of his brother-in-law. But he certainly did not do so. I was conscious of a sharp and instinctive disappointment at having had, as I fancied, wealth so near my grasp, and at seeing it all cast violently into the sea of my Father's scruples.

Not one of my village friends attended the boarding-school to which I was now attached, and I arrived there without an acquaintance. I should soon, however, have found a corner of my own if my Father had not unluckily stipulated that I was not to sleep in the dormitory with the boys of my own age, but in the room occupied by the two elder sons of a prominent Plymouth Brother whom he knew. From a social point of view, this was an unfortunate arrangement, since these youths were some years older and many years riper than I ; the eldest, in fact, was soon to leave ; they had enjoyed their independence, and they now greatly resented being saddled with the presence of an unknown urchin. The supposition had been that they would protect and foster my religious practices ; would encourage me, indeed, as my Father put it, to approach the Throne of Grace with them at morning and evening prayer. They made no pretence, however, to be considered godly ; they looked upon me as an intruder ; and after a while the younger, and ruder, of them openly let me know that they believed I had been put into their room to " spy upon " them ; it had been a plot, they knew, between their father and mine : and he darkly warned me that I should suffer if " anything got out." I had, however, no wish to trouble them, nor any faint interest in their affairs. I soon discovered that they were absorbed in a silly kind of amorous correspondence with the girls of a neighbouring academy, but " what were all such toys to me ? "

These young fellows, who ought long before to have left the school, did nothing overtly unkind to me, but they condemned me to silence. They ceased to address me except with an occasional command. By reason of my youth,

I was in bed and asleep before my companions
arrived upstairs, and in the morning I was
always routed up and packed about my business while they still were drowsing. But the
fact that I had been cut off from my coevals
by night, cut me off from them also by day—
so that I was nothing to them, neither a boarder
nor a day-scholar, neither flesh, fish nor fowl.
The loneliness of my life was extreme, and that
I always went home on Saturday afternoon and
returned on Monday morning still further checked
my companionships at school. For a long time,
round the outskirts of that busy throng of opening lives, I " wandered lonely as a cloud," and
sometimes I was more unhappy than I had ever
been before. No one, however, bullied me, and
though I was dimly and indefinably witness to
acts of uncleanness and cruelty, I was the victim
of no such acts and the recipient of no dangerous
confidences. I suppose that my queer reputation for sanctity, half dreadful, half ridiculous,
surrounded me with a non-conducting atmosphere.

We are the victims of hallowed proverbs,
and one of the most classic of these tells us
that " the child is father of the man." But
in my case I cannot think that this was true.
In mature years I have always been gregarious,
a lover of my kind, dependent upon the company
of friends for the very pulse of moral life. To
be marooned, to be shut up in a solitary cell, to
inhabit a lighthouse, or to camp alone in a forest,
these have always seemed to me afflictions too

heavy to be borne, even in imagination. A state in which conversation exists not, is for me an air too empty of oxygen for my lungs to breathe it.

Yet when I look back upon my days at boarding-school, I see myself unattracted by any of the human beings around me. My grown-up years are made luminous to me in memory by the ardent faces of my friends, but I can scarce recall so much as the names of more than two or three of my schoolfellows. There is not one of them whose mind or whose character made any lasting impression upon me. In later life, I have been impatient of solitude, and afraid of it; at school, I asked for no more than to slip out of the hurly-burly and be alone with my reflections and my fancies. That magnetism of humanity which has been the agony of mature years, of this I had not a trace when I was a boy. Of those fragile loves to which most men look back with tenderness and passion, emotions to be explained only as Montaigne explained them, "parceque c'était lui, parceque c'était moi," I knew nothing. I, to whom friendship has since been like sunlight and like sleep, left school unbrightened and unrefreshed by commerce with a single friend.

If I had been clever, I should doubtless have attracted the jealousy of my fellows, but I was spared this by the mediocrity of my success in the classes. One little fact I may mention, because it exemplifies the advance in observation which has been made in forty years. I was extremely nearsighted and in consequence was placed at a gross disadvantage, by being unable to see the slate or the black-board on which our tasks were explained. It seems almost incredible, when one reflects upon it, but during the whole of my school life, this fact was never commented upon or taken into account by a single person, until the Polish lady who taught us the elements of German and French drew some one's attention to it in my sixteenth year. I was not quick, but I passed for being denser than I was because of the myopic haze that enveloped me. But this is not an autobiography, and with the cold and shrouded details of my uninteresting school life I will not fatigue the reader.

I was not content, however, to be the cipher that I found myself, and when I had been at school for about a year, I " broke out," greatly, I think, to my own surprise, in a popular act. We had a young usher whom we disliked. I suppose, poor half-starved phthisic lad, that he was the most miserable of us all. He was, I think, unfitted for the task which had been forced upon him ; he was fretful, unsympathetic, agitated. The school-house, an old rambling place, possessed a long cellar-like room that opened from our general corridor and was lighted by deep windows, carefully barred, which looked into an inner garden. This vault was devoted to us and to our play-boxes : by a tacit law, no master entered it. One evening, just at dusk, a great number of us were here

when the bell for night-school rang, and many
of us dawdled at the summons. Mr. B., tactless
in his anger, bustled in among us, scolding in a
shrill voice, and proceeded to drive us forth. I
was the latest to emerge, and as he turned away
to see if any other truant might not be hiding,
I determined upon action. With a quick movement, I drew the door behind me and bolted it,
just in time to hear the imprisoned usher scream
with vexation. We boys all trooped upstairs and
it is characteristic of my isolation that I had not
one "chum" to whom I could confide my feat.

That Mr. B. had been shut in became, however, almost instantly known, and the night-
class, usually so unruly, was awed by the event
into exemplary decorum. There, with no master
near us, in a silence rarely broken by a giggle or
a cat-call, we sat diligently working, or pretending to work. Through my brain, as I hung
over my book, a thousand new thoughts began
to surge. I was the liberator, the tyrannicide ;
I had freed all my fellows from the odious op-
pressor. Surely, when they learned that it was
I, they would cluster round me ; surely, now,
I should be somebody in the school-life, no
longer a mere trotting shadow or invisible
presence. The interval seemed long ; at length
Mr. B. was released by a servant, and he came
up into the school-room to find us in that ominous
condition of suspense.

At first he said nothing. He sank upon a
chair in a half-fainting attitude, while he pressed
his hand to his side ; his distress and silence

redoubled the boys' surprise, and filled me with
something like remorse. For the first time,
I reflected that he was human, that perhaps he
suffered. He rose presently and took a slate,
upon which he wrote two questions : " Did you
do it ? " " Do you know who did ? " and these
he propounded to each boy in rotation. The
prompt, redoubled " No " in every case seemed
to pile up his despair.

One of the last to whom he held, in silence,
the trembling slate was the perpetrator. As I
saw the moment approach, an unspeakable
timidity swept over me. I reflected that no
one had seen me, that no one could accuse
me. Nothing could be easier or safer than
to deny, nothing more perplexing to the enemy,
nothing less perilous for the culprit. A flood
of plausible reasons invaded my brain ; I seemed
to see this to be a case in which to tell the truth
would be not merely foolish, it would be wrong.
Yet when the usher stood before me, holding the
slate out in his white and shaking hand, I seized
the pencil, and, ignoring the first question, I
wrote " Yes " firmly against the second. I
suppose that the ambiguity of this action puzzled
Mr. B. He pressed me to answer : " Did *you*
do it ? " but to that I was obstinately dumb ;
and away I was hurried to an empty bedroom,
where for the whole of that night and the next
day I was held a prisoner, visited at intervals by
the head-master and other inquisitorial persons,
until I was gradually persuaded to make a full
confession and apology.

This absurd little incident had one effect,
it revealed me to my schoolfellows as an existence. From that time forth I lay no longer
under the stigma of invisibility ; I had produced my material shape and had thrown my
shadow for a moment into a legend. But, in
other respects, things went on much as before :
curiously uninfluenced by my surroundings, I
in my turn failed to exercise influence, and my
practical isolation was no less than it had been
before. It was thus that it came about that
my social memories of my boarding-school life
are monotonous and vague. It was a period
during which, as it appears to me now on looking back, the stream of my spiritual nature
spread out into a shallow pool which was
almost stagnant. I was labouring to gain those
elements of conventional knowledge, which had,
in many cases, up to that time been singularly
lacking. But my brain was starved, and my
intellectual perceptions were veiled. Elder persons who in later years would speak to me frankly
of my school-days assured me that, while I had
often struck them as a smart and quaint and
even interesting child, all promise seemed to
fade out of me as a school-boy, and that those
who were most inclined to be indulgent gave
up the hope that I should prove a man in a way
remarkable. This was particularly the case
with the most indulgent of my protectors, my
refined and gentle stepmother.

As this record can, however, have no value
that is not based on its rigorous adhesion to

the truth, I am bound to say that the dreariness and sterility of my school-life were more
apparent than real. I was pursuing certain
lines of moral and mental development all the
time, and since my schoolmasters and my
schoolfellows combined in thinking me so dull,
I will display a tardy touch of " proper spirit "
and ask whether it may not partly have been because they were themselves so commonplace.
I think that if some drops of sympathy, that
magic dew of Paradise, had fallen upon my
desert, it might have blossomed like the rose,
or, at all events, like that chimerical flower, the
Rose of Jericho. As it was, the conventionality around me, the intellectual drought, gave
me no opportunity of outward growth. They
did not destroy, but they cooped up, and ren-
dered slow and inefficient, that internal life
which continued, as I have said, to live on
unseen. This took the form of dreams and
speculations, in the course of which I went
through many tortuous processes of the mind,
the actual aims of which were futile, although
the movements themselves were useful. If I
may more minutely define my meaning, I would
say that in my schooldays, without possessing
thoughts, I yet prepared my mind for thinking,
and learned how to think.

The great subject of my curiosity at this
time was words, as instruments of expression.
I was incessant in adding to my vocabulary,
and in finding accurate and individual terms
for things. Here, too, the exercise preceded

the employment, since I was busy providing
myself with words before I had any ideas to
express with them. When I read Shakespeare
and came upon the passage in which Prospero
tells Caliban that he had no thoughts till his
master taught him words, I remember starting
with amazement at the poet's intuition, for such
a Caliban had I been :

> I pitied thee,
> Took pains to make thee speak, taught thee each hour
> One thing or other, when thou didst not, savage,
> Know thine own meaning, but wouldst gabble, like
> A thing most brutish ; I endow'd thy purposes
> With words that made them know.

For my Prosperos I sought vaguely in such
books as I had access to, and I was conscious
that as the inevitable word seized hold of me,
with it out of the darkness into strong light
came the image and the idea.

My Father possessed a copy of Bailey's
"Etymological Dictionary," a book published
early in the eighteenth century. Over this I
would pore for hours, playing with the words
in a fashion which I can no longer reconstruct,
and delighting in the savour of the rich, old-
fashioned country phrases. My Father finding
me thus employed, fell to wondering at the
nature of my pursuit, and I could offer him,
indeed, no very intelligible explanation of it.
He urged me to give up such idleness, and to
make practical use of language. For this purpose he conceived an exercise which he obliged
me to adopt, although it was hateful to me. He

sent me forth, it might be, up the lane to Warbury
Hill and round home by the copses ; or else
down one chine to the sea and along the shingle
to the next cutting in the cliff, and so back by way
of the village ; and he desired me to put down,
in language as full as I could, all that I had seen
in each excursion. As I have said, this practice
was detestable and irksome to me, but, as I look
back, I am inclined to believe it to have been
the most salutary, the most practical piece of
training which my Father ever gave me. It
forced me to observe sharply and clearly, to
form visual impressions, to retain them in the
brain, and to clothe them in punctilious and
accurate language.

It was in my fifteenth year that I became
again, this time intelligently, acquainted with
Shakespeare. I got hold of a single play,
"The Tempest," in a school edition, prepared, I
suppose, for one of the university examinations
which were then being instituted in the provinces. This I read through and through, not
disdaining the help of the notes, and revelling
in the glossary. I studied "The Tempest" as I
had hitherto studied no classic work, and it
filled my whole being with music and romance.
This book was my own hoarded possession ;
the rest of Shakespeare's works were beyond
my hopes. But gradually I contrived to borrow
a volume here and a volume there. I completed
"The Merchant of Venice," read "Cymbeline,"
"Julius Cæsar" and "Much Ado" ; most of the
others, I think, remained closed to me for a long

time. But these were enough to steep my horizon with all the colours of sunrise. It was due, no doubt, to my bringing up, that the plays never appealed to me as bounded by the exigencies of a stage or played by actors. The images they raised in my mind were of real people moving in the open air, and uttering, in the natural play of life, sentiments that were clothed in the most lovely, and yet, as it seemed to me, the most obvious and the most inevitable language.

It was while I was thus under the full spell of the Shakespearean necromancy that a significant event occurred. My Father took me up to London for the first time since my infancy. Our visit was one of a few days only, and its purpose was that we might take part in some enormous Evangelical conference. We stayed in a dark hotel off the Strand, where I found the noise by day and night very afflicting. When we were not at the conference, I spent long hours, among crumbs and blue-bottle flies, in the coffee-room of this hotel, my Father being busy at the British Museum and the Royal Society. The conference was held in an immense hall, somewhere in the north of London. I remember my short-sighted sense of the terrible vastness of the crowd, with rings on rings of dim white faces fading in the fog. My Father, as a privileged visitor, was obliged with seats on the platform, and we were in the heart of the first really large assemblage of persons that I had ever seen.

The interminable ritual of prayers, hymns

and addresses left no impression on my memory,
but my attention was suddenly stung into life
by a remark. An elderly man, fat and greasy,
with a voice like a bassoon, and an imperturb-
able assurance, was denouncing the spread of
infidelity, and the lukewarmness of professing
Christians, who refrained from battling the
wickedness at their doors. They were like the
Laodiceans, whom the angel of the Apocalypse
spewed out of his mouth. For instance, who,
the orator asked, is now rising to check the
outburst of idolatry in our midst? " At this
very moment," he went on, " there is proceeding, unreproved, a blasphemous celebration of
the birth of Shakespeare, a lost soul now suffering
for his sins in hell ! " My sensation was that
of one who has suddenly been struck on the head ;
stars and sparks beat round me. If some person
I loved had been grossly insulted in my presence,
I could not have felt more powerless in anguish.
No one in that vast audience raised a word of
protest, and my spirits fell to their nadir. This,
be it remarked, was the earliest intimation that
had reached me of the tercentenary of the Birth
at Stratford, and I had not the least idea what
could have provoked the outburst of outraged
godliness.

But Shakespeare was certainly in the air.
When we returned to the hotel that noon, my
Father of his own accord reverted to the subject.
I held my breath, prepared to endure fresh tor-
ment. What he said, however, surprised and
relieved me. " Brother So-and-so," he re-

marked, "was not, in my judgment, justified in saying what he did. The uncovenanted mercies of God are not revealed to us. Before so rashly speaking of Shakespeare as 'a lost soul in hell,' he should have remembered how little we know of the poet's history. The light of salvation was widely disseminated in the land during the reign of Queen Elizabeth, and we cannot know that Shakespeare did not accept the atonement of Christ in simple faith before he came to die." The concession will to-day seem meagre to gay and worldly spirits, but words cannot express how comfortable it was to me. I gazed at my Father with loving eyes across the cheese and celery, and if the waiter had not been present I believe I might have hugged him in my arms.

This anecdote may serve to illustrate the attitude of my conscience, at this time, with regard to theology. I was not consciously in any revolt against the strict faith in which I had been brought up, but I could not fail to be aware of the fact that literature tempted me to stray up innumerable paths which meandered in directions at right angles to that direct strait way which leadeth to salvation. I fancied, if I may pursue the image, that I was still safe up these pleasant lanes if I did not stray far enough to lose sight of the main road. If, for instance, it had been quite certain that Skakespeare had been irrecoverably damnable and damned, it would scarcely have been possible for me to have justified myself in going on read-

ing "Cymbeline."   One who broke bread with
the Saints every Sunday morning, who "took a
class" at Sunday school, who made, as my
Father loved to remind me, a public weekly confession of his willingness to bear the Cross of
Christ, such an one could hardly, however be-
wildering and torturing the thought, continue
to admire a lost soul.   But that happy possibility
of an ultimate repentance, how it eased me !   I
could always console myself with the belief
that when Shakespeare wrote any passage
of intoxicating beauty, it was just then that
he was beginning to breathe the rapture
that faith in Christ brings to the anointed
soul.   And it was with a like casuistry that
I condoned my other intellectual and personal
pleasures.

My Father continued to be under the impression that my boarding-school, which he
never again visited after originally leaving me
there, was conducted upon the same principles
as his own household.   I was frequently tempted
to enlighten him, but I never found the courage
to do so.   As a matter of fact the piety of the
establishment, which collected to it the sons of
a large number of evangelically minded parents
throughout that part of the country, resided
mainly in the prospectus.   It proceeded no
further than the practice of reading the Bible
aloud, each boy in successive order one verse,
in the early morning before breakfast.   There
was no selection and no exposition ; where the
last boy sat, there the day's reading ended, even

if it were in the middle of a sentence, and there
it began next morning.

Such reading of " the chapter " was followed
by a long dry prayer. I do not know that this
morning service would appear more perfunc-
tory than usual to other boys, but it astounded
and disgusted me, accustomed as I was to the
ministrations at home, where my Father read
" the word of God " in a loud passionate voice,
with dramatic emphasis, pausing for commentary and paraphrase, and treating every phrase
as if it were part of a personal message or of
thrilling family history. At school, " morning
prayer " was a dreary, unintelligible exercise,
and with this piece of mumbo-jumbo, religion
for the day began and ended. The discretion
of little boys is extraordinary. I am quite
certain no one of us ever revealed this fact to
our godly parents at home.

If any one was to do this, it was of course I
who should first of all have " testified." But I
had grown cautious about making confidences.
One never knew how awkwardly they might
develop or to what disturbing excesses of zeal
they might precipitously lead. I was on my
guard against my Father, who was, all the
time, only too openly yearning that I should
approach him for help, for comfort, for ghostly
counsel. Still " delicate," though steadily gaining in solidity of constitution, I was liable to
severe chills and to fugitive neuralgic pangs.
My Father was, almost maddeningly, desirous
that these afflictions should be sanctified to

me, and it was in my bed, often when I was much bowed in spirit by indisposition, that he used to triumph over me most pitilessly. He retained the singular superstition, amazing in a man of scientific knowledge and long human experience, that all pains and ailments were directly sent by the Lord in chastisement for some definite fault, and not in relation to any physical cause. The result was sometimes quite startling, and in particular I recollect that my stepmother and I exchanged impressions of astonishment at my Father's action when Mrs. Goodyer, who was one of the "Saints" and the wife of a young journeyman cobbler, broke her leg. My Father, puzzled for an instant as to the meaning of this accident, since Mrs. Goodyer was the gentlest and most inoffensive of our church members, decided that it must be because she had made an idol of her husband, and he reduced the poor thing to tears by standing at her bed-side and imploring the Holy Spirit to bring this sin home to her conscience.

When, therefore, I was ill at home with one of my trifling disorders, the problem of my spiritual state always pressed violently upon my Father, and this caused me no little mental uneasiness. He would appear at my bed-side, with solemn solicitude, and sinking on his knees would earnestly pray aloud that the purpose of the Lord in sending me this affliction might graciously be made plain to me ; and then, rising, and standing by my pillow, he would put me through a searching spiritual inquiry as to

the fault which was thus divinely indicated to
me as observed and reprobated on high.

It was not on points of moral behaviour that
he thus cross-examined me ; I think he dis-
dained such ignoble game as that. But un-
certainties of doctrine, relinquishment of faith
in the purity of this dogma or of that, lukewarm
zeal in " taking up the cross of Christ," growth
of intellectual pride,—such were the insidious
offences in consequence of which, as he supposed, the cold in the head or the toothache
had been sent as heavenly messengers to recall
my straggling conscience to its plain path of
duty.

What made me very uncomfortable on these
occasions was my consciousness that confine-
ment to bed was hardly an affliction at all. It
kept me from the boredom of school, in a fire-
lit bed-room at home, with my pretty, smiling
stepmother lavishing luxurious attendance upon
me, and it gave me long, unbroken days for
reading. I was awkwardly aware that I simply
had not the effrontery to " approach the Throne
of Grace " with a request to know for what sin
I was condemned to such a very pleasant disposition of my hours.

The current of my life ran, during my school-
days, most merrily and fully in the holidays,
when I resumed my out-door exercises with
those friends in the village of whom I have
spoken earlier. I think they were more refined
and better bred than any of my schoolfellows,
at all events it was among these homely com-

panions alone that I continued to form congenial
and sympathetic relations. In one of these
boys,—one of whom I have heard or seen
nothing now for nearly a generation,—I found
tastes singularly parallel to my own, and we
scoured the horizon in search of books in prose
and verse, but particularly in verse.

As I grew stronger in muscle, I was capable
of adding considerably to my income by an
exercise of my legs. I was allowed money for
the railway ticket between the town where the
school lay and the station nearest to my home.
But, if I chose to walk six or seven miles along
the coast, thus more than halving the distance
by rail from school house to home, I might
spend as pocket-money the railway fare I thus
saved. Such considerable sums I fostered in
order to buy with them editions of the poets.
These were not in those days, as they are now,
at the beck and call of every purse, and the attainment of each little masterpiece was a separate
triumph. In particular I shall never forget the
excitement of reaching at length the exorbitant
price the bookseller asked for the only, although
imperfect, edition of the poems of S. T. Coleridge.
At last I could meet his demand, and my friend
and I went down to consummate the solemn
purchase. Coming away with our treasure,
we read aloud from the orange-coloured volume,
in turns, as we strolled along, until at last we
sat down on the bulging root of an elm-tree
in a secluded lane. Here we stayed, in a sort
of poetical *nirvana*, reading, reading, forgetting

the passage of time, until the hour of our neglected mid-day meal was a long while past, and
we had to hurry home to bread and cheese and
a scolding.

There was occasionally some trouble about
my reading, but now not much nor often. I
was rather adroit, and careful not to bring
prominently into sight anything of a literary
kind which could become a stone of stumbling.
But, when I was nearly sixteen, I made a purchase which brought me into sad trouble, and
was the cause of a permanent wound to my self-
respect. I had long coveted in the book-shop
window a volume in which the poetical works
of Ben Jonson and Christopher Marlowe were
said to be combined. This I bought at length,
and I carried it with me to devour as I trod
the desolate road that brought me along the
edge of the cliff on Saturday afternoons. Of
Ben Jonson I could make nothing, but when I
turned to " Hero and Leander," I was lifted
to a heaven of passion and music. It was a
marvellous revelation of romantic beauty to
me, and as I paced along that lonely and exquisite highway, with its immense command
of the sea, and its peeps every now and then,
through slanting thickets, far down to the
snow-white shingle, I lifted up my voice, singing
the verses, as I strolled along :

> Buskins of shells, all silver'd, usèd she,
> And branch'd with blushing coral to the knee,
> Where sparrows perched, of hollow pearl and gold,
> Such as the world would wonder to behold,—

so it went on, and I thought I had never read anything so lovely,—

> Amorous Leander, beautiful and young,
> Whose tragedy divine Musaeus sung,—

it all seemed to my fancy intoxicating beyond anything I had ever even dreamed of, since I had not yet become acquainted with any of the modern romanticists.

When I reached home, tired out with enthusiasm and exercise, I must needs, so soon as I had eaten, search out my stepmother that she might be a partner in my joys. It is remarkable to me now, and a disconcerting proof of my still almost infantile innocence, that, having induced her to settle to her knitting, I began, without hesitation, to read Marlowe's voluptuous poem aloud to that blameless Christian gentlewoman. We got on very well in the opening, but at the episode of Cupid's pining, my stepmother's needles began nervously to clash, and when we launched on the description of Leander's person, she interrupted me by saying, rather sharply, " Give me that book, please, I should like to read the rest to myself." I resigned the reading in amazement, and was stupefied to see her take the volume, shut it with a snap and hide it under her needlework. Nor could I extract from her another word on the subject.

The matter passed from my mind, and I was therefore extremely alarmed when, soon after my going to bed that night, my Father came into my room with a pale face and burning eyes, the prey of violent perturbation. He set down the candle and stood by the bed, and it was some time before he could resolve on a form of speech. Then he denounced me, in unmeasured terms, for bringing into the house, for possessing at all or reading, so abominable a book. He explained that my stepmother had shown it to him, and that he had looked through it, and had burned it.

The sentence in his tirade which principally affected me was this. He said, "You will soon be leaving us, and going up to lodgings in London, and if your landlady should come into your room, and find such a book lying about, she would immediately set you down as a profligate." I did not understand this at all, and it seems to me now that the fact that I had so very simply and childishly volunteered to read the verses to my stepmother should have proved to my Father that I connected it with no ideas of an immoral nature.

I was greatly wounded and offended, but my indignation was smothered up in the alarm and excitement which followed the news that I was to go up to live in lodgings, and, as it was evident, alone, in London. Of this no hint or whisper had previously reached me. On reflection, I can but admit that my Father, who was little accustomed to seventeenth-century literature, must have come across some startling exposures in Ben Jonson, and probably never reached "Hero and Leander" at all. The artistic effect of such poetry on an innocently pagan mind did not come within the circle of his experience. He judged the outspoken Elizabethan poets, no doubt, very much in the spirit of the problematical landlady.

Of the world outside, of the dim wild whirlpool of London, I was much afraid, but I was now ready to be willing to leave the narrow Devonshire circle, to see the last of the red mud, of the dreary village street, of the plethoric elders, to hear the last of the drawling voices of the " Saints." Yet I had a great difficulty in persuading myself that I could ever be happy away from home, and again I compared my lot with that of one of the speckled soldier-crabs that roamed about in my Father's aquarium, dragging after them great whorlshells. They, if by chance they were turned out of their whelk-habitations, trailed about a pale soft body in search of another house, visibly broken-hearted and the victims of every ignominious accident.

My spirits were divided pathetically between the wish to stay on, a guarded child, and to proceed into the world, a budding man, and, in my utter ignorance, I sought in vain to conjure up what my immediate future would be. My Father threw no light upon the subject, for he had not formed any definite idea of what I could possibly do to earn an honest living. As a matter of fact I was to stay another year at school and home.

This last year of my boyish life passed rapidly

and pleasantly. My sluggish brain waked up
at last and I was able to study with application.
In the public examinations I did pretty well,
and may even have been thought something of
a credit to the school. Yet I formed no close
associations, and I even contrived to avoid, as
I had afterwards occasion to regret, such lessons
as were distasteful to me, and therefore particularly valuable. But I read with unchecked
voracity, and in several curious directions.
Shakespeare now passed into my possession
entire, in the shape of a reprint more hideous
and more offensive to the eyesight than would
in these days appear conceivable. I made
acquaintance with Keats, who entirely captivated
me ; with Shelley, whose "Queen Mab" at
first repelled me from the threshold of his
edifice ; and with Wordsworth, for the exercise
of whose magic I was still far too young. My
Father presented me with the entire bulk of
Southey's stony verse, which I found it impossible to penetrate, but my stepmother lent me
"The Golden Treasury," in which almost everything seemed exquisite.

Upon this extension of my intellectual powers,
however, there did not follow any spirit of
doubt or hostility to the faith. On the contrary,
at first there came a considerable quickening
of fervour. My prayers became less frigid and
mechanical ; I no longer avoided as far as
possible the contemplation of religious ideas ; I
began to search the Scriptures for myself with
interest and sympathy, if scarcely with ardour.

FATHER AND SON   281

I began to perceive, without animosity, the
strange narrowness of my Father's system,
which seemed to take into consideration only
a selected circle of persons, a group of disciples
peculiarly illuminated, and to have no message
whatever for the wider Christian community.

On this subject I had some instructive conversations with my Father, whom I found not
reluctant to have his convictions pushed to
their logical extremity. He did not wish to
judge, he protested ; but he could not admit
that a single Unitarian (or "Socinian," as he
preferred to say) could possibly be redeemed ;
and he had no hope of eternal salvation for
the inhabitants of Catholic countries. I recollect
his speaking of Austria. He questioned whether
a single Austrian subject, except, as he said,
here and there a pious and extremely ignorant
individual, who had not comprehended the
errors of the Papacy, but had humbly studied
his Bible, could hope to find eternal life. He
thought that the ordinary Chinaman or savage
native of Fiji had a better chance of salvation
than any cardinal in the Vatican. And even in
the priesthood of the Church of England he
believed that while many were called, few
indeed would be found to have been chosen.

I could not sympathise, even in my then
state of ignorance, with so rigid a conception
of the Divine mercy. Little inclined as I was
to be sceptical, I still thought it impossible,
that a secret of such stupendous importance
should have been entrusted to a little group of

K

Plymouth Brethren, and have been hidden from
millions of disinterested and pious theologians.
That the leaders of European Christianity were
sincere, my Father did not attempt to question.
But they were all of them wrong, *incorrect*;
and no matter how holy their lives, how self-
sacrificing their actions, they would have to
suffer for their inexactitude through æons of
undefined torment. He would speak with a
solemn complacency of the aged nun, who, after
a long life of renunciation and devotion, died at
last, " only to discover her mistake."

He who was so tender-hearted that he could
not bear to witness the pain or distress of any
person, however disagreeable or undeserving,
was quite acquiescent in believing that God
would punish human beings, in millions, for
ever, for a purely intellectual error of comprehension. My Father's inconsistencies of perception seem to me to have been the result of
a curious irregularity of equipment. Taking
for granted, as he did, the absolute integrity
of the Scriptures, and applying to them his
trained scientific spirit, he contrived to stifle,
with a deplorable success, alike the function of
the imagination, the sense of moral justice,
and his own deep and instinctive tenderness of
heart.

There presently came over me a strong desire
to know what doctrine indeed it was that the
other Churches taught. I expressed a wish to
be made aware of the practices of Rome, or
at least of Canterbury, and I longed to attend

the Anglican and the Roman services. But
to do so was impossible. My Father did not,
indeed, forbid me to enter the fine parish church
of our village, or the stately Puginesque cathedral
which Rome had just erected at its side, but I
knew that I could not be seen at either service
without his immediately knowing it, or without
his being deeply wounded. Although I was
sixteen years of age, and although I was treated
with indulgence and affection, I was still but a
bird fluttering in the net-work of my Father's
will, and incapable of the smallest independent
action. I resigned all thought of attending any
other services than those at our " Room," but
I did no longer regard this exclusion as a final
one. I bowed, but it was in the house of
Rimmon, from which I now knew that I must
inevitably escape. All the liberation, however,
which I desired or dreamed of was only just so
much as would bring me into communion with
the outer world of Christianity, without divesting
me of the pure and simple principles of faith.

Of so much emancipation, indeed, I now
became ardently desirous, and in the contemplation of it I rose to a more considerable
degree of religious fervour than I had ever
reached before or was ever to experience later.
Our thoughts were at this time abundantly
exercised with the expectation of the immediate coming of the Lord, who, as my Father
and those who thought with him believed,
would suddenly appear, without the least warning, and would catch up to be with Him in

everlasting glory all whom acceptance of the Atonement had sealed for immortality. These were, on the whole, not numerous, and our belief was that the world, after a few days' amazement at the total disappearance of these persons, would revert to its customary habits of life, merely sinking more rapidly into a moral corruption due to the removal of these souls of salt. This event an examination of prophecy had led my Father to regard as absolutely imminent, and sometimes, when we parted for the night, he would say with a sparkling rapture in his eyes, " Who knows ? We may meet next in the air, with all the cohorts of God's saints ! "

This conviction I shared, without a doubt ; and, indeed,—in perfect innocency, I hope, but perhaps with a touch of slyness too,—I proposed at the end of the summer holidays that I should stay at home. " What is the use of my going to school ? Let me be with you when we rise to meet the Lord in the air ! " To this my Father sharply and firmly replied that it was our duty to carry on our usual avocations to the last, for we knew not the moment of His coming, and we should be together in an instant on that day, how far soever we might be parted upon earth. I was ashamed, but his argument was logical, and, as it proved, judicious. My father lived for nearly a quarter of a century more, never losing the hope of " not tasting death," and as the last moments of mortality approached, he was

bitterly disappointed at what he held to be a
scanty reward of his long faith and patience.
But if my own life's work had been, as I proposed, shelved in expectation of the Lord's
imminent advent, I should have cumbered the
ground until this day.

To school, therefore, I returned with a brain
full of strange discords, in a huddled mixture
of " Endymion " and the Book of Revelation,
John Wesley's hymns and "Midsummer Night's
Dream." Few boys of my age, I suppose,
carried about with them such a confused throng
of immature impressions and contradictory hopes.
I was at one moment devoutly pious, at the
next haunted by visions of material beauty and
longing for sensuous impressions. In my hot
and silly brain, Jesus and Pan held sway together,
as in a wayside chapel discordantly and impishly
consecrated to Pagan and to Christian rites.
But for the present, as in the great chorus which
so marvellously portrays our double nature,
"the folding-star of Bethlehem" was still
dominant. I became more and more pietistic.
Beginning now to versify, I wrote a tragedy in
pale imitation of Shakespeare, but on a Biblical
and evangelistic subject; and odes that were
parodies of those in "Prometheus Unbound,"
but dealt with the approaching advent of our
Lord and the rapture of His saints. My unwholesome excitement, bubbling up in this
violent way, reached at last a climax and
foamed over.

It was a summer afternoon, and, being now

left very free in my movements, I had escaped
from going out with the rest of my schoolfellows in their formal walk in charge of an
usher. I had been reading a good deal of
poetry, but my heart had translated Apollo
and Bacchus into terms of exalted Christian
faith. I was alone, and I lay on a sofa, drawn
across a large open window at the top of the
school-house, in a room which was used as a
study by the boys who were " going up for
examination." I gazed down on a labyrinth of
gardens sloping to the sea, which twinkled
faintly beyond the towers of the town. Each
of these gardens held a villa in it, but all the
near landscape below me was drowned in
foliage. A wonderful warm light of approaching sunset modelled the shadows and set the
broad summits of the trees in a rich glow.
There was an absolute silence below and around
me ; a magic of suspense seemed to keep every
topmost twig from waving.

Over my soul there swept an immense wave
of emotion. Now, surely, now the great final
change must be approaching. I gazed up into
the tenderly-coloured sky, and I broke irresistibly into speech. " Come now, Lord Jesus,"
I cried, " come now and take me to be for ever
with Thee in Thy Paradise. I am ready to come.
My heart is purged from sin, there is nothing
that keeps me rooted to this wicked world. Oh,
come now, now, and take me before I have
known the temptations of life, before I have
to go to London and all the dreadful things

that happen there ! '' And I raised myself on the sofa, and leaned upon the window-sill, and waited for the glorious apparition.

This was the highest moment of my religious life, the apex of my striving after holiness. I waited awhile, watching ; and then I felt a faint shame at the theatrical attitude I had adopted, although I was alone. Still I gazed and still I hoped. Then a little breeze sprang up, and the branches danced. Sounds began to rise from the road beneath me. Presently the colour deepened, the evening came on. From far below there rose to me the chatter of the boys returning home. The tea-bell rang,—last word of prose to shatter my mystical poetry. '' The Lord has not come, the Lord will never come,'' I muttered, and in my heart the artificial edifice of extravagant faith began to totter and crumble. From that moment forth my Father and I, though the fact was long successfully concealed from him and even from myself, walked in opposite hemispheres of the soul, with '' the thick o' the world between us.''

EPILOGUE

THIS narrative, however, must not be allowed to close with the Son in the foreground of the piece. If it has a value, that value consists in what light it may contrive to throw upon the unique and noble figure of the Father. With the advance of years, the characteristics of this figure became more severely outlined, more rigorously confined within settled limits. In relation to the Son—who presently departed, at a very immature age, for the new life in London—the attitude of the Father continued to be one of extreme solicitude, deepening by degrees into disappointment and disenchantment. He abated no jot or tittle of his demands upon human frailty. He kept the spiritual cord drawn tight ; the Biblical bearing-rein was incessantly busy, jerking into position the head of the dejected neophyte. That young soul, removed from the Father's personal inspection, began to blossom forth crudely and irregularly enough, into new provinces of thought, through fresh layers of experience. To the painful mentor at home in the West, the centre of anxiety was still the meek and docile heart, dedicated to the Lord's service, which must, at all hazards and with all defiance of the rules of life, be kept unspotted from the world.

The torment of a postal inquisition began

directly I was settled in my London lodgings. To my Father—with his ample leisure, his palpitating apprehension, his ready pen—the flow of correspondence offered no trouble at all ; it was a grave but gratifying occupation. To me the almost daily letter of exhortation, with its string of questions about conduct, its series of warnings, grew to be a burden which could hardly be borne, particularly because it involved a reply as punctual and if possible as full as itself. At the age of seventeen, the metaphysics of the soul are shadowy, and it is a dreadful thing to be forced to define the exact outline of what is so undulating and so shapeless. To my Father there seemed no reason why I should hesitate to give answers of full metallic ring to his hard and oft-repeated questions ; but to me this correspondence was torture. When I feebly expostulated, when I begged to be left a little to myself, these appeals of mine automatically stimulated, and indeed blew up into fierce flames, the ardour of my Father's alarm.

The letter, the only too-confidently expected letter, would lie on the table as I descended to breakfast. It would commonly be, of course, my only letter, unless tempered by a cosy and chatty note from my dear and comfortable stepmother, dealing with such perfectly tranquillising subjects as the harvest of roses in the garden or the state of health of various neighbours. But the other, the solitary letter, in its threatening whiteness, with its exquisitely penned address—there it would lie awaiting me, destroying the taste of the bacon, reducing the flavour of the tea to insipidity. I might fatuously dally with it, I might pretend not to observe it, but there it lay. Before the morning's exercise began, I knew that it had to be read, and what was worse, that it had to be answered. Useless the effort to conceal from myself what it contained. Like all its precursors, like all its followers, it would insist, with every variety of appeal, on a reiterated declaration that I still fully intended, as in the days of my earliest childhood, " to be on the Lord's side " in everything.

In my replies, I would sometimes answer precisely as I was desired to answer ; sometimes I would evade the queries, and write about other things ; sometimes I would turn upon the tormentor, and urge that my tender youth might be let alone. It little mattered what form of weakness I put forth by way of baffling my Father's direct, firm, unflinching strength. To an appeal against the bondage of a correspondence of such unbroken solemnity I would receive—with what a paralysing promptitude !—such a reply as this :—

" Let me say that the ' solemnity ' you complain of has only been the expression of tender anxiousness of a father's heart, that his only child, just turned out upon the world, and very far out of his sight and hearing, should be walking in God's way. Recollect that it is

not now as it was when you were at school,
when we had personal communication with
you at intervals of five days : — we now know
absolutely nothing of you, save from your
letters, and if they do not indicate your spiritual
prosperity, the deepest solicitudes of our hearts
have nothing to feed on. But I will try henceforth to trust you, and lay aside my fears ; for
you are worthy of my confidence ; and your
own God and your father's God will hold you
with His right hand."

Over such letters as these I am not ashamed
to say that I sometimes wept ; the old paper
I have just been copying shows traces of tears
shed upon it more than forty years ago, tears
commingled of despair at my own feebleness,
distraction at my want of will, pity for my
Father's manifest and pathetic distress. He
would "try henceforth to trust" me, he said.
Alas ! the effort would be in vain ; after a day
or two, after a hollow attempt to write of other
things, the importunate subject would recur ;
there would intrude again the inevitable questions about the Atonement and the Means of
Grace, the old anxious fears lest I was "yielding"
my intimacy to agreeable companions who were
not "one with me in Christ," fresh passionate
entreaties to be assured, in every letter, that I
was walking in the clear light of God's presence.
It seems to me now profoundly strange,
although I knew too little of the world to
remark it at the time, that these incessant

exhortations dealt, not with conduct, but with
faith. Earlier in this narrative I have noted
how disdainfully, with what an austere pride,
my Father refused to entertain the subject of
personal shortcomings in my behaviour. There
were enough of them to blame, Heaven knows,
but he was too lofty-minded a gentleman to
dwell upon them, and, though by nature deeply
suspicious of the possibility of frequent moral
lapses, even in the very elect, he refused to
stoop to anything like espionage.

I owe him a deep debt of gratitude for his
beautiful faith in me in this respect, and now
that I was alone in London, at this tender time
of life, "exposed," as they say, to all sorts of
dangers, as defenceless as a fledgling that has
been turned out of its nest, yet my Father did
not, in his uplifted Quixotism, allow himself
to fancy me guilty of any moral misbehaviour,
but concentrated his fears entirely upon my
faith.

"Let me know more of your inner light.
Does the candle of the Lord shine on your
soul?" This would be the ceaseless inquiry.
Or, again, "Do you get any spiritual companionship with young men? You passed over
last Sunday without even a word, yet this day
is the most interesting to me in your whole
week. Do you find the ministry of the Word
pleasant, and, above all, profitable? Does it
bring your soul into exercise before God?
The Coming of Christ draweth nigh. Watch,
therefore and pray always, that you may be

counted worthy to stand before the Son of
Man.''

If I quote such passages as this from my
Father's letters to me, it is not that I seek
entertainment in a contrast between his earnestness and the casuistical inattention and provoked
distractedness of a young man to whom the
real world now offered its irritating and stimulating scenes of animal and intellectual life, but
to call out sympathy, and perhaps wonder, at
the spectacle of so blind a Roman firmness as
my Father's spiritual attitude displayed.

His aspirations were individual and metaphysical. At the present hour, so complete
is the revolution which has overturned the
puritanism of which he was perhaps the latest
surviving type, that all classes of religious
persons combine in placing philanthropic activity,
the objective attitude, in the foreground. It is
extraordinary how far-reaching the change has
been, so that nowadays a religion which does
not combine with its subjective faith a strenuous
labour for the good of others is hardly held to
possess any religious principle worth proclaiming.

This propaganda of beneficence, this constant
attention to the moral and physical improvement of persons who have been neglected, is
quite recent as a leading feature of religion,
though indeed it seems to have formed some
part of the Saviour's original design. It was
unknown to the great preachers of the seventeenth century, whether Catholic or Protestant,
and it offered but a shadowy attraction to my

Father, who was the last of their disciples.
When Bossuet desired his hearers to listen to
the " cri de misère à l'entour de nous, qui
devrait nous fondre le cœur," he started a
new thing in the world of theology. We may
search the famous " Rule and Exercises of
Holy Living " from cover to cover, and not
learn that Jeremy Taylor would have thought
that any activity of the district-visitor or the
Salvation lassie came within the category of
saintliness.

My Father, then, like an old divine, concentrated his thoughts upon the intellectual part
of faith. In his obsession about me, he
believed that if my brain could be kept un-
affected by any of the seductive errors of the
age, and my heart centred in the adoring love
of God, all would be well with me in perpetuity.
He was still convinced that by intensely directing
my thoughts, he could compel them to flow in
a certain channel, since he had not begun to
learn the lesson, so mournful for saintly men of
his complexion, that " virtue would not be
virtue, could it be given by one fellow creature
to another." He had recognised, with reluctance, that holiness was not hereditary, but he
continued to hope that it might be compulsive.
I was still " the child of many prayers," and it
was not to be conceded that these prayers could
remain unanswered.

The great panacea was now, as always, the
study of the Bible, and this my Father never
ceased to urge upon me. He presented to me

a copy of Dean Alford's edition of the Greek
New Testament, in four great volumes, and
these he had had so magnificently bound in full
morocco that the work shone on my poor shelf
of sixpenny poets like a duchess among dairy-
maids. He extracted from me a written promise
that I would translate and meditate upon a
portion of the Greek text every morning before
I started for business. This promise I presently
failed to keep, my good intentions being under-
mined by an invincible *ennui ;* I concealed
the dereliction from him, and the sense that I
was deceiving my Father ate into my conscience
like a canker. But the dilemma was now before
me that I must either deceive my Father in
such things or paralyse my own character.

My growing distaste for the Holy Scriptures
began to occupy my thoughts, and to surprise
as much as it scandalised me. My desire was
to continue to delight in those sacred pages,
for which I still had an instinctive veneration.
Yet I could not but observe the difference
between the zeal with which I snatched at a
volume of Carlyle or Ruskin — since these
magicians were now first revealing themselves
to me—and the increasing languor with which
I took up Alford for my daily "passage."
Of course, although I did not know it, and
believed my reluctance to be sinful, the real
reason why I now found the Bible so difficult
to read was my familiarity with its contents.
These had the colourless triteness of a story
retold a hundred times. I longed for some-

thing new, something that would gratify curiosity and excite surprise. Whether the facts and doctrines contained in the Bible were true or false was not the question that appealed to me ; it was rather that they had been presented to me so often and had sunken into me so far that, as some one has said, they " lay bedridden in the dormitory of the soul," and made no impression of any kind upon me.

It often amazed me, and I am still unable to understand the fact, that my Father, through his long life—or till nearly the close of it— continued to take an eager pleasure in the text of the Bible. As I think I have already said, before he reached middle life, he had committed practically the whole of it to memory, and if started anywhere, even in a Minor Prophet, he could go on without a break as long as ever he was inclined for that exercise. He, therefore, at no time can have been assailed by the satiety of which I have spoken, and that it came so soon to me I must take simply as an indication of difference of temperament. It was not possible, even through the dark glass of corre- spondence, to deceive his eagle eye in this matter, and his suspicions accordingly took another turn. He conceived me to have become, or to be becoming, a victim of " the infidelity of the age."

In this new difficulty, he appealed to forms of modern literature by the side of which the least attractive pages of Leviticus or Deuter- onomy struck me as even thrilling. In parti-

cular, he urged upon me a work, then just
published, called "The Continuity of Scripture" by William Page Wood; afterwards Lord
Chancellor Hatherley. I do not know why he
supposed that the lucubrations of an exemplary
lawyer, delivered in a style that was like
the trickling of sawdust, would succeed in
rousing emotions which the glorious rhetoric
of the Orient had failed to awaken ; but
Page Wood had been a Sunday School teacher
for thirty years, and my Father was always
unduly impressed by the acumen of pious
barristers.

As time went on, and I grew older and
more independent in mind, my Father's anxiety
about what he called "the pitfalls and snares
which surround on every hand the thoughtless
giddy youth of London" became extremely
painful to himself. By harping in private upon
these "pitfalls"—which brought to my imagination a funny rough woodcut in an old edition
of Bunyan, where a devil was seen capering
over a sort of box let neatly into the ground—
he worked himself up into a frame of mind
which was not a little irritating to his hapless
correspondent, who was now "snared" indeed,
limed by the pen like a bird by the feet, and
could not by any means escape. To a peck
or a flutter from the bird the implacable fowler
would reply :

"You charge me with being suspicious, and
I fear I cannot deny the charge. But I can

appeal to your own sensitive and thoughtful mind for a considerable allowance. My deep and tender love for you ; your youth and inexperience ; the examples of other young men ; your distance from parental counsel ; our absolute and painful ignorance of all the details of your daily life, except what you yourself tell us :—try to throw yourself into the standing of a parent, and say if my suspiciousness is unreasonable. I rejoicingly acknowledge that from all I see you are pursuing a virtuous, steady, worthy course. One good thing my suspiciousness does :—ever and anon it brings out from you assurances, which greatly refresh and comfort me. And again, it carries me ever to God's Throne of Grace on your behalf. Holy Job *suspected* that his sons might have sinned, and cursed God in their heart. Was not his suspicion much like mine, grounded on the same reasons, and productive of the same results ? For it drove him to God in intercession. I have adduced the example of this Patriarch before, and he will endure being looked at again."

In fact, Holy Job continued to be frequently looked at, and for this Patriarch I came to experience a hatred which was as venomous as it was undeserved. But what youth of eighteen would willingly be compared with the sons of Job ? And indeed, for my part, I felt much more like that justly exasperated character, Elihu the Buzite, of the kindred of Ram.

As time went on, the peculiar strain of inquisition was relaxed, and I endured fewer and fewer of the torments of religious correspondence. Nothing abides in one tense projection, and my Father, resolute as he was, had other preoccupations. His orchids, his microscope, his physiological researches, his interpretations of prophecy, filled up the hours of his active and strenuous life, and, out of his sight, I became not indeed out of his mind, but no longer ceaselessly in the painful foreground of it. Yet, although the reiteration of his anxiety might weary him a little as it had wearied me well nigh to groans of despair, there was not the slightest change in his real attitude towards the subject or towards me.

I have already had occasion to say that he had nothing of the mystic or the visionary about him. At certain times and on certain points, he greatly desired that signs and wonders, such as had astonished and encouraged the infancy of the Christian Church, might again be vouchsafed to it, but he did not pretend to see such miracles himself, nor give the slightest credence to others who asserted that they did. He often congratulated himself on the fact that although his mind dwelt so constantly on spiritual matters it was never betrayed into any suspension of the rational functions.

Cross-examination by letter slackened, but on occasion of my brief and usually summer visits to Devonshire I suffered acutely from my Father's dialectical appetites. He was surrounded by peasants, on whom the teeth of his arguments could find no purchase. To him, in that intellectual Abdera, even an unwilling youth from London offered opportunities of pleasant contest. He would declare himself ready, nay eager, for argument. With his mental sleeves turned up, he would adopt a fighting attitude, and challenge me to a round on any portion of the Scheme of Grace. His alacrity was dreadful to me, his well-aimed blows fell on what was rather a bladder or a pillow than a vivid antagonist.

He was, indeed most unfairly handicapped, —I was naked, he in a suit of chain armour,— for he had adopted a method which I thought, and must still think, exceedingly unfair. He assumed that he had private knowledge of the Divine Will, and he would meet my temporising arguments by asseverations,—" So sure as my God liveth ! " or by appeals to a higher authority,—" But what does *my* Lord tell me in Paul's Letter to the Philippians ? " It was the prerogative of his faith to know, and of his character to overpower objection ; between these two millstones I was rapidly ground to powder.

These " discussions," as they were rather ironically called, invariably ended for me in disaster. I was driven out of my *papier-mâché* fastnesses, my canvas walls rocked at the first peal from my Father's clarion, and the foe pursued me across the plains of Jericho until I lay down ignominiously and covered

my face. I seemed to be pushed with horns
of iron, such as those which Zedekiah the son
of Chenaanah prepared for the encouragement
of Ahab.

When I acknowledged defeat and cried for
quarter, my Father would become radiant,
and I still seem to hear the sound of his full
voice, so thrilling, so warm, so painful to my
over-strained nerves, bursting forth in a sort
of benediction at the end of each of these one-
sided contentions, with " I bow my knees unto
the Father of our Lord Jesus Christ, that He
would grant you, according to the riches of His
glory, to be strengthened with might by His
Spirit in the inner man; that Christ may dwell
in your heart by faith ; that you, being rooted
and grounded in love, may be able to comprehend
with all saints what is the breadth, and length,
and depth, and height, and to know the love of
Christ which passeth knowledge, that you might
be filled with the fullness of God."

Thus solemn and thus ceremonious was my
Father apt to become, without a moment's
warning, on plain and domestic occasions ;
abruptly brimming over with emotion like a
basin which an unseen flow of water has filled
and over-filled.

I earnestly desire that no trace of that absurd
self-pity which is apt to taint recollections
of this nature should give falsity to mine.
My Father, let me say once more, had other
interests than those of his religion. In particular, at this time, he took to painting in

water-colours in the open air, and he resumed
the assiduous study of botany. He was no
fanatical monomaniac. Nevertheless, there was,
in everything he did and said, the central
purpose present. He acknowledged it plainly ;
"with me," he confessed, "every question
assumes a Divine standpoint and is not ade-
quately answered if the judgment-seat of Christ
is not kept in sight."

This was maintained whether the subject
under discussion was poetry, or society, or the
Prussian war with Austria, or the stamen of a
wild flower. Once, at least, he was himself conscious of the fatiguing effect on my temper of
this insistency, for, raising his great brown eyes
with a flash of laughter in them, he closed the
Bible suddenly after a very lengthy disquisition,
and quoted his Virgil to startling effect :—

> Claudite jam rivos, pueri : Sat prata biberunt.

The insistency of his religious conversation
was, probably, the less incomprehensible to me
on account of the evangelical training to which
I had been so systematically subjected. It was,
however, none the less intolerably irksome, and
would have been exasperating, I believe, even
to a nature in which a powerful and genuine
piety was inherent. To my own, in which a
feeble and imitative faith was expiring, it was
deeply vexatious. It led, alas ! to a great deal
of bowing in the house of Rimmon, to much
hypocritical ingenuity in drawing my Father's
attention away, if possible, as the terrible subject
was seen to be looming and approaching. In

this my stepmother would aid and abet, sometimes producing incongruous themes, likely to
attract my Father aside, with a skill worthy of a
parlour conjurer, and much to my admiration.
If, however, she was not unwilling to come, in
this way, to the support of my feebleness, there
was no open collusion between us. She always
described my Father, when she was alone with
me, admiringly, as one " whose trumpet gave
no uncertain sound." There was not a tinge
of infidelity upon her candid mind, but she was
human, and I think that now and then she was
extremely bored.

My Father was entirely devoid of the prudence
which turns away its eyes and passes as rapidly
as possible in the opposite direction.   The
peculiar kind of drama in which every sort of
social discomfort is welcomed rather than that
the characters should be happy when guilty of
" acting a lie," was not invented in those days,
and there can hardly be imagined a figure more
remote from my Father than Ibsen. Yet when
I came, at a far later date, to read " The Wild
Duck," memories of the embarrassing household
of my infancy helped me to realise Gregers
Werle, with his determination to pull the veil
of illusion away from every compromise that
makes life bearable.

I was docile, I was plausible, I was anything
but combative ; if my Father could have
persuaded himself to let me alone, if he could
merely have been willing to leave my subterfuges
and my explanations unanalysed, all would have

been well.   But he refused to see any difference
in temperament between a lad of twenty and a
sage of sixty.   He had no vital sympathy for
youth, which in itself had no charm for him.
He had no compassion for the weaknesses of
immaturity, and his one and only anxiety was
to be at the end of his spiritual journey, safe
with me in the house where there are many
mansions.   The incidents of human life upon
the road to glory were less than nothing to
him.

My Father was very fond of defining what
was his own attitude at this time, and he was
never tired of urging the same ambition upon
me.   He regarded himself as the faithful steward
of a Master who might return at any moment,
and who would require to find everything ready
for his convenience.   That master was God,
with whom my Father seriously believed himself
to be in relations much more confidential than
those vouchsafed to ordinary pious persons.   He
awaited, with anxious hope, " the coming of the
Lord," an event which he still frequently
believed to be imminent.   He would calculate,
by reference to prophecies in the Old and New
Testament, the exact date of this event ; the
date would pass, without the expected Advent,
and he would be more than disappointed,—he
would be incensed.   Then he would understand
that he must have made some slight error in
calculation, and the pleasures of anticipation
would recommence.

Me in all this he used as a kind of inferior

coadjutor, much as a responsible and upper servant might use a footboy. I, also, must be watching ; it was not important that I should be seriously engaged in any affairs of my own. I must be ready for the Master's coming ; and my Father's incessant cross-examination was made in the spirit of a responsible servant who fidgets lest some humble but essential piece of household work has been neglected.

My holidays, however, and all my personal relations with my Father were poisoned by this insistency. I was never at my ease in his company ; I never knew when I might not be subjected to a series of searching questions which I should not be allowed to evade. Meanwhile, on every other stage of experience I was gaining the reliance upon self and the respect for the opinion of others which come naturally to a young man of sober habits who earns his own living and lives his own life. For this kind of independence my Father had no respect or consideration, when questions of religion were introduced, although he handsomely conceded it on other points. And now first there occurred to me the reflection, which in years to come I was to repeat over and over, with an ever sadder emphasis,—what a charming companion, what a delightful parent, what a courteous and engaging friend my Father would have been, and would pre-eminently have been to me, if it had not been for this stringent piety which ruined it all.

Let me speak plainly. After my long ex-

perience, after my patience and forbearance, I
have surely the right to protest against the
untruth (would that I could apply to it any
other word !) that evangelical religion, or any
religion in a violent form, is a wholesome or
valuable or desirable adjunct to human life.
It divides heart from heart. It sets up a vain,
chimerical ideal, in the barren pursuit of which
all the tender, indulgent affections, all the
genial play of life, all the exquisite pleasures
and soft resignations of the body, all that en-
larges and calms the soul, are exchanged for
what is harsh and void and negative. It en-
courages a stern and ignorant spirit of condemnation ; it throws altogether out of gear the
healthy movement of the conscience ; it invents
virtues which are sterile and cruel ; it invents
sins which are no sins at all, but which darken
the heaven of innocent joy with futile clouds
of remorse. There is something horrible, if
we will bring ourselves to face it, in the
fanaticism that can do nothing with this pathetic
and fugitive existence of ours but treat it as if
it were the uncomfortable ante-chamber to a
palace which no one has explored and of the
plan of which we know absolutely nothing. My
Father, it is true, believed that he was intimately
acquainted with the form and furniture of this
habitation, and he wished me to think of nothing
else but of the advantages of an eternal residence
in it.

Then came a moment when my self-suffi-
ciency revolted against the police-inspection to

which my " views " were incessantly subjected.
There was a morning, in the hot-house at
home, among the gorgeous waxen orchids which
reminded my Father of the tropics in his youth,
when my forbearance or my timidity gave way.
The enervated air, soaked with the intoxicating
perfumes of all those voluptuous flowers, may
have been partly responsible for my outburst.
My Father had once more put to me the customary interrogatory. Was I " walking closely
with God " ? Was my sense of the efficacy of
the Atonement clear and sound ? Had the Holy
Scriptures still their full authority with me ?
My replies on this occasion were violent and
hysterical. I have no clear recollection what it
was that I said,—I desire not to recall the
whimpering sentences in which I begged to be
let alone, in which I demanded the right to think
for myself, in which I repudiated the idea that
my Father was responsible to God for my secret
thoughts and my most intimate convictions.

He made no answer ; I broke from the odor-
ous furnace of the conservatory, and buried my
face in the cold grass upon the lawn. My
visit to Devonshire, already near its close, was
hurried to an end. I had scarcely arrived in
London before the following letter, furiously
despatched in the track of the fugitive, buried
itself like an arrow in my heart :

" When your sainted Mother died, she not
only tenderly committed you to God, but left
you also as a solemn charge to me, to bring

you up in the nurture and admonition of the
Lord. That responsibility I have sought constantly to keep before me : I can truly aver
that it *has* been ever before me—in my choice
of a housekeeper, in my choice of a school, in
my ordering of your holidays, in my choice
of a second wife, in my choice of an occupation
for you, in my choice of a residence for you ;
and in multitudes of lesser things—I have sought
to act for you, not in the light of this present
world, but with a view to Eternity.

"Before your childhood was past, there
seemed God's manifest blessing on our care ;
for you seemed truly converted to Him ; you
confessed, in solemn baptism, that you had
died and had been raised with Christ ; and
you were received with joy into the bosom of
the Church of God, as one alive from the dead.

"All this filled my heart with thankfulness
and joy, whenever I thought of you :—how
could it do otherwise ? And when I left you
in London, on that dreary winter evening, my
heart, full of sorrowing love, found its refuge
and its resource in this thought,—that you
were one of the lambs of Christ's flock ; sealed
with the Holy Spirit as His ; renewed in heart
to holiness, in the image of God.

"For a while, all appeared to go on fairly
well : we yearned, indeed, to discover more of
heart in your allusions to religious matters,
but your expressions towards us were filial and
affectionate ; your conduct, so far as we could
see, was moral and becoming ; you mingled

with the people of God, spoke of occasional
delight and profit in His ordinances ; and employed your talents in service to Him.

"But of late, and specially during the past
year, there has become manifest a rapid progress towards evil. (I must beg you here to
pause, and again to look to God for grace to
weigh what I am about to say ; or else wrath
will rise.)

"When you came to us in the summer, the
heavy blow fell full upon me ; and I discovered
how very far you had departed from God. It
was not that you had yielded to the strong tide
of youthful blood, and had fallen a victim to
fleshly lusts ; in that case, however sad, your
enlightened conscience would have spoken loudly,
and you would have found your way back to
the blood which cleanseth us from all sin, to
humble confession and self-abasement, to for-
giveness and to re-communion with God. It
was not this ; it was worse. It was that horrid,
insidious infidelity, which had already worked
in your mind and heart with terrible energy.
Far worse, I say, because this was sapping the
very foundations of faith, on which all true
godliness, all real religion, must rest.

"Nothing seemed left to which I could
appeal. We had, I found, no common ground.
The Holy Scriptures had no longer any authority : you had taught yourself to evade their
inspiration. Any particular Oracle of God which
pressed you, you could easily explain away ;
even the very character of God you weighed

in your balance of fallen reason, and fashioned it accordingly. You were thus sailing down the rapid tide of time towards Eternity, without a single authoritative guide (having cast your chart overboard), except what you might fashion and forge on your own anvil,—except what you might *guess*, in fact.

"Do not think I am speaking in passion, and using unwarrantable strength of words. If the written Word is not absolutely authoritative, what do we know of God? What more than we can infer, that is, guess,—as the thoughtful heathens guessed,—Plato, Socrates, Cicero,—from dim and mute surrounding phenomena? What do we know of Eternity? Of our relations to God? Especially of the relations of a *sinner* to God? What of reconciliation? What of the capital question—How can a God of perfect spotless rectitude deal with me, a corrupt sinner, who have trampled on those of His laws which were even written on my conscience? . . .

"This dreadful conduct of yours I had intended, after much prayer, to pass by in entire silence; but your apparently sincere inquiries after the cause of my sorrow have led me to go to the root of the matter, and I could not stop short of the development contained in this letter. It is with pain, not in anger, that I send it; hoping that you may be induced to review the whole course, of which this is only a stage, before God. If this grace were granted to you, oh! how joyfully should I bury all the

past, and again have sweet and tender fellowship
with my beloved Son, as of old."

The reader who has done me the favour to
follow this record of the clash of two temperaments will not fail to perceive the crowning
importance of the letter from which I have
just made a long quotation. It sums up, with
the closest logic, the whole history of the
situation, and I may leave it to form the
epigraph of this little book.

All that I need further say is to point out
that when such defiance is offered to the intelligence of a thoughtful and honest young
man with the normal impulses of his twenty-
one years, there are but two alternatives.
Either he must cease to think for himself ; or
his individualism must be instantly confirmed,
and the necessity of religious independence
must be emphasised.

No compromise, it is seen, was offered ; no
proposal of a truce would have been acceptable.   It was a case of "Everything or
Nothing" ; and thus desperately challenged,
the young man's conscience threw off once for
all the yoke of his "dedication," and, as
respectfully as he could, without parade or
remonstrance, he took a human being's privilege
to fashion his inner life for himself.